IT Risk Fundamentals

Study Guide

IT RISK
FUNDAMENTALS
An ISACA Certificate

ISACA®

About ISACA

For more than 50 years, ISACA® (*www.isaca.org*) has advanced the best talent, expertise and learning in technology. ISACA equips individuals with knowledge, credentials, education and community to progress their careers and transform their organizations, and enables enterprises to train and build quality teams. Among those credentials, ISACA advances and validates business-critical skills and knowledge through the globally respected Certified Information Systems Auditor® (CISA®), Certified in Risk and Information Systems Control™ (CRISC™), Certified Information Security Manager® (CISM®) and Certified in the Governance of Enterprise IT® (CGEIT®) credentials. ISACA is a global professional association and learning organization that leverages the expertise of its 145,000 members who work in information security, governance, assurance, risk and privacy to drive innovation through technology. It has a presence in 188 countries, including more than 220 chapters worldwide.

Disclaimer

ISACA has designed and created *IT Risk Fundamentals Study Guide* (the "Work") primarily as an educational resource for professionals. ISACA makes no claim that use of any of the Work will assure a successful outcome. The Work should not be considered inclusive of all proper information, procedures and tests or exclusive of other information, procedures and tests that are reasonably directed to obtaining the same results. In determining the propriety of any specific information, procedure or test, professionals should apply their own professional judgment to the specific circumstances presented by the particular systems or information technology environment.

Reservation of Rights

ISACA

1700 E. Golf Road, Suite 400
Schaumburg, IL 60173, USA
Phone: +1.847.660.5505
Fax: +1.847.253.1755
Contact us: https://support.isaca.org
Website: www.isaca.org

Participate in the ISACA Online Forums: https://engage.isaca.org/onlineforums

Twitter: http://twitter.com/ISACANews
LinkedIn: www.linkedin.com/company/isaca
Facebook: www.facebook.com/ISACAGlobal
Instagram: www.instagram.com/isacanews/

ISBN 978-1-60420-726-2
IT Risk Fundamentals Study Guide
Printed in the United States of America

Acknowledgments

ISACA would like to recognize:

Expert Reviewers

Urs Fischer, CISA, CRISC, CPA (Swiss), UBS Business Solutions AG, Switzerland
Jack Freund, Ph.D., CISA, CRISC, CISM, CGEIT, CDPSE, Moody's/Team8 Cyber Risk Assessment Venture, USA
Mike Hughes, CISA, CRISC, CGEIT, MIoD, Prism RA, United Kingdom
Jack Jones, Chief Risk Scientist, RiskLens, USA
Linda Kostic, CISA, CISSP, Doctor of IT-Cybersecurity & Information Assurance, PRMIA Complete Course in Risk Management, George Washington University, Citi, USA
Katsumi Sakagawa, CISA, CRISC, Japan
James C. Samans, CISA, CRISC, CISM, CBCP, CISSP-ISSEP, CPP, PMP, American Institutes for Research, USA
Peter C. Tessin, CISA, CRISC, CISM, CGEIT, Discover Financial Services, USA
Alok Tuteja, Ph.D., CRISC, CGEIT, CIA, CISSP, BRS Ventures, India
Evan Wheeler, CRISC, IASO, Edelman Financial Engines, USA
Prometheus Yang, CISA, CRISC, CISM, CFE, Standard Chartered Bank, Hong Kong
Lisa Young, CISA, CISM, CISSP, Axio, USA

Page intentionally left blank

Table of Contents

List of Figures 11

About this Study Guide 15

Intended Audience 16

Study Guide Scope and Organization 17

Chapter 1:

Risk Introduction and Overview 19

Learning Objectives 20

Risk Introduction and Overview 21

1.1 Risk Terminology 21
1.1.1 Common Risk Terms 21
1.2 Business Risk 22
1.2.1 Types of Business Risk 22
Strategic Risk 23
Environmental Risk 23
Market Risk 23
Credit Risk 24
Operational Risk 24
Compliance Risk 24
Project Risk 25
1.2.2 Levels of Risk 25
Strategic Level 25
Program and Project Level 25
Operational Level 26
1.3 I&T-related Risk 26
1.3.1 I&T Risk Types 26
I&T Benefit/Value Enablement Risk 27
I&T Program and Project Delivery Risk 27
Project Risk 28
I&T Operations and Service Delivery Risk 28
Change Risk 28
Cyber and Information Security Risk 28
1.3.2 Risk Standards and Guidance 28
1.3.3 Risk IT Framework 29
1.3.4 Risk-Related Business Functions 29
Risk and Business Continuity 30
Risk and Audit 30
Risk and Information Security 30
1.3.5 Three Lines of Defense 30
1.4 Controls 31
1.4.1 Policies, Standards and Procedures 31
1.4.2 Risk Relationship to Control 32
Control Risk 33
1.4.3 General Controls 33
1.4.4 I&T Controls 34
Input Controls 34
Processing Controls 35
Application Controls 35
1.5 Summary of Terminology 35

Chapter 1 Knowledge Check 37

Chapter 2:
Risk Governance and Management 39

Learning Objectives 40

Risk Governance and Management 41
- **2.1 Risk Governance** 41
  - 2.1.1 Governance Objectives 41
    - Benefits Realization 41
    - Risk Optimization 41
    - Resource Optimization 41
  - 2.1.2 Risk Governance Objectives 42
- **2.2 Risk Management** 43
  - 2.2.1 Risk Management Overview 44
  - 2.2.2 I&T Risk Governance and Management 44
    - Connect to Enterprise Business or Mission 46
    - Align with Enterprise Risk Management 46
    - Balance Costs and Benefits 46
    - Promote Ethical and Open Communication 46
    - Establish Tone at the Top and Accountability 47
    - Consistent Approach Aligned to Strategy 47
  - 2.2.3 Risk Universe 47
- **2.3 Positioning Risk** 49
  - 2.3.1 Risk Appetite, Risk Tolerance and Risk Capacity 50
    - Risk Appetite 50
    - Risk Tolerance 51
    - Risk Capacity 52
- **2.4 Risk Stakeholders, Roles and Culture** 52
  - 2.4.1 I&T Risk Management Stakeholders 52
  - 2.4.2 Risk Roles 55
  - 2.4.3 Risk Culture 56
- **2.5 Risk Communication, Policy, Scope and Workflow** 59
  - 2.5.1 Risk Communication 59
  - 2.5.2 Risk Policy 61
  - 2.5.3 Risk Scope 63
  - 2.5.4 Risk Management Workflow 64
- **2.6 Summary of Terminology** 65

Chapter 2 Knowledge Check 67

Chapter 3:
Risk Identification 69

Learning Objectives 70

Risk Identification 71
- **3.1 Asset Types** 71
  - 3.1.1 People 71
  - 3.1.2 Information 71
  - 3.1.3 Business Processes 71
  - 3.1.4 Infrastructure 72
  - 3.1.5 Finances 72
  - 3.1.6 Reputation 72
- **3.2 Asset Classification (Criticality and Sensitivity)** 72
- **3.3 Asset Valuation** 74
- **3.4 Information Asset Valuation** 75

3.5 Threats ... 76
3.5.1 Threat Types ... 77
External Threats ... 77
Advanced Persistent Threats (APTs) ... 78
Internal Threats ... 79
Emerging Threats ... 80
3.5.2 Threat Intelligence ... 80
3.5.3 Threat Assessment ... 81
3.6 Vulnerabilities ... 81
3.6.1 Vulnerability Types ... 82
Networks ... 82
Physical Access ... 82
Applications and Web-facing Services ... 83
Utilities ... 83
Supply Chain ... 83
Processes ... 83
Equipment ... 84
Cloud Computing Services ... 84
Big Data ... 84
Cybersecurity ... 84
3.6.2 Vulnerability Assessment and Penetration Testing ... 85
3.7 Likelihood ... 86
3.8 Risk Awareness ... 88
3.9 I&T-related Risk ... 88
3.9.1 IT Components and Areas of Concern ... 89
Hardware ... 89
Software ... 90
Operating Systems ... 91
Applications ... 91
Software Utilities ... 91
Environmental Systems ... 92
Platforms ... 92
Networks ... 93
3.9.2 Risk Identification Overview ... 93
3.9.3 Risk Identification Sources ... 94
Interviews ... 95
3.10 Risk Scenarios ... 95
3.10.1 Risk Scenario Approaches ... 96
Top-down Approach ... 96
Bottom-up Approach ... 97
Contextual Factors ... 98
Capability Factors ... 98
3.10.2 Risk Scenario Benefits ... 98
3.10.3 I&T-related Risk Scenario Development ... 98
3.11 Summary of Terminology ... 103

Chapter 3 Knowledge Check ... 105

Chapter 4:
Risk Assessment and Analysis ... 107

Learning Objectives ... 108

Risk Assessment and Analysis ... 109
4.1 Risk Assessment Processes ... 109
4.1.1 Risk Assessment ... 109
4.1.2 Risk Analysis ... 109
4.1.3 Risk Evaluation ... 110

4.2 Risk Scenario Evaluation 110
4.2.1 Frequency Analysis 110
4.2.2 Impact Criteria 111
4.2.3 Business Impact Analysis 112
4.3 Risk Analysis Process, Approaches and Methods 113
4.3.1 Risk Analysis Process 113
4.3.2 Risk Analysis Approaches 114
Qualitative Approach 114
Operationally Critical Threat Asset and Vulnerability Evaluation® (OCTAVE®) 117
Quantitative Approach 117
Quantitative Approach Uses and Examples 118
Annual Loss Expectancy 118
Value at Risk 118
Earnings at Risk 118
Cost-benefit Analysis 119
Hybrid Approach 119
Practical Guidance on Choosing Methods 119
4.3.3 Risk Analysis Methods (Techniques) 119
4.4 Risk Ranking, Prioritization and Aggregation 121
4.4.1 Risk Map 121
4.4.2 Risk Aggregation 123
4.4.3 Risk Aggregation Guidelines 124
4.5 Risk Documentation 125
4.5.1 Addressing Bypassed Risk 126
4.5.2 Risk Register 126
4.5.3 Risk Owner 129
4.6 Control Assessment 130
4.6.1 Current State of Controls Sources 133
4.6.2 Control Self-Assessment 133
4.6.3 Control Owner 134
4.7 Summary of Terminology 134

Chapter 4 Knowledge Check 137

Chapter 5:
Risk Response 139

Learning Objectives 140

Risk Response 141
5.1 Risk Response and Strategies 141
5.1.1 Purpose and Business Objective Alignment 141
5.1.2 Risk Response Strategies 142
Risk Acceptance 142
Risk Acceptance Framework 143
Risk Mitigation 144
Awareness Education and Training 145
Risk Transfer (Sharing) 145
Risk Avoidance 146
5.2 Control Design and Implementation 146
5.2.1 Control Design 146
5.2.2 Control Matrix 147
5.2.3 Control Management 147
5.3 Incident Management, Business Continuity and Disaster Recovery 148
5.3.1 Incident Management 148
5.3.2 Business Continuity Planning 149
5.3.3 Disaster Recovery 150

5.4 Risk States 150
5.4.1 Risk and Control 151
5.5 Risk Response Selection, Prioritization and Communication 153
5.5.1 Risk Response Selection Parameters 153
5.5.2 Risk Response Options 154
5.5.3 Business Case Development 155
Cost-benefit Analysis 156
Return on Investment 156
5.5.4 Risk Response Prioritization 157
5.5.5 Risk Response Communication 157
5.5.6 Risk Response Plan 158
5.6 Summary of Terminology 158

Chapter 5 Knowledge Check 161

Chapter 6:

Risk Monitoring, Reporting and Communication 165

Learning Objectives 166

Risk Monitoring, Reporting and Communication 167
6.1 Risk Monitoring Process 167
6.1.1 Risk Monitoring Stakeholders 168
6.1.2 Risk Monitoring Status 168
6.2 Key Risk Indicators 168
6.2.1 Types of Key Risk Indicators 169
Lag Risk Indicator 169
Lead Risk Indicator 169
6.2.2 Developing Risk Indicators 169
Root Cause Analysis 169
6.2.3 KRI Selection 170
KRI Attributes 171
KRI Selection Benefits 171
KRI Selection Challenges 171
6.2.4 Examples of Key Risk Indicators 172
6.2.5 Using KRIs for Gap Analysis 174
6.2.6 KRI Optimization, Communication and Maintenance 174
6.3 Key Performance Indictors 175
6.3.1 Using KPIs with KRIs 175
KPI and KRI Example 176
6.4 Risk and Control Monitoring and Testing 176
6.4.1 Continuous Monitoring 176
6.4.2 Control Monitoring 177
6.4.3 Control Assessment and Testing 177
Control Self-Assessment 178
Internal Audit Control Review 178
Vulnerability Assessment 178
Vulnerability Scan 178
Penetration Test 178
Third-party Assurance 179
6.4.4 Risk and Control Monitoring Effectiveness 179
6.4.5 Monitoring Control Exceptions 180
6.5 Risk Reporting and Communication 181
6.5.1 Reporting Principles 181
6.5.2 Risk Report/Communication Types 182
6.5.3 Risk Reporting Channels 185
6.6 Summary of Terminology 187

Chapter 6 Knowledge Check 189

APPENDIX A: GLOSSARY 191

LIST OF FIGURES

Chapter 1. Risk Introduction and Overview

Figure 1.1—Simple View of Threats, Vulnerabilities and Risk 22
Figure 1.2—Business/Enterprise Risk Types 23
Figure 1.3—Levels of Risk 25
Figure 1.4—I&T-related Risk Relative to Business/Enterprise Risk 27
Figure 1.5—Three Lines of Defense 31
Figure 1.6—Risk in Relation to Control 32
Figure 1.7—Control Types 33
Figure 1.8— Chapter 1 Terminology 35

Chapter 2. Risk Governance and Management

Figure 2.1—Risk Governance 42
Figure 2.2—Risk Governance Objectives 43
Figure 2.3—I&T Risk Management Principles 45
Figure 2.4—Risk Universe 48
Figure 2.5—Value Chain 49
Figure 2.6—Risk Capacity, Risk Appetite and Actual Risk 52
Figure 2.7—I&T Risk Management Stakeholders 53
Figure 2.8—Stakeholders for I&T Risk Management 53
Figure 2.9—RACI Model 56
Figure 2.10—Sample RACI Chart 56
Figure 2.11—Risk Governance and Management Behaviors 57
Figure 2.12—Risk Communication 59
Figure 2.13—Stakeholder Communication (about Risk) 60
Figure 2.14—Risk Policy Types 61
Figure 2.15—Risk Management Workflow 65
Figure 2.16—Chapter 2 Terminology 66

Chapter 3. Risk Identification

Figure 3.1—Intellectual Property Examples ...73
Figure 3.2—Loss Scenario Matrix ...75
Figure 3.3—Risk Factors ...77
Figure 3.4—Typical APT Sources ...79
Figure 3.5—Cybersecurity Vulnerabilities ...85
Figure 3.6—Factors Influencing Risk ...87
Figure 3.7—I&T-related Business Risk Types ...89
Figure 3.8—I&T-related Risk Scenario Approaches ...97
Figure 3.9—I&T-related Risk Scenario Development Structure ...99
Figure 3.10—Risk Scenario Technique Main Focus Areas ...100
Figure 3.11—Chapter 3 Terminology ...103

Chapter 4. Risk Assessment and Analysis

Figure 4.1—Impact Criteria ...112
Figure 4.2—Qualitative Approach ...116
Figure 4.3—Generic Risk Map ...122
Figure 4.4—Risk Map with Risk Appetite Example ...122
Figure 4.5—Aggregated Risk Map ...123
Figure 4.6—Risk Register Part 1 ...128
Figure 4.7—Risk Register Part 2 ...129
Figure 4.8—Control Intent ...130
Figure 4.9—Threat Event Control Interactions ...132
Figure 4.10—Chapter 4 Terminology ...135

Chapter 5. Risk Response

Figure 5.1—Risk Response Process Phases ...141
Figure 5.2—Risk Acceptance Framework ...143
Figure 5.3—Control Matrix ...147
Figure 5.4—Risk States ...150
Figure 5.5—How Residual Risk Relates to Inherent Risk ...152
Figure 5.6—Risk Response Selection and Prioritization ...155
Figure 5.7—Chapter 5 Terminology ...159

Chapter 6. Risk Monitoring, Reporting and Communication

Figure 6.1—KRI Selection Guidance 172
Figure 6.2—Stakeholder KRIs (Example) 173
Figure 6.3—Reducing the Gap 174
Figure 6.4—Example of KRI and KPI Use 176
Figure 6.5—Risk Reporting Principles 181
Figure 6.6—Types of Risk Reports/Communication 182
Figure 6.7—Risk Report 184
Figure 6.8—Risk Reporting Channels 186
Figure 6.9—Chapter 6 Terminology 187

Page intentionally left blank

About This Study Guide

The *IT Risk Fundamentals Study Guide* is a reference guide designed to assist individuals in acquiring a base-level knowledge of risk that is related to information and technology (I&T) and in preparing to earn the ISACA IT Risk Fundamentals certificate. The topics and explanatory content presented in this guide are intended to represent a body of knowledge of risk that every information technology (IT) and business professional should possess. The material presented in this guide is from many sources, including ISACA frameworks, guides, certification review manuals and white papers that discuss I&T-related risk. The primary references that were used to develop this guide include the ISACA:

- *Risk IT Framework, 2nd Edition*[1]
- *Risk IT Practitioner Guide, 2nd Edition*[2]
- *COBIT® 2019 Framework: Introduction and Methodology*[3]
- *COBIT® 2019 Framework: Governance and Management Objectives*[4]
- *CRISC Review Manual, 6th Edition*[5]
- *CGEIT Review Manual, 8th Edition*[6]
- *CISA Review Manual, 27th Edition*[7]
- *CISM Review Manual, 15th Edition*[8]
- *Cybersecurity Fundamentals Study Guide, 2nd Edition*[9]
- *Cybersecurity Audit Certificate Study Guide*[10]
- *Glossary*[11]

[1] ISACA, *Risk IT Framework, 2nd Edition*, USA, 2020, *www.isaca.org/bookstore/bookstore-risk-digital/ritf2*
[2] ISACA, *Risk IT Practitioner Guide, 2nd Edition*, USA, 2020, *www.isaca.org/bookstore/bookstore-risk-digital/ritpg2*
[3] ISACA, *COBIT® 2019 Framework: Introduction and Methodology,* USA, 2018, *www.isaca.org/bookstore/bookstore-cobit_19-digital/wcb19fim*
[4] ISACA, *COBIT® 2019 Framework: Governance and Management Objectives,* USA, 2018, *www.isaca.org/bookstore/bookstore-cobit_19-digital/wcb19fgm*
[5] ISACA, *CRISC Review Manual, 6th Edition,* USA, 2015, *www.isaca.org/bookstore/crisc-exam-resources/crr6ed*
[6] ISACA, *CGEIT Review Manual, 8th Edition,* USA, 2020, *www.isaca.org/bookstore/cgeit-exam-resources/cgm8ed*
[7] ISACA, *CISA Review Manual, 27th Edition,* USA, 2019, *www.isaca.org/bookstore/cisa-exam-resources/crm27ed*
[8] ISACA, *CISM Review Manual, 15th Edition*, USA, 2019, *https://www.isaca.org/bookstore/cism-exam-resources/cm15ed*
[9] ISACA, *Cybersecurity Fundamentals Study Guide, 2nd Edition*, USA, 2017, *www.isaca.org/bookstore/csx-certificate-exam-resources/csxg2*
[10] *Ibid.*
[11] ISACA, *Glossary*, *www.isaca.org/resources/glossary*

Intended Audience

Topics in this guide are presented at a foundational level and include basic terminology, concepts, examples, general practices and explanations of risk and I&T-related risk that prepare professionals to earn the ISACA IT Risk Fundamentals certificate. This guide is intended for professionals who wish to learn about risk and I&T-related risk, currently interact with risk professionals, or are new to risk and interested in working as a risk or IT-risk professional.

Study Guide Scope and Organization

The *IT Risk Fundamentals Study Guide* provides the IT or business professional with a conversational knowledge of risk and I&T-related risk, and a thorough understanding of the enterprise risk management process. The guide delivers this essential risk knowledge in the following main content areas:

- Risk introduction and overview
- Governance and management of risk
- Identifying risk
- Assessing and analyzing risk
- Responding to risk
- Monitoring, reporting and communicating risk

Every chapter contains the following sections:

- Learning Objectives—knowledge that learners should understand after reading the chapter
- Chapters and Sections—knowledge content
- Summary of Terminology and Knowledge Check—glossary of terms that were introduced in the chapter and a quiz on the chapter knowledge

Note: Throughout this guide, the term **IT** refers to the enterprise function that has the primary responsibility for technology. The term **I&T**, in this guide, refers to all the information the enterprise generates, processes and uses to achieve its goals, and the technology to support that throughout the enterprise.

Page intentionally left blank

Chapter 1:

Risk Introduction and Overview

Learning Objectives 20

Risk Introduction and Overview

1.1 Risk Terminology 21
1.2 Business Risk 22
1.3 I&T-related Risk 26
1.4 Controls 31
1.5 Summary of Terminology 35

Chapter 1 Knowledge Check 37

Learning Objectives

This chapter introduces and provides a high-level overview of risk and I&T-related risk, including:

- Common risk terminology and types of risk
- Risk-related business functions
- How the three lines of defense are important to the risk management process
- General and I&T controls and their role in the risk management process

Learning objectives include the following:

- Define terms that an enterprise uses to express and describe risk, and explain how they relate to each other.
- Describe how risk management relates to other business functions, such as business continuity, IT audit and information security.
- Explain the different types of risk that an enterprise may encounter.
- Appraise I&T-related risk and how it is a part of overall enterprise risk.
- Describe common standards and frameworks that apply to risk management.
- Identify control principles and the types of controls that support the achievement of business objectives.

Risk Introduction and Overview

1.1 Risk Terminology

Every enterprise experiences risk. Risk is the result of uncertainties to which an enterprise is exposed that threaten its ability to achieve its business goals and objectives. To identify, measure, assess and manage risk, risk-related professionals are expected to know and use an extensive, common, risk vocabulary that allows a consistent approach to address and openly communicate about risk within an enterprise.

Key risk terms are explained throughout this study guide. When a new term is introduced and defined, it is included in the "Terminology" section at the end of each chapter and the summary "Glossary" at the end of the guide. These glossaries are a useful tool for grasping a thorough knowledge of risk terminology and understanding the relationships among the terms.

1.1.1 Common Risk Terms

There are many definitions of risk that exist today. ISACA uses the following definition of risk.

Risk is the combination of the likelihood of an event and its impact. Risk is most often associated with uncertainties and deviations from expected results that can have an adverse impact to an enterprise and threaten its ability to meet its business objectives.

Risk refers to the likelihood and impact that exists from a combination of assets, threats and control conditions.

Likelihood describes the potential of a risk event. Likelihood is the probability of something happening. Other terms used to describe the potential of a risk event include:

- **Frequency**—A measure of the rate by which events occur over a certain period of time.
- **Probability** — A mathematical-driven measure of the possibility of a specific outcome as a ratio of all possible outcomes. Probability represents the extent to which an event is likely to occur, measured by the ratio of the studied cases or cases in question to the whole number of cases.

Impact is the term that is used to describe the result of a risk event. Impact is defined as the magnitude of loss resulting from a threat exploiting a vulnerability. Other terms used to describe the result of a risk event include:

- **Magnitude** — A measure of the potential severity of loss or the potential gain from realized events/scenarios.
- **Consequence** — The magnitude of loss resulting from a threat exploiting a vulnerability (used interchangeably with impact).

An event is something that happens at a specific place and/or time. Other terms used to describe an event include:

- **Incident** — Any event that is not part of the ordinary (standard) operation of a service and that causes, or may cause, an interruption to, or a reduction in, the quality of that service.
- **Exploit** — An event where the attacker takes advantage of a vulnerability.
- **Attack** — An attempt to gain unauthorized access or make use of an asset.

To better appreciate risk, the various elements within an enterprise that can affect risk must be well understood. Having a strong grasp of risk terminology is essential to understanding risk management and for being able to properly communicate about risk.

It is important to be able to distinguish between a risk, a threat and a vulnerability, because these terms are often used incorrectly as synonyms (see **figure 1.1**). This figure is built-on throughout the study guide as additional terms and factors are introduced.

Figure 1.1—Simple View of Threats, Vulnerabilities and Risk

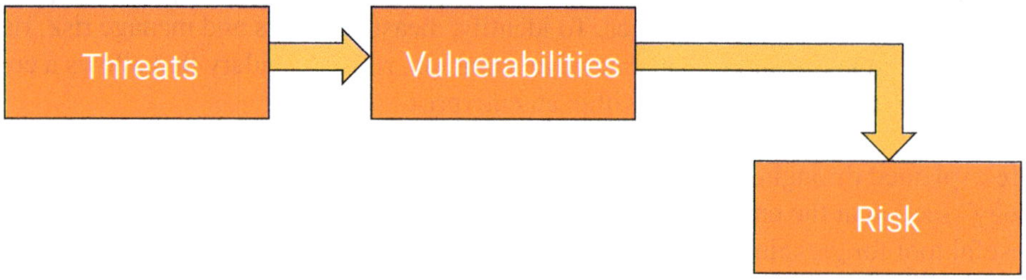

Source: ISACA, *CRISC Review Manual, 6th Edition*, USA, 2015, figure 1.9, *www.isaca.org/bookstore/crisc-exam-resources/crr6ed*

A threat is anything that is capable of acting against an asset in a manner that can result in harm. Threats are aimed at exploiting enterprise vulnerabilities.

A vulnerability is a control condition that is deemed to be deficient relative to requirements of the threat levels being faced by the enterprise.

Vulnerabilities represent a weakness in the design, implementation, operation or internal control of a process that could expose the system to adverse threats from threat events.

1.2 Business Risk

Risk is a critical part of business. Unless an enterprise is willing to take a risk, it will not be able to realize the benefits associated with risk.

Business risk is the probability a situation with uncertain frequency and magnitude of loss (or gain) that could prevent the enterprise from meeting its business objectives. Taking too much risk may lead to an increased likelihood of business failure and/or financial loss.

1.2.1 Types of Business Risk

An enterprise can be subject to a number of different types of business risk (**figure 1.2**). The following business/enterprise risk types are common to most enterprises:

- Strategic risk
- Environmental risk
- Market risk
- Credit risk
- Operational risk
- Compliance risk
- Project Risk

Figure 1.2—Business/Enterprise Risk Types

Source: Adapted from ISACA, *Risk IT Framework, 2nd Edition*, USA, 2020, figure 1.1, *www.isaca.org/bookstore/bookstore-risk-digital/ritf2*

Strategic risk

Strategic risk is associated with future business plans and strategies of an enterprise. These can include planning for expansion, entering new markets and enhancing the business infrastructure. Examples of events that can cause strategic risk include:

- Sudden changes in customer preferences
- Executive turnover
- Game-changing technological disruptions
- Erosion of brand power
- Large-scale initiatives that do not deliver as expected
- Commoditization of enterprise products or business mode (e.g., product or mode no longer considered unique)

Environmental Risk

Environmental risk represents threats to natural resources, human health and wildlife. Examples of events that can cause environmental risk include:

- Exploiting oil reserves discovered in a national park, which could harm or destroy some of the park wildlife
- Carcinogenic risk caused by airborne pollutants
- Pollution from factories and vehicles
- Use of household pesticides
- Discharge of hazardous chemicals into local water bodies

Market Risk

Market risk comprises pressures on an asset class. Market risk can be broken down into subcategories according to the type of pressured asset, including:

- Currency risk
- Interest-rate risk
- Equity risk
- Property risk
- Foreign-exchange risk
- Commodity risk

Examples of events that can cause market risk include:

- Recession and depression
- War
- Inflation

Credit Risk

Credit risk is the potential that a borrower or creditor will fail to meet financial obligations in accordance with agreed terms. Examples of events that can cause credit risk include:

- Poor or falling cash flow from operations
- Rising interest rates
- Callable loans
- Changes in the nature of the marketplace that adversely affect the enterprise
- Technological changes
- Increase in competitors
- Regulatory changes
- Sociopolitical situation within a country, or among countries in a global market
- Stability and regulatory practices of a government, or governments in a global market
- Damage to assets for which the enterprise is the insurer

Operational Risk

Operational risk is the potential for losses caused by inadequate systems or controls, human error, mismanagement, or natural disasters. Examples of events that can cause operational risk include:

- Employee errors
- Systems failures
- Fire, floods and other physical losses
- Epidemics and pandemics
- Fraud, theft and other criminal activity

Compliance Risk

Compliance risk is the probability and consequences of an enterprise failing to comply with laws, regulations or the ethical standards or codes of conduct applicable to the enterprise industry. Compliance risk represents the potential for financial loss, sanctions or damage to reputation and brand value caused by a failure to comply with legal or regulatory requirements.

Examples of events that can cause compliance risk include:

- Failing to comply with laws or regulations
- Failing to adhere to ethical standards or codes of conduct applicable to the enterprise's industry

Understanding how these types of risk can affect an enterprise and how to assess risk is important to the risk management process.

Project Risk

Project risk is risk that the project will fail to meet its intended objectives and deliver results according to the project charter.

Even the smallest IT project can get very complex due to internal and external variables. An IT project has many inter-connected attributes and one small delay in one area can easily affect the entire initiative. In all projects, there are events that no one can predict. However, some adverse events are common and result in project risks that should be clear to an experienced risk manager and project manager.

1.2.2 Levels of Risk

Risk can exist at four levels within an enterprise, as shown in **figure 1.3**.

Figure 1.3—Levels of Risk

Source: ISACA, *IT Governance Domain Practices and Competencies: Information Risks: Whose Business Are They?*, USA, 2005, figure 1

Strategic Level

The strategic level is where choices are made about risk in relation to innovation and plans for delivering the business strategy. At the strategic level, it needs to be understood that accepting risk is an essential element of business today and success comes to those enterprises that detect, identify and manage risk most effectively.

The program, project and operational levels are concerned with delivery of the enterprise strategy.

Program and Project Level

The focus at the program and project levels is on medium-term goals to deliver the enterprise strategic objectives. These are the levels at which choices about risk are made. At any time during the life of a program, there may be circumstances or situations that can have a detrimental impact on the program. Such circumstances or situations are the risk and issues that the program must manage and resolve. Dealing with issues at the project level requires a program risk policy or a strategic-level risk policy to give overall guidance and direction on how risk should be managed.

Operational Level

The emphasis at the operational level is on short-term goals to ensure ongoing continuity of business services. The context of risk management varies significantly from the strategic (enterprise) level to the IT operations level. At a minimum, risk needs to be properly analyzed, even if no immediate action is taken, because the awareness of risk often influences strategic decisions for the better. Often, the most damaging I&T-related risk is one that is not well understood or communicated. At the operational level, risk management involves responding to the potential impact on the business, identifying the issues and making sure that the risk that has the highest likelihood and impact of occurring is being addressed.

1.3 I&T-related Risk

I&T-related risk is a part of overall business risk and is associated with the use, ownership, operation, involvement, influence and adoption of I&T within an enterprise. Most enterprises are highly dependent on their IT systems. The more an enterprise relies on its IT systems, the more serious the potential consequences of an I&T-related failure. An IT system failure can have a great impact on the business supported by the IT system.

1.3.1 I&T Risk Types

The I&T-related risk types include:

- I&T benefit/value enablement risk
- I&T program and project delivery risk
- I&T operations and service delivery risk
- Cyber and information security risk

The relationship between business/enterprise risk and I&T-related risk is depicted in **figure 1.4**.

Figure 1.4—I&T-related Risk Relative to Business/Enterprise Risk

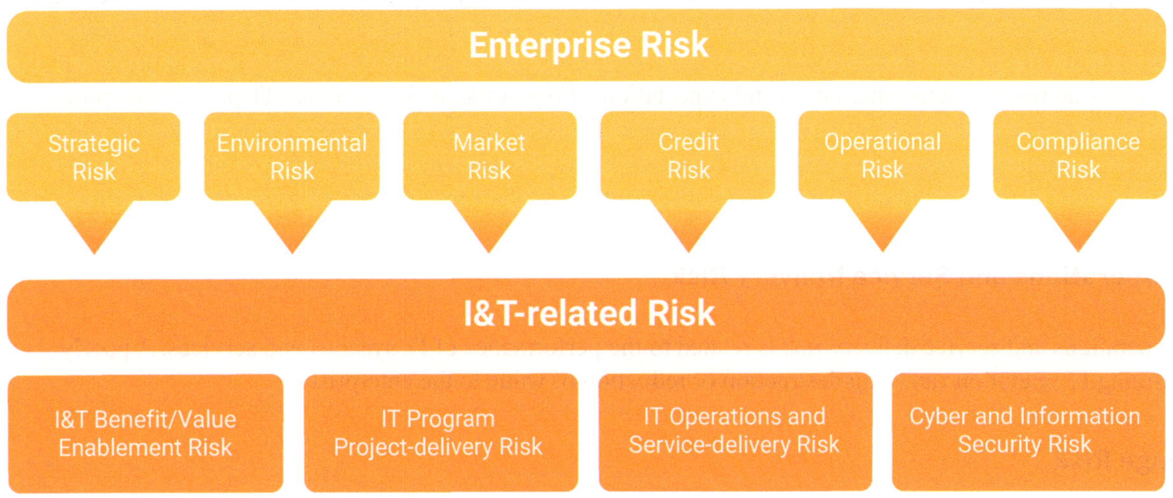

Source: ISACA, *Risk IT Framework, 2nd Edition*, USA, 2020, figure 1.1, *www.isaca.org/bookstore/bookstore-risk-digital/ritf2*

I&T Benefit/Value Enablement Risk

I&T benefit/value enablement risk refers to the opportunities to use technology to improve the efficiency or effectiveness of business processes or as an enabler for new business initiatives. Conversely, this I&T-related risk type also includes the risk of missing new business opportunities because of inadequate I&T-related capabilities. IT involvement is critical and can play different roles in the risk-opportunity relationship, as an enabler of value and as an impediment.

- **Value enabler**—New business initiatives almost always depend on some involvement of IT. In this role, IT can:
  - Enable successful I&T-related projects, support new initiatives and, thus, create value
  - Apply new technology in innovative ways, enable new business initiatives and create value
  - Protect assets and resources from threats that may impact delivery of products and services
- **Value impediment**—I&T-related activities and processes can result in an array of negative consequences, such as:
  - IT-enabled business projects or investments often fail to deliver expected results, so value is not delivered.
  - The enterprise may fail to identify or capture opportunities for new business initiatives arising from new technology.

I&T Program and Project Delivery Risk

I&T program and project delivery risk refers to the contribution of IT to new or improved business solutions, usually in the form of projects and programs.

Project Risk

Many projects fail; numerous studies of IT projects indicate that a majority of IT projects can be considered failures. Failure of a particular project may be defined as going over the allotted budget or the allotted time scheduled, or not delivering what the project promised. A project may also be deemed a failure if it delivers what it promised, but the deliverables do not meet customer needs and expectations. Project risk is from a failed IT project that poses a significant risk to an enterprise, manifesting as lost market share, failure to seize new opportunities or other adverse impacts on customers, shareholders and staff. Identifying the risk associated with a project and successfully managing that risk are very likely to result in higher levels of project success and stakeholder satisfaction.

I&T Operations and Service Delivery Risk

I&T operations and service delivery risk is related to the performance of IT systems and services. A poorly performing IT operation can bring destruction or reduction of value to the enterprise.

Change Risk

Risk is not static. Change risk is a change in technology, regulations, business processes, functionality, architecture, users and other variables that affect the enterprise business and technical environments and the levels of risk associated with systems in operation. For instance, when intentional changes are made to the configuration or architecture of a system, that change may result in controls that were originally effective as designed becoming ineffective.

Cyber and Information Security Risk

Cyber and information security risk is the danger, harm or loss related to the use of, or dependence on, information and communications technology, electronic data, and digital or electronic communications. Typically, the realization of cyber and information security risk involves unauthorized access and/or unauthorized use of information and communications technology.

I&T-related risk often arises at critical nodes between (or among) interconnected environments, including points of access to the Internet. These interconnections are vital to business and mission, and, therefore, often entail the most acute information security and cybersecurity risk.

1.3.2 Risk Standards and Guidance

Many authoritative risk management standards and guidance are available as sources of good practice for the management of I&T-related risk. These references are managed and published by authoritative bodies and kept current. They help to form a basis for a risk management program, but require an enterprise to tailor the practices to meet its specific enterprise goals. Among the most recognized risk management reference sources are:

- *ISACA Risk IT Framework, 2nd Edition*
- *Committee of Sponsoring Organizations of the Treadway Commission (COSO), Enterprise Risk Management — Integrated Framework*
- *International Organization for Standardization (ISO®)*
  - *ISO/IEC 27005:2018 Information technology — Security techniques — Information security risk management*
  - *ISO 31000: 2018 Risk Management — Guidelines*
  - *IEC 31010:2019 Risk Management —Risk Assessment Techniques*

- *National Institute of Standards and Technology (NIST) Special Publications (SPs)*
  - *SP 800-37 Revision 2: Risk Management Framework for Information Systems and Organizations: A System Life Cycle Approach for Security and Privacy*
  - *SP 800-39: Managing Information Security Risk*
  - *Framework for Improving Critical Infrastructure Cybersecurity*
- *Operationally Critical Threat, Asset and Vulnerability Evaluation (OCTAVE) Framework*

1.3.3 Risk IT Framework

An I&T risk framework is a useful reference for a comprehensive view of I&T-related risk to help understand and manage it. The ISACA *Risk IT Framework, 2nd Edition*[12] explains I&T-related risk and helps to:

- Identify current and emerging risk throughout the extended enterprise
- Develop appropriate operational capabilities to ensure that business processes continue operating through adverse events
- Leverage investments in compliance or internal control systems already in place to optimize I&T-related risk
- Recognize I&T-related risk that exceeds the scope of technical controls and IT-related tools and techniques to integrate into the risk management program
- Raise awareness of the balance between the benefits of technology and external partners (on the one hand), and the potential impact of cyberthreats, internal control failures, and risk introduced by vendors, suppliers and partners (on the other hand)
- Promote risk awareness, accountability and responsibility throughout the enterprise
- Frame I&T-related risk within a business context to understand aggregate exposure in terms of enterprise value
- Focus internal and external risk management resources to maximize enterprise objectives

1.3.4 Risk-Related Business Functions

Risk management is an all-encompassing, strategic requirement in any enterprise. Risk management requires the involvement of:

- Top executives and board members who set strategic direction and monitor risk at the enterprise level
- Managers of IT, OT and business departments who are responsible for day-to-day operational decision making and the integration of risk management processes into daily work
- Risk management professionals
- External stakeholders, such as clients, regulators, suppliers and partners

Many other functions within an enterprise are involved in the risk management process. These include but are not limited to:

- Business continuity
- Audit
- Information security

[12] *Op cit* ISACA, *Risk IT Framework, 2nd Edition*

Risk and Business Continuity

The management of I&T-related risk is closely linked with business continuity. This business function is concerned with the preservation of critical business functions and the ability of the enterprise to survive an adverse event that may impact the ability of the enterprise to meet its mission and goals. Through risk management, the enterprise attempts to reduce all I&T-related risk to an acceptable level. It is important that incident management and business continuity teams work together to identify possible threats and put in place the mechanism to detect, contain and recover from an adverse event. If the business continuity plan (BCP) is inadequate or inaccurate, the enterprise may not be able to meet its goals for recovery after an incident.

Risk and Audit

An audit is a formal inspection and verification to check whether a standard or set of guidelines is being followed, records are accurate, or efficiency and effectiveness targets are being met. An audit is a methodical and structured review that requires competence and knowledge in the subject matter of the area being audited. As such, an auditor must be familiar with the technology being used, the significance of operating conditions and the requirements of the enterprise.

The audit function is an important part of governance that provides management with assurance regarding the effectiveness of the control framework, risk management program and compliance efforts. An enterprise must diligently demonstrate an adequate control environment and risk management program. For that reason, audits should be conducted by objective, skilled and independent personnel able to assess risk, identify vulnerabilities, document findings and provide recommendations on how to address issues that are discovered.

Risk and Information Security

Risk management drives the selection of controls and justifies their initial and continued operation. If the management of I&T-related risk is not conducted properly, information security controls are almost certain to be incorrectly designed, poorly implemented and improperly operated. Every control should be traceable back to a specific I&T-related risk that the control is designed to mitigate.

1.3.5 Three Lines of Defense

The governance and management of I&T-related risk require an enterprise to establish a proper defense system comprising the three lines of defense.

- The first line of defense owns and manages risk. Within the first line of defense, control functions are established, such as IT control within the IT department.
- The second line of defense oversees risk and monitors controls. It is independent of the first line of defense and can challenge the effectiveness of controls and management of risk across the enterprise.
- The third line of defense is internal audit, which provides independent testing and assurance.

Figure 1.5 provides examples of the functions in the three lines of defense. These processes and/or the three lines of defense participate in the risk management process by identifying risk, gathering information and conducting tests and reviews.

Figure 1.5—Three Lines of Defense

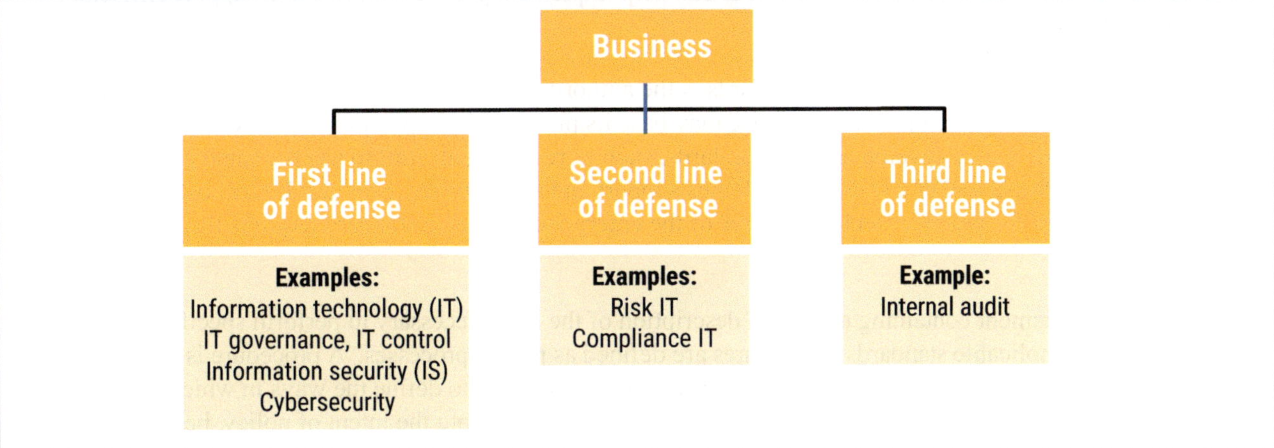

1.4 Controls

Controls are a means of responding to risk and are normally composed of processes, policies, procedures, practices, infrastructure, applications and organizational structures.

1.4.1 Policies, Standards and Procedures

A policy is a document that records a high-level principle or course of action that has been decided on. The intended purpose is to influence and guide present and future decision making to be in line with the philosophy, objectives and strategic plans that the enterprise management teams establish.

Policies empower risk management and should clearly state the position of senior management toward the protection of information, which allows the development of procedures, standards and baselines that reflect management priorities. Executive sponsorship also provides a mandate that all departments comply with policy requirements.

An enterprise may have several layers of policy to allow delegation of authority. A high-level policy may be issued by senior management as a way to address the objectives of the enterprise mission and vision statement. This overarching policy does not have a technical focus, which prevents the policy from becoming outdated when technology changes. High-level policy may direct compliance with laws and good practices, and is likely to state the goal of managing risk through protecting the enterprise assets, including the I&T systems that support business operations. High-level policies are instrumental in determining the approach of the enterprise toward risk management and acceptable levels of risk.

Technical and functional policies include specifics regarding technology use, such as remote access, acceptable use and passwords. These policies are subject to change as technology changes and new systems are developed.

Policies must be developed and communicated. If not, the enterprise has no means of enforcing standards of behavior, which increases the risk that the behavior that occurs may be inappropriate. A lack of enforcement may also lead to circumvention of controls or increased liability, because the enterprise recognizes the need for a policy but does not follow its own rules.

A standard is a requirement, code of practice or specification approved by a recognized external body, such as the International Organization for Standardization (ISO) or a regulatory agency. A standard mandates not only what must be done but also the way in which an enterprise must comply,[13] and organizations meeting the requirements of standards may be certified as compliant. Standards can help implement policy, limit risk and support efficient business operations.

Many enterprises believe that the value of standards is the authority and perception of excellence that they provide., which In lieu of formal certification, an enterprise may base its practices and operations on external standards such as an ISO standard, or it may develop its own standards, such as requiring all staff to use the same product, operating system or desktop. Proper use of a standard facilitates support and maintenance, provides better cost control, and provides authority for the practices and procedures of the enterprise because a standard requires the implementation of certain practices.

A procedure is a document containing a detailed description of the steps necessary to perform specific operations in conformance with applicable standards. Procedures are defined as part of processes. A procedure is more granular than standards and supports their implementation. Procedures are created to define the ways in which the processes should be carried out. Procedures are invaluable as a means of implementing the intent of policy, because they define the tasks that people perform. By defining actions in consistent and measurable ways, the enterprise can greatly increase the probability that an operation is conducted according to good practice and that any abnormal operations are detected. A lack of standards and procedures makes it difficult to carry out activities in a systematic manner and may result in undependable, inconsistent operations and elevated risk. Procedures should be published and used. It is common for procedures to be followed for only a short time, after which point, experienced staff begin to work from memory. This practice should be discouraged in any environment in which precision is important, such as shutdown procedures for power plants or industrial machinery, or complex monetary transactions.

1.4.2 Risk Relationship to Control

There is a direct relationship between risk and control that demonstrates that risk is addressed through control and control is justified by the risk it addresses. This relationship is shown in **figure 1.6**.

Figure 1.6—Risk in Relation to Control

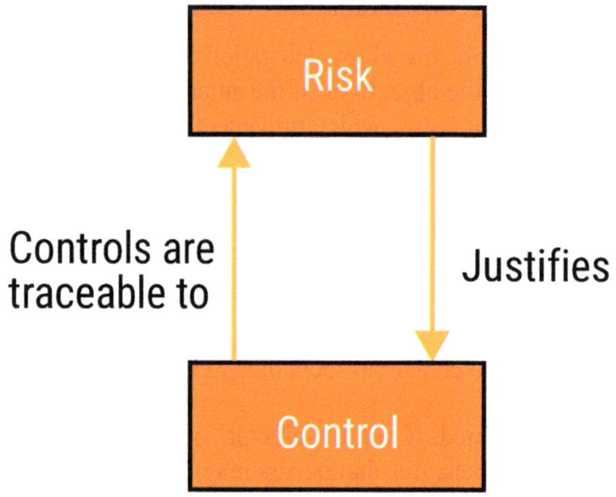

Source: ISACA, *CRISC Review Manual, 6th Edition*, USA, 2015, figure 1.30, *www.isaca.org/bookstore/crisc-exam-resources/crr6ed*

[13] Standards differ from frameworks, which state only what is to be accomplished and not how to do it.

Control Risk

A control is chosen to manage and mitigate risk. Control risk is risk to an enterprise from a control that is not operating correctly and may not prevent a failure or compromise. The selection of the wrong control, the incorrect configuration of the control, the improper operation of the control, the failure to monitor and review the control, or the inadequacy of the control to address new threats can introduce the risk of control failure. Control risk is discussed in more detail in Section 5.4 Risk States.

1.4.3 General Controls

It is important that an enterprise maintain a correct balance between technical, managerial (administrative) and physical control types (see **figure 1.7**).

Figure 1.7—Control Types

Category	Description
Managerial (administrative)	These are related to the oversight, reporting, procedures and operations of a process. These include controls such as policy, procedures, balancing, employee development and compliance reporting.
Technical	Technical controls are also known as logical controls and are provided through the use of a technology, piece of equipment or device. Examples of technical controls include firewalls, network or host-based intrusion detection systems (IDSs), passwords and antivirus software. A technical controls requires proper managerial (administrative) controls to operate correctly.
Physical	Physical controls are locks, fences, closed-circuit TV (CCTV) and devices that are installed to physically restrict access to a facility or hardware. Physical controls require maintenance.

Source: ISACA, *CISA Review Manual, 27th Edition*, USA, 2019, figure 5.4, *www.isaca.org/bookstore/cisa-exam-resources/crm27ed*

Implementation of a technical control, such as a firewall, requires training for the staff who manage or operate it, correct procedures for its configuration, assignment of responsibilities for its monitoring, and schedules for regular testing. If these coinciding controls are not in place, stakeholders may develop a false sense of security, resulting in unidentified vulnerabilities, an ineffective use of resources and greater risk than anticipated or intended.

Controls can be:

- **Preventive**—Preventive controls directly address risk.
- **Detective**—Detective controls warn of violations or attempted violations
- **Corrective**—Corrective controls remediate impact

If a control weakness exists, a compensating control should be implemented. Compensating controls are internal controls that reduce the risk of an existing or potential control weakness, resulting in errors and omissions.

The use of controls to mitigate and manage risk is described throughout this study guide. Specifically, the use of, and examples of preventive, detective, corrective and compensating controls is covered in Section 4.6 Control Assessment.

1.4.4 I&T Controls

General controls can be translated into I&T controls. A well-designed information system should have controls built in for all its sensitive or critical functions. For example, the general procedure to ensure that adequate safeguards over access to assets and facilities can be translated into an IT-related set of control procedures, covering access safeguards over computer programs, data and equipment.

I&T control procedures should include:[14]

- Strategy and direction of the IT function
- General organization and management of the IT function
- Access to IT resources, including data and programs
- Systems development methodologies and change control
- Operations procedures
- Systems programming and technical support functions
- Quality assurance (QA) procedures
- Physical access controls
- Business continuity planning/Disaster recovery planning
- Networks and communication technology (e.g., local area networks, wide area networks, wireless)
- Database administration
- Protection and detective mechanisms against internal and external attacks

I&T controls are in place to maintain information integrity and the security of information assets handled within business processes within an enterprise or its outsourced operation. I&T controls are generally classified as:

- Input
- Processing
- Output
- Application

Input Controls

Input controls are techniques and procedures used to verify, validate and edit data to ensure that only correct data are entered into the computer.

Input control procedures must ensure that every transaction to be processed is entered, processed and recorded accurately and completely. These controls should ensure that only valid and authorized information is input and these transactions are processed only once. These include machine and manual inputs.

[14] ISACA, *COBIT® 2019 Framework: Governance and Management Objectives,* USA, 2018, *www.isaca.org/bookstore/bookstore-cobit_19-digital/wcb19fgm,* also offers a complete and good overview of general IT controls.

Processing Controls

Processing controls (and procedures) are used to ensure the reliability of application program processing. Processing controls are meant to ensure the completeness and accuracy of accumulated data. They ensure that data in a file/database remain complete and accurate until changed as a result of authorized processing or modification routines.

Application Controls

Application controls are the policies, procedures and activities designed to provide reasonable assurance that objectives relevant to a given automated solution (application) are achieved. These controls help ensure data accuracy, completeness, validity, verifiability and consistency, thus achieving data integrity and data reliability. Implementation of these controls helps ensure that systems maintain integrity; applicable system functions operate as intended; and information contained by the system is relevant, reliable, secure and available when needed.

1.5 Summary of Terminology

It is important to recognize and understand I&T-related risk terminology. The following terms were introduced in this chapter (**figure 1.8**).

Figure 1.8— Chapter 1 Terminology

Term	Definition
Attack	An event or attempt to gain unauthorized access or use of an asset
Audit	A formal inspection and verification to check whether a standard or set of guidelines is being followed, records are accurate, or efficiency and effectiveness targets are being met
Business risk	Business risk is the probability a situation with uncertain frequency and magnitude of loss (or gain) that could prevent the enterprise from meeting its business objectives.
Change risk	A change in technology, regulation, business process, functionality, architecture, user and other variables that affect the enterprise business and technical environments and the level of risk associated with systems in operation
Compliance risk	The probability and consequences of an enterprise failing to comply with laws, regulations or the ethical standards or codes of conduct applicable to the enterprise's industry
Consequence	The magnitude of loss resulting from a threat exploiting a vulnerability (used interchangeably with impact)
Control	The means of managing risk, including policies, procedures, guidelines, practices or organizational structures
Credit risk	The potential that a borrower or creditor will fail to meet financial obligations in accordance with agreed terms
Cyber and information security risk	The danger, harm or loss related to the use of, or dependence on, information and communications technology, electronic data, and digital or electronic communications
Environmental risk	Threats to natural resources, human health and wildlife
Event	Something that happens at a specific place and/or time
Exploit	An event where the attacker takes advantage of a vulnerability

Figure 1.8— Chapter 1 Terminology *(cont.)*	
Term	**Definition**
Frequency	A measure of the rate by which events occur over a certain period of time
Incident	Any event that is not part of the ordinary operation of a service that causes, or may cause, an interruption to, or a reduction in, the quality of that service
Impact	Magnitude of loss resulting from a threat exploiting a vulnerability
I&T operations and service delivery risk	Risk related to the performance of IT systems and services. A poorly performing IT operation can bring destruction or reduction of value to the enterprise.
I&T-related risk	A part of overall business risk associated with the use, ownership, operation, involvement, influence and adoption of I&T within an enterprise
Likelihood	The probability of something happening
Magnitude	A measure of the potential severity of loss or the potential gain from realized events/scenarios
Market risk	Pressures on an asset class
Operational risk	The potential for losses caused by inadequate systems or controls, human error or mismanagement and natural disasters
Policy	A document that records a high-level principle or course of action that has been decided on
Probability	A mathematically driven measure of the possibility of a specific outcome as a ratio of all possible outcomes
Procedure	A document containing a detailed description of the steps necessary to perform specific operations in conformance with applicable standards
Project risk	A failed IT project that poses a significant risk to an enterprise, manifesting as lost market share, failure to seize new opportunities or other adverse impacts on customers, shareholders and staff
Risk	The combination of the likelihood of an event and its impact
Standard	A mandatory requirement, code of practice or specification approved by a recognized external standards organization
Strategic risk	The risk associated with an enterprise's future business plans and strategies
Threat	Anything that is capable of acting against an asset in a manner that can result in harm. Threats are aimed at exploiting enterprise vulnerabilities.
Threat agent	Methods and things used to exploit a vulnerability.
Uncertainty	The difficulty of predicting an outcome due to limited knowledge of all components
Vulnerability	Control condition that is deemed to be deficient relative to requirements of the threat levels being faced by the enterprise. Vulnerabilities represent a weakness in the design, implementation, operation or internal control of a process that could expose the system to adverse threats from threat events.

Chapter 1 Knowledge Check

Review questions are provided as a means to support the content presented within this study guide and serve as a gauge or assessment of knowledge of I&T-related risk topics. One question is provided for each topic.

For individuals intending to earn the ISACA IT Risk Fundamentals Certificate, these questions are written to depict the type of questions that may appear on the exam. These questions will not specifically appear on the exam, but similar ones may appear.

REVIEW QUESTIONS

1. Which of the following statements **BEST** describes the relationship between threats and vulnerabilities?

   A. Threats are aimed to exploit vulnerabilities.
   B. Threats and vulnerabilities both represent control weaknesses.
   C. Threats are initiated externally, while vulnerabilities exist internally.

2. The risk of a sudden and impactful change in customer preferences for an enterprise's core products is a primary example of:

   A. Strategic risk
   B. Operational risk
   C. Market risk

3. Which of the following I&T-risk related activities is part of the second line of defense within a good governance structure?

   A. Establishing I&T controls to mitigate risk
   B. Monitoring I&T control effectiveness
   C. Managing I&T-related risk

4. Which of the following documents empowers risk management and clearly describes how IT will be governed and managed within an enterprise?

   A. IT standard
   B. IT procedure
   C. IT policy

Answers on page 38

Chapter 1 ANSWER KEY

Review Questions

1. **A. Threats are aimed at exploiting enterprise vulnerabilities, which are control conditions that are deemed to be deficient relative to requirements of the threat levels being faced by the enterprise.**
   B. Vulnerabilities alone are control conditions that are deemed to be deficient relative to requirements of the threat levels being faced by the enterprise.
   C. Threats can be external or internal, while vulnerabilities exist within IT systems.

2. **A. Strategic risk involves an enterprise's future business plans and strategies. A sudden and impactful change in customer preferences for an enterprise's core products would represent a risk to these future plans and strategies, either positively or negatively.**
   B. Operational risk represents the potential for losses caused by inadequate systems or controls, human error or mismanagement, and natural disasters. Although a sudden and impactful change in customer preferences for an enterprise's core products can be caused by mismanagement, this type of event is most associated with strategic risk.
   C. Market risk results from pressures on an asset class, such as financial assets, property and equity assets. Although a sudden and impactful change in customer preferences for an enterprise's core products can result in a financial hardship, it is not typically associated with this type of risk.

3. A. Establishing I&T controls, such as IT control within the IT department, is part of the first line of defense, which is responsible for owning and managing risk.
   B. The second line of defense oversees risk and monitors I&T-related controls. It is independent of the first line of defense and can challenge the effectiveness of controls and management of risk across the enterprise.
   C. The ownership and management of I&T-related risk takes place within the first line of defense. As described in the explanation to choice A, this is also where I&T-related controls are established.

4. A. An IT standard is a mandatory requirement, code of practice or specification. IT standards are implemented to comply with the requirements and direction of an IT policy to limit risk and support efficient business operations.
   B. An IT procedure is a document containing a detailed description of the steps necessary to perform specific operations in conformance with applicable standards. IT procedures are invaluable as a means of implementing the intent of an IT policy, A lack of IT standards and IT procedures makes it difficult to carry out activities in a systematic manner and may result in undependable, inconsistent operations and elevated risk.
   C. An IT policy represents a high-level principle or course of action that has been decided on. IT policies empower risk management and should clearly state the position of senior management toward the protection of information, which allows the development of procedures, standards and baselines that reflect management priorities.

Chapter 2:

Risk Governance and Management

Learning Objectives 40

Risk Governance and Management

2.1 Risk Governance 41
2.2 Risk Management 43
2.3 Positioning Risk 49
2.4 Risk Stakeholders, Roles and Culture 52
2.5 Risk Communication, Policy, Scope and Workflow 59
2.6 Summary of Terminology 65

Chapter 2 Knowledge Check 67

Learning Objectives

This chapter explains the elements and structures of risk governance and management, and how risk is embraced and treated within an enterprise. Risk appetite, risk tolerance and risk capacity are described, and risk roles, culture and communication are presented. Risk scope is also discussed and a risk management process workflow is introduced.

Learning objectives include the following:

- Articulate the purpose, objectives and importance of risk governance and risk management.
- Summarize how risk management fits within an enterprise governance strategy.
- Explain how an enterprise decides the amount of risk it is willing to accept (risk appetite, tolerance and capacity).
- Describe the structure, roles and responsibilities of risk stakeholders.
- Summarize the risk management process and workflow.

Risk Governance and Management

2.1 Risk Governance

Governance ensures that:

- Stakeholder needs, conditions and options are evaluated to determine balanced, agreed-on enterprise objectives
- Direction is set through prioritization and decision making
- Performance and compliance are monitored against agreed-on direction and objectives

In most enterprises, overall governance is the responsibility of the board of directors, under the leadership of the chairperson. Specific governance responsibilities may be delegated to special enterprise structures at an appropriate level, particularly in larger, complex enterprises.

2.1.1 Governance Objectives

The objective of any governance system is to enable an enterprise to create value for its stakeholders or to promote value creation. Value creation, in turn, comprises:

- Benefits realization
- Risk optimization
- Resource optimization

Benefits Realization

Benefits realization consists of creating value for the enterprise through I&T, maintaining and increasing value derived from existing I&T investments, and eliminating IT initiatives and assets that are not creating sufficient value. The basic principle of I&T value are delivery of fit-for-purpose services and solutions, on time and within budget, that generate the intended financial and nonfinancial benefits. The value that I&T delivers should be aligned directly with the values on which the business is focused. IT value should also be measured in a way that shows the impact and contributions of IT-enabled investments in the value creation process of the enterprise.

Risk Optimization

Risk optimization involves addressing the business risk associated with the use, ownership, operation, involvement, influence and adoption of I&T within an enterprise. I&T-related business risk consists of I&T-related events that could potentially impact the business. While value delivery focuses on the creation of value, risk management focuses on the preservation of value. The management of I&T-related risk should be integrated within the enterprise risk management approach to ensure a focus on IT by the enterprise. It should also be measured in a way that shows the impact and contributions of optimizing I&T-related business risk on preserving value. Risk optimization is an essential part of any governance system and cannot be seen in isolation from benefits realization or resource optimization.

Resource Optimization

Resource optimization ensures that the appropriate capabilities are in place to execute the strategic plan and sufficient, appropriate and effective resources are provided. Resource optimization ensures that an integrated, economical IT infrastructure is provided, new technology is introduced as required by the business, and obsolete systems are updated or replaced. Because it recognizes the importance of people, in addition to hardware and software, it focuses on providing training, promoting retention and ensuring competence of key IT personnel. An important resource is data and information, and exploiting data and information to gain optimal value is another key element of resource optimization.

2.1.2 Risk Governance Objectives

Risk governance:

- Sets the direction and strategy of risk management efforts
- Defines risk culture and acceptable levels of risk
- Makes risk-aware business decisions
- Ensures that the risk management function is operating effectively to identify, manage, monitor and report on current and potential risk facing the enterprise

Risk governance ensures that:

- Stakeholder needs, conditions and options are evaluated to determine balanced, agreed-on enterprise objectives to be achieved.
- Direction is set through prioritization and decision making.
- Performance, compliance and progress are monitored against agreed-on direction and objectives.

In most enterprises, risk governance is the responsibility of the board of directors under the leadership of the chairperson, as shown in **figure 2.1**.

Figure 2.1—Risk Governance

Source: ISACA, *Risk IT Practitioner Guide, 2nd Edition*, USA, 2020, figure 3.1, *https://www.isaca.org/bookstore/bookstore-risk-digital/ritpg2*

Good risk governance means that risk optimization is part of the arrangements that are put in place, and risk information is included in the decision-making process. At the same time, the risk function needs to be governed, i.e., provided with direction and monitored. Effective risk governance helps ensure that risk management practices are embedded in the enterprise, enabling it to secure optimal risk-adjusted return.

Figure 2.2 describes the four main objectives of risk governance.

Figure 2.2—Risk Governance Objectives

Objective	Description
1. Establish and maintain a common risk view.	Effective risk governance establishes the common view of risk for the enterprise. This determines which controls are necessary to mitigate risk and how risk-based controls are integrated into business processes and information security. The risk governance function sets the tone of the business regarding how to determine an acceptable level of risk tolerance. Risk governance is a continuous life cycle that requires regular reporting and ongoing review. The risk governance function must oversee the operations of the risk management team.
2. Integrate risk management into the enterprise.	Integrating risk management into the enterprise enforces a holistic enterprise risk management (ERM) approach across the entire enterprise. It requires the integration of risk management into every department, function, system and geographic location. Understanding that risk in one department or system may pose an unacceptable risk to another department or system requires that all business processes be compliant with a baseline level of risk management. The objective of ERM is to establish the authority to require all business processes to undergo a risk analysis on a periodic basis or when there is a significant change to the internal or external environment.
3. Make risk-aware business decisions.	To make risk-aware business decisions, the risk governance function must consider the full range of opportunities and consequences of each such decision and its impact on the enterprise, society and the environment.
4. Ensure that risk management controls are implemented and operating correctly.	Governance requires oversight and due diligence to ensure that the enterprise is following up on the implementation and monitoring of controls to ensure that the controls are effective to mitigate risk and protect organizational assets.
Source: ISACA, *CRISC Review Manual, 6th Edition*, USA, 2015, figure 0.2, *www.isaca.org/bookstore/crisc-exam-resources/crr6ed*	

2.2 Risk Management

The governing board should ensure there is a risk management process. Managers require accurate information to be able to correctly understand risk and address circumstances that indicate the need for a risk response.

There is a clear distinction between governance and management. Management focuses on planning, building, running and monitoring activities in alignment with the direction set by the governance body to create value by achieving objectives. A well-managed enterprise that is subject to poor governance creates and executes clear, effective plans to attain objectives that do not create value. Similarly, risk management foresees the challenges to achieving objectives and attempts to lower the probabilities of negative outcomes occurring and/or their impacts if they do occur, but the effectiveness of risk management depends in large part on decisions made by managers who are responsible for risk governance.

2.2.1 Risk Management Overview

Risk management encompasses the coordinated activities to direct and control an enterprise with regard to risk. Risk can be viewed as a challenge to achieving objectives, and risk management as the activity undertaken to predict challenges and lower their chances of occurring and/or their impact. Effective risk management can also assist in maximizing opportunities. For example, a risk decision can take the form of potential benefits that may accrue if opportunities are taken, versus missed benefits if those same opportunities are foregone.

The dual nature of risk is a result of its use in different contexts by business and IT, and it is not always easy to draw the distinction.

Risk management starts with understanding the enterprise and the environment in which it operates. This understanding includes evaluating the:

- Intentional and unintentional threats and capabilities
- Relative value of assets or resources, and the trust that must be placed in them
- Presence and extent of vulnerabilities that might be exploited to intercept, interrupt, modify or fabricate data in information assets
- Intentional and intentional human errors
- Acts of nature

Other factors that must be evaluated include the:

- Dependency of the enterprise on a supply chain, especially one based in another geographic region or reliant on just-in-time delivery
- Influences of financing, debt, and partners or substantial stakeholders
- Susceptibility to changes in economic or political conditions
- Susceptibility to changes in market trends and patterns
- Emergence of new competition
- Impact of new legislation
- Existence of potential natural disasters or events
- Constraints caused by legacy systems and antiquated technology
- Likelihood of strained labor relations and inflexible management

2.2.2 I&T Risk Governance and Management

I&T risk governance and management is the implementation of a risk strategy that:

- Reflects the culture, appetite and tolerance levels of enterprise management
- Considers technology and budgets
- Addresses the requirements of regulation and compliance

An effective I&T risk management strategy is critical to the enterprise ability to effectively and efficiently execute its overall business strategy. Any I&T-related risk that jeopardizes the enterprise business or mission should be managed from the perspective of overall enterprise objectives and should (see **figure 2.3**):

- Connect management of I&T-related risk to business or mission objectives.
- Align the management of I&T business or mission risk with ERM when possible.
- Balance the costs and benefits of managing I&T-related risk.
- Promote ethical and open communication of all I&T-related risk
- Establish the tone at the top, while defining and enforcing personal accountability for operating within acceptable and well-defined tolerance levels.
- Use a consistent approach, integrated into daily activities, that is standard, repeatable and aligned to strategy.

Figure 2.3—I&T Risk Management Principles

Source: ISACA, *COBIT® 5 for Risk*, USA, 2013, figure 15, *www.isaca.org/bookstore/cobit-5/wcb5rk*

Connect to Enterprise Business or Mission

I&T risk governance and management should connect to business or mission objectives, which means that:

- I&T-related risk, including cyberrisk, is treated as a business risk, not as a separate type of risk, and the approach to management is comprehensive and cross-functional.
- Governance of I&T-related risk contributes to business or mission outcomes. I&T supports the achievement of business objectives, and any associated risk is expressed in terms of the impact and probability it may have on business objectives or strategy. Analysis of I&T-related risk considers the connection between business processes and supporting I&T assets, applications or infrastructure, and/or third-party dependencies.
- I&T risk management, including practices in information security and cybersecurity, strives to advance the business or mission, rather than limit or inhibit it.

Align with Enterprise Risk Management

The effective enterprise governance of I&T-related risk aligns its management with overall enterprise risk management (ERM), which means that:

- Business or mission objectives and risk appetite are clearly defined.
- Enterprise decision-making processes consider the full range of potential consequences and opportunities from I&T-related risk.
- The defined and stated risk appetite reflects the enterprise risk management policy and tone at the top, and influences the culture of the enterprise.
- I&T-related risk assessment is coordinated and consolidated across the enterprise (e.g., across information security and cybersecurity).

Balance Costs and Benefits

The effective enterprise governance of I&T-related risk balances its costs and benefits, which means that:

- I&T-related risk is prioritized and addressed in line with risk appetite and risk tolerance. Risk appetite and risk tolerance are described in Section 2.3.
- Risk responses are implemented on the basis of cost/benefit analysis, analysis of alternatives and prioritization of risk that has the greatest potential impact on enterprise objectives.
- Existing controls and risk response actions are leveraged to address risk as efficiently as possible.

Promote Ethical and Open Communication

The effective management of I&T-related risk promotes ethical and open communication, which means that:

- Open, accurate, timely and transparent information on I&T-related risk is freely exchanged and informs risk-related decisions.
- Risk culture and risk management methods are integrated across the enterprise.
- Technical findings are translated into relevant and understandable business and financial terms.
- Information about an incident and the associated response is communicated openly to stakeholders, government and/or regulatory authorities, customers, and (as necessary) the public.

Establish Tone at the Top and Accountability

The effective management of I&T-related risk establishes an engaged tone from the top while defining and enforcing personal accountability for operating within acceptable and well-defined tolerance levels, which means that:

- Business owners, the board of directors and executive leadership are engaged in risk management.
- There is clear accountability and assignment of risk ownership.
- Risk assumptions are understood and supported by appropriate business leaders and are clearly stated in documentation of risk appetite, tolerances, culture, policies and guidelines for enforcement.
- Risk management performance is measured and integrated into the performance management of those accountable and responsible.
- Risk-aware culture and personal responsibility are promoted.
- Risk-informed decisions are made at the right level in the enterprise, by authorized individuals, in line with tolerances.
- Risk management practices are appropriately prioritized and embedded into enterprise decision making.

Consistent Approach Aligned to Strategy

The effective management of I&T risk promotes continuous improvement and is part of daily activities, which means that:

- The dynamic nature of risk requires the enterprise to prepare by giving advance consideration to changes in:
  - The enterprise itself (mergers and acquisitions)
  - Risk landscape
  - Applicable laws and regulations
  - Information and technology, as they evolve
  - The industry at large
- Risk assessment methods, scales of measurement and criteria are consistent across the enterprise, especially as applied to:
  - Identification of key processes and associated risk
  - Identification of impacts on objectives
  - Identification of triggers that indicate when risk is out of tolerance, when an update of the framework or components in the framework are required, etc.
  - Monitoring and testing of operating controls
  - Actions to prevent risk from materializing
  - Risk response (if adverse events occur)
  - Identification and, to the extent possible, mitigation of assessor bias in the quantitative risk measurement process

2.2.3 Risk Universe

Managing I&T-related risk requires defining the boundaries of the enterprise risk universe. The risk universe:

- Encompasses the overall risk environment
- Defines the areas that risk management activities address
- Provides a structure for I&T-related risk management

The risk universe (see **figure 2.4**):

- Considers the overall mission and the enterprise objectives, business processes and their dependencies throughout the enterprise. Identification of I&T dependencies aids in understanding the risk that cut across different functions and operations of the enterprise.
- Describes the I&T components, processes, assets and infrastructure that support the business and mission objectives.
- Understands that I&T-related risk involves IT operations, project management, application development, disaster recovery, security, etc.
- Describes risk in a complete and comprehensive language so that risk can be viewed from an end-to-end business or mission perspective.
- Considers the full value chain of the enterprise (subsidiaries, business units, clients, suppliers and service providers)
- Views all I&T-related business activities, including transformation programs, investments, projects and operations
- Includes a logical and workable segmentation of the overall risk landscape in which the enterprise operates (e.g., business units and subunits; business processes or services; geographic locations; technology types, i.e., internal IT function versus cloud components; and other areas where there may be an opportunity to align differing views across the enterprise).
- Aligns the strategic planning of the enterprise with the identification of the risk types that have the greatest impact on meeting the business strategy and objectives
- Requires regular reviewing and updating to navigate the constantly changing internal and external environment.
- Is influenced by the business climate or geopolitical environment in which the enterprise operates

Figure 2.4—Risk Universe

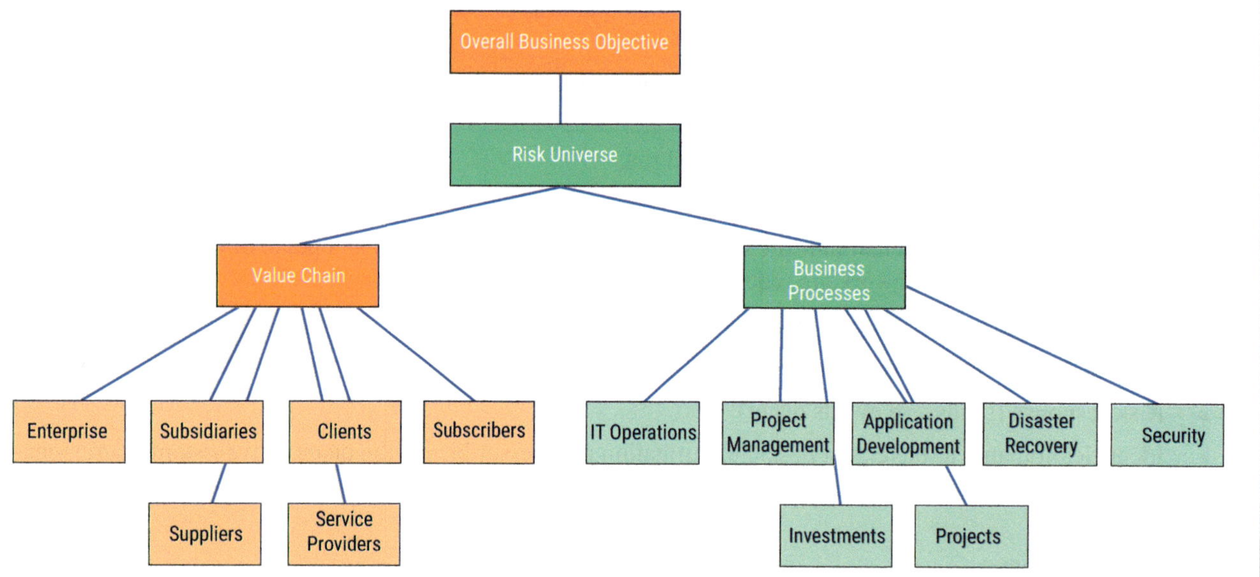

The value chain of an enterprise is the sequential set of primary and support activities performed by an enterprise to turn inputs into value-added outputs for its external customers. The risk universe should include value chain activities (see **figure 2.5**).

Figure 2.5—Value Chain

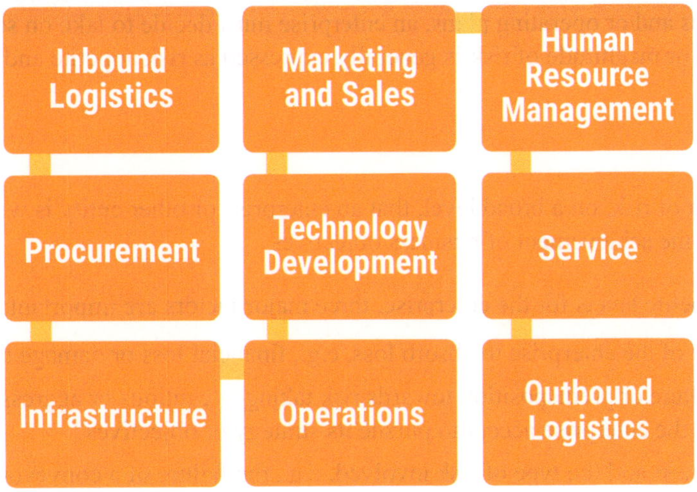

Value chain activities include:

- **Inbound logistics**—Activities that facilitate receiving and storing materials from external sources
- **Procurement**—Processes by which an enterprise acquires resources (e.g., sourcing and negotiating with materials suppliers)
- **Infrastructure**—Concerned with a wide range of support systems and functions (e.g., finance, planning, quality control, general senior management, etc.)
- **Operations**—The manufacture of products and services; the processes by which the enterprise converts resource inputs (e.g., materials) to outputs (e.g., products)
- **Technology development**—Activities concerned with managing information processing and the development and protection of knowledge in an enterprise
- **Marketing and sales**—An information activity; informing buyers and consumers about products and services (e.g., benefits, use, price)
- **Human resource management**—Recruiting, developing, motivating and rewarding the workforce of an enterprise
- **Service**—Activities associated with maintaining a product, following its sale
- **Outbound logistics**—Activities associated with transferring finished goods and services to buyers

2.3 Positioning Risk

Before an enterprise can begin to govern and manage risk, the enterprise must position risk in the context of the enterprise mission, strategy and objectives. Pairing a risk-based approach with a strategic view of the enterprise enables communication and clarification of the risk (uncertainties) that has the highest potential to prevent the enterprise from meeting its intended targets, objectives and mission.

Establishing the criteria against which the identified risk is evaluated is an important part of the overall risk management process. The development of risk appetite and risk tolerances can assist in quickly evaluating and understanding the risk that is in alignment with risk appetite and the risk that may need further analysis or investigation to make that determination.

2.3.1 Risk Appetite, Risk Tolerance and Risk Capacity

When developing strategies and/or operating plans, an enterprise must decide to take on some level of risk to achieve its objectives. The amount or magnitude of risk is generally expressed as risk appetite and risk tolerance.

Risk Appetite

Risk appetite is the amount of risk, on a broad level, that an enterprise or other entity is willing to accept in pursuit of its mission (or vision) and the achievement of business objectives.

When considering risk appetite levels for the enterprise, three major factors are important:

- The objective capacity of the enterprise to absorb loss, e.g., financial loss or damage to reputation.
- The (management) culture or predisposition towards risk taking— cautious or aggressive. What amount or magnitude of loss will the enterprise accept to pursue its strategy or objectives?
- The nature of the business and the type of risk involved, e.g., the failure of a conveyor belt system in a candy factory vs. the failure of a flight-control system on a commercial airliner

Risk appetite is different in each enterprise, and there is no absolute norm or standard of what constitutes acceptable and unacceptable risk.

Risk appetite is presented in a risk statement. A risk statement is a description of the current conditions that may lead to the loss; and a description of the loss.[15] For risk to be understandable, it must be expressed clearly. Such a treatment must include a description of the current conditions that may lead to a loss; and a description of the loss.

Risk statements that are too broad, are difficult to cascade down through the enterprise as management directives and should be avoided. Risk statements should also avoid absolute prohibitions on risk, such as:

- "The enterprise will not accept the risk of noncompliance."
- "The enterprise will not accept I&T-related risk."

Absolute prohibitions on risk are impossible to maintain and therefore impractical. Under such a prohibition against risk, every control deficiency is fixed, and every business endeavor with risk is declined. In practice, this approach is not a productive or efficient use of resources. Instead, enterprises should attempt to determine a loss amount that is acceptable and manage to that amount.

An example of a more practical, concrete, quantified risk appetite statement follows:

> *Although the enterprise desires to have no appetite for I&T risk, it recognizes that this is impractical in the achievement of its objectives. Therefore, the enterprise will remediate loss scenarios whereby aggregate losses of $1 million or more are at risk.*

Large enterprises may find it useful to have a risk appetite statement for each line of business or business risk type. However, a risk appetite statement that covers the entire enterprise should reflect (or aggregate) all the line-of-business or business risk type statements.

[15] Software Engineering Institute (SEI) cited in the ISACA Glossary

Every enterprise must define its own risk appetite levels and review them on a regular basis. Risk appetite should align with the overall risk culture that the enterprise wants to express (i.e., ranging from very risk averse to risk taking/opportunity seeking). Although there is no universal right or wrong, risk appetite needs to be defined, well understood and communicated throughout the enterprise.

When evaluating, testing and improving risk appetite statements over time an enterprise should consider the following:

- Are the management and governance entities of the enterprise aligned on the business outcomes that are unacceptable to the enterprise? What is the process to periodically evaluate the enterprise risk appetite statements if there are significant changes in its business, mission, or other conditions?
- Are unacceptable outcomes clear and communicated to everyone in the enterprise who needs to know? Is there a clear distinction between the types of risk that the enterprise is willing to accept versus those to avoid?
- Are processes in place that allow a potential risk or concern to be raised before a negative event occurs? Are reviews conducted to determine the effectiveness of the enterprise process for identifying, assessing, and reporting risk in relation to the stated risk appetite?
- Do the people on the front line of the enterprise know the boundaries, parameters, control limits, or other constraints on risk-taking decisions for their role? In many businesses, there are upper and lower limits on decision making that are integrated into the workflow that assist in making sure the optimal risk appetite is maintained.
- Are there published financial loss limits, regulatory compliance, business interruption, operational performance, life, health, or safety impacts that are clearly defined and communicated? Do these published limits exist for information security, cybersecurity, technology, events or incidents?

Risk Tolerance

Risk tolerance is the acceptable level of variation that management is willing to allow for any particular risk as the enterprise pursues its objectives. Risk tolerance is the acceptable deviation from the level set by the risk appetite and business objectives.

Risk appetite and tolerance are defined at the enterprise level, reviewed and/or influenced by the board of directors, and reflected in strategy and policies set by executives. At lower (tactical) levels of the enterprise, or perhaps within certain enterprise entities or subsidiaries, exceptions can be tolerated (or different thresholds defined), as long as overall exposure at the enterprise level does not exceed the determined risk appetite. Any business initiative includes a risk component, so management should have discretion to pursue new opportunities in the context of risk. Enterprises that have a conservative risk appetite and tolerance policies can lack the agility or innovation to exploit new business opportunities. Conversely, risk appetite and tolerance policies can be dictated by legal, regulatory or industry requirements, and it may be appropriate to have no risk tolerance for failure to meet such mandates.

Risk appetite and tolerances should be defined, reviewed and updated periodically (as determined by the enterprise), and clearly communicated to all stakeholders. New market conditions, changing risk landscape, revised strategy and many other factors require the enterprise to reconfirm its risk appetite at regular intervals, triggering risk policy reviews. In this respect, the enterprise should understand that risk management can provide value to the enterprise by allowing it to pursue risk-inclusive strategies and optimize allocation of resources. Risk appetite and risk tolerance should be applied to all I&T-related decision making.

Risk Capacity

Risk capacity is typically defined as the objective magnitude or amount of loss that an enterprise can tolerate without risking its continued existence. As such, it differs from risk appetite, which generally reflects a board or management decision regarding how much risk is desirable, as illustrated in **figure 2.6**.

Figure 2.6—Risk Capacity, Risk Appetite and Actual Risk

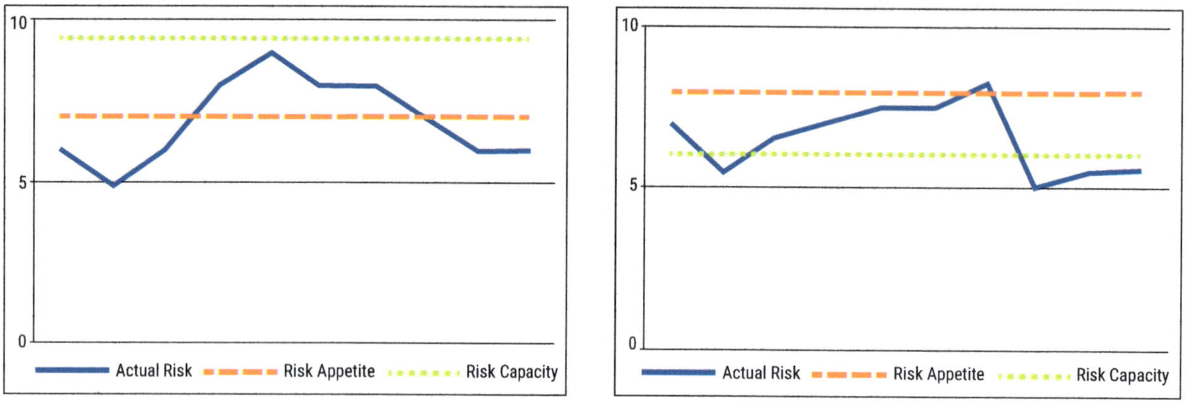

Source: ISACA, *COBIT® 5 for Risk*, USA, 2013, figure 68, *www.isaca.org/bookstore/cobit-5/wcb5rk*

- The left diagram shows a relatively sustainable situation in which risk appetite is lower than risk capacity, and actual risk exceeds risk appetite in several situations, but always remains below the risk capacity.
- The right diagram shows a rather unsustainable situation, where risk appetite is defined by management at a level beyond risk capacity. Management is prepared to accept risk well over the objective capacity to absorb loss. As a result, actual risk routinely exceeds risk capacity, despite remaining below the risk appetite level most of the time.

Defining risk capacity and risk appetite at the enterprise level has benefits that include:

- Supporting and providing evidence of the risk-based decision-making processes
- Supporting the understanding of how each component of the enterprise contributes to the overall risk profile
- Showing how different resource allocation strategies can add to or lessen the burden of risk by simulating different risk response options
- Supporting the prioritization and approval process of risk response actions through risk budgets
- Identifying specific areas where a risk response should be made

2.4 Risk Stakeholders, Roles and Culture

2.4.1 I&T Risk Management Stakeholders

To be effective, an I&T-related risk management effort should hold as its principal goal the protection of the enterprise and its ability to meet its business objectives. To this end, I&T-related risk management must consider IT as an integrated component of the enterprise and target the protection of all assets and processes, not just those belonging to IT.

A stakeholder is anyone who has a responsibility for, an expectation from, or some other interest in, the enterprise. Stakeholders protect enterprise assets and their value, and minimize risk by establishing control objectives and establishing controls in an effort to achieve the business objectives of the enterprise. A control objective is a statement of the desired result or purpose to be achieved by implementing control procedures in a particular process.

Stakeholders in the I&T risk management process include business management who determine what IT needs to do to support their business. This includes enterprise roles, business-line leaders and support functions (see **figure 2.7**).

Figure 2.7—I&T Risk Management Stakeholders

Across enterprises, the stakeholders for I&T risk management may differ in name and structure. **Figure 2.8** describes typical enterprise roles that are involved in the management of I&T-related risk.

Figure 2.8—Stakeholders for I&T Risk Management

Role/Structure	Description
Board of Directors	Group of the most senior executives and/or nonexecutive directors accountable for governance and overall control of enterprise resources
Executive Committee	Group of senior executives appointed by the board to ensure that the board is involved in, and kept informed of, major decisions. (The executive committee is accountable for managing the portfolios of I&T-enabled investments and I&T-related services and assets, ensuring the value is delivered, and managing risk. The committee is normally chaired by a board member.)
Chief Executive Officer (CEO)	Highest-ranking officer charged with the total management of the enterprise
Chief Financial Officer (CFO)	Most senior official accountable for all aspects of financial management, including financial risk and controls and reliable and accurate accounts.
Chief Operating Officer (COO)	Most senior official accountable for operation of the enterprise
Chief Risk Officer (CRO)	Most senior official accountable for all aspects of risk management across the enterprise (An I&T risk officer function may be established to oversee I&T-related risk.)
Chief Information Officer (CIO)	Most senior official responsible for aligning IT and business strategies and accountable for planning, resourcing and managing delivery of I&T-related services and solutions.

Figure 2.8—Stakeholders for I&T Risk Management *(cont.)*	
Role/Structure	Description
Chief Technology Officer (CTO)	Most senior official tasked with technical aspects of I&T, including managing and monitoring decisions related to I&T services, solutions and infrastructures. (This role may be assumed by the CIO.)
Chief Digital Officer (CDO)	Most senior official tasked with putting into practice the digital ambition of the enterprise or business unit. (This role may be assumed by the CIO or another member of the executive committee.)
I&T Governance Board	Group of stakeholders and experts accountable for guiding I&T-related matters and decisions, including managing IT-enabled investments, delivering value and monitoring risk
Architecture Board	Group of stakeholders and experts accountable for guiding enterprise-related matters and decisions and for setting architectural policies and standards
Enterprise Risk Committee	Group of executives accountable for enterprise-level collaboration and consensus required to support enterprise risk management (ERM) activities and decisions (An I&T risk council may be established to consider I&T-related risk in more detail and advise the enterprise risk committee.)
Chief Information Security Officer (CISO)	Most senior official accountable for all aspects of security management across the enterprise
Business Process Owner	Individual accountable for performing processes and/or realizing process objectives, driving process improvement and approving process changes
Portfolio Manager	Individual responsible for guiding portfolio management, ensuring selection of correct programs and projects, managing and monitoring programs and projects for optimal value, and realizing long-term strategic objectives effectively and efficiently
Steering Committee (Programs/Projects)	Group of stakeholders and experts accountable for guiding programs and projects, including managing and monitoring plans, allocating resources, delivering benefits and value, and managing program and project risk
Program Manager	Individual responsible for guiding a specific program (including articulating and following up on goals and objectives of the program) and managing risk and impact on the business
Project Manager	Individual responsible for guiding a specific project, including coordinating and delegating time, budget, resources and tasks across the project team
Project Management Office	Function responsible for supporting program and project managers and for gathering, assessing and reporting information about the conduct of programs and constituent projects
Data Management Function	Function responsible for supporting enterprise data assets across the data life cycle and managing data strategy, infrastructure and repositories
Head Human Resources	Most senior official accountable for planning and policies regarding human resources in the enterprise
Relationship Manager	Senior individual responsible for overseeing and managing the internal interface and communications between business and I&T functions
Head Architect	Senior individual accountable for the enterprise architecture process
Head Development	Senior individual accountable for the I&T-related solution development process
Head IT Operations	Senior individual accountable for IT operational environments and infrastructure
Head IT Administration	Senior individual accountable for I&T-related records and responsible for supporting I&T-related administrative matters

Figure 2.8—Stakeholders for I&T Risk Management *(cont.)*	
Role/Structure	Description
Service Manager	Individual who manages the development, implementation, evaluation and ongoing maintenance of new and existing products and services for a specific customer (user) or group of customers (users)
Information Security Manager	Individual who manages, designs, oversees and/or assesses an enterprise's information security
Business Continuity Manager	Individual who manages, designs, oversees and/or assesses an enterprise's business continuity capability, to ensure that the enterprise's critical functions continue to operate following disruptive events
Privacy Officer	Individual responsible for monitoring risk and business impact of privacy laws and for guiding and coordinating the implementation of policies and activities that ensure compliance with privacy directives (In some enterprises, the role may be referenced as the data protection officer.)
Legal Counsel	Function responsible for guidance on legal and regulatory matters
Compliance	Function responsible for all guidance on external compliance
Audit	Function responsible for provision of internal audits

Source: Adapted from ISACA, *COBIT® 2019 Framework: Governance and Management Objectives*, USA, 2019, Appendix B, *www.isaca.org/bookstore/bookstore-cobit_19-digital/wcb19fgm*

2.4.2 Risk Roles

The effectiveness of the risk management effort is often influenced by the positioning of the risk management function. Ideally, risk management should be a function with enterprise scope, able to reach into all the parts of the enterprise and provide leadership, advice and direction. An effective risk management program provides a consistent way to manage risk and creates a risk process that serves as a foundation for risk management for all departments and business functions.

The enterprise should establish three lines of defense with the first line of defense managing risk; the second line of defense guiding, directing, influencing and/or assessing risk; and the third line of defense independently overseeing, reviewing and monitoring risk.

Risk management may be applied to an entire enterprise as one or more formal risk management teams, or it may be practiced separately in each level of the enterprise or in regard to specific functions, projects and activities.

Each function within the three lines of defense should be explicitly mapped to at least one of the roles in the RACI chart. A RACI chart illustrates individuals who are:

- Responsible (R) for managing the risk
- Accountable (A) for the risk management effort
- Consulted (C) and provide support and assistance to the risk management effort
- Informed (I) of the risk management effort but may not necessarily be involved in its execution

A RACI model often serves as a method to define and depict roles and responsibilities. The purpose of a RACI model is to clearly show the relationships and interactions between the various roles.

Ideally, only one person should be held accountable (assigned an A) for each key activity. This person should have the authority and resources required to successfully support the activity. Depending on the activity scope, responsibility may fall to one or more people. Depending on the enterprise industry, regulatory requirements may require responsibilities to be assigned to specific roles. Banking regulations, for example, require boards to be responsible for activities that may not receive such a high level of attention in another industry, and a business continuity leader may be responsible for specific activities because of financial market regulations.

Figure 2.9 describes the components of a RACI model and **figure 2.10** provides an example of a RACI chart.

Figure 2.9—RACI Model

Assigned Role and Responsibility	Description
Responsible	Individuals tasked with getting the job done, performing the actual work effort to meet stated objectives.
Accountable	The single person liable or answerable for the completion of the task, who oversees and manages the person(s) responsible for performing the work effort, who may also play a role in the project. Accountability for a particular task should be assigned to a specific person in order to be effective.
Consulted	Individuals who provide input data, advice, feedback or approvals. Consulted personnel may be from other departments, from all layers of the organization, from external sources or from regulators.
Informed	Individuals who are informed of the status, achievement and/or deliverables of the task but who are often not directly responsible for the work effort.

Source: ISACA, *CRISC Review Manual, 6th Edition*, USA, 2015, figure 1.16, *www.isaca.org/bookstore/crisc-exam-resources/crr6ed*

Figure 2.10—Sample RACI Chart

Task	Senior Management	Steering Committee (Chair)	Department Managers	Risk Practitioner
Collect risk data	I	A	C	R
Deliver the risk report	I	A	I	R
Prioritize risk response	A	I	R	C
Monitor risk	I	A	R	C

Source: ISACA, *CRISC Review Manual, 6th Edition*, USA, 2015, figure 1.17, *www.isaca.org/bookstore/crisc-exam-resources/crr6ed*

2.4.3 Risk Culture

Risk culture is the set of shared values and beliefs that governs attitudes toward risk-taking, care and integrity, and determines how openly risk and losses are reported and discussed.

A risk-aware culture:

- Begins at the top (board members and business executives set the direction, communicate risk-aware decision making and reward effective risk management behaviors)
- Promotes an open discussion of risk
- Ensures acceptable levels of risk are understood and maintained

Risk culture is not easy to describe. It consists of a series of behaviors, as shown in **figure 2.11**.

Figure 2.11—Risk Governance and Management Behaviors

General Enterprise Behavior	
Has a risk- and compliance-aware culture throughout, including the proactive identification and escalation of risk	The enterprise defines an approach to risk management and risk appetite and establishes a policy of zero tolerance for noncompliance with legal and regulatory requirements.
Has defined policies that have been communicated and that drive behavior	All personnel understand and implement the requirements of the enterprise as defined in relevant policies.
Shows active receptivity towards raising issues and acknowledging negative outcomes	Whistle-blowers are regarded as positive contributors to the enterprise. The blame culture is avoided. Personnel understand the need for risk awareness and reporting of potential exposures.
Recognizes the value of risk	Personnel understand the importance of maintaining risk awareness and the value that managing risk adds to their roles.
Has transparent and participative culture	Communication is open and facts are not omitted, misrepresented or understated. The negative impact of hidden agendas is avoided.
Shows mutual respect	Stakeholders and risk assessors are encouraged to collaborate, respected as professionals and treated as experts in their roles.
Accepts ownership of risk	Risk practices are incorporated throughout the enterprise. Accountability is clearly assigned and accepted. I&T-related risk is owned by the enterprise and not viewed solely as the responsibility of the IT department or IT risk function.
Allows risk acceptance as a valid option	Management understands the consequences of risk acceptance. Impact is determined to be within the enterprise's risk appetite.
Risk Professional Behavior	
Shows effort to understand what risk is for each stakeholder and how it impacts their objectives	Risk professionals understand the business impact of risk, including competitive, operational, regulatory and compliance requirements. Although risk may be common across a given industry, each enterprise is unique in terms of how risk affects its objectives.
Creates awareness and understanding of risk policy	Alignment of risk capacity, risk appetite and enterprise policy leads to effective risk strategy.
Fosters collaboration and two-way communication during risk assessment	Risk assessment is fundamentally accurate and complete, and addresses stakeholder needs.
Defines risk appetite clearly and communicates in a timely fashion with relevant stakeholders	Stakeholders manage risk more effectively and there is appropriate alignment with organizational strategy and objectives.
Sets policies that reflect risk appetite and risk tolerance	Employees and management operate within risk tolerance. Business lines apply formal risk appetite and tolerance to daily practice. There is a clear process for proposing and making changes to risk appetite levels, with senior management consideration and approval.

Figure 2.11—Risk Governance and Management Behaviors *(cont.)*	
Supports effective risk practice	Stakeholders understand risk from common portfolio view (product, process) and apply risk-based decision making to daily practice.
Uses KRIs effectively as an early warning	KRIs are associated with valid metrics and can be used as an indicator of process or control failure. KRI metrics are available and accessible for regular reporting and relate to objectives.
Acts promptly on the basis of risk indicators or events that fall outside of appetite and tolerance	Risk indicators are linked to the management risk response and remediation activities.
Management Behavior	
Sets direction and demonstrates visible and genuine support for risk practices	Quality risk management practices are maintained through genuine support from senior management.
Engages with all relevant stakeholders to agree on actions and follow up on action plans	The correct stakeholders are appropriately involved in ensuring timely resolution of issues and achievement of business plans.
Obtains genuine commitment and assigns resources for execution of actions	Personnel are empowered to execute actions required by risk management decisions.
Aligns policies and actions to risk appetite	Management makes appropriate risk decisions in complying with policies. Risk adjusted revenue aligns with management expectations.
Monitors risk and progress against action plans	Remediation plans are completed within expected business time frames and have a positive impact on enterprise objectives.
Reports risk trends to senior executives and board	The timely reporting of risk trends proactively manages risk and avoids lost opportunities.
Rewards effective risk management	Good risk practice is acknowledged. Employees' performance goals and reward structures stimulate effective risk management practices and appropriate execution of mitigation actions.
Source: Adapted from ISACA, *COBIT® 5 for Risk*, USA, 2013, figure 26, *www.isaca.org/bookstore/cobit-5/wcb5rk*	

The best indicator of the enterprise risk culture is how the enterprise handles risk. Risk culture reflects a balance between weighing the negative, positive and regulatory elements of risk.

Risk culture includes:

- **Behavior toward taking risk**—What are the norms and attitudes towards risk-taking, identification of risk and analysis of risk?
- **Behavior toward policy**—Is policy something that exists but is not followed? Do policies drive behavior? Are policies easy to read, understand and follow?
- **Behavior toward negative outcomes**—How does the enterprise deal with negative outcomes, policy exceptions, loss events, cyberincidents, missed opportunities and incident investigations? Will it learn from them and try to adjust, or will blame be assigned without treating the root cause?

Symptoms of an inadequate or problematic risk culture include:

- Misalignment of actual risk appetite, stated tolerances and risk policies

- Failure to align risk policy with management direction and/or enterprise norms regarding compliance with policy
- Existence of a blame culture. This type of culture should be avoided, because it inhibits relevant and efficient communication. In a blame culture, business units tend to point the finger at the IT department—or at each other—when projects are not delivered on time or do not meet expectations. In doing so, they fail to realize how the business unit's involvement up front affects project success. In extreme cases, the business unit may assign blame for failure to meet expectations that it never clearly communicated. Blame diminishes effective communication across units, further exacerbating delays. Executive leadership must identify and quickly rectify a blame culture to foster collaboration throughout the enterprise.

2.5 Risk Communication, Policy, Scope and Workflow

2.5.1 Risk Communication

Risk communication plays a key role in defining and understanding the risk culture of an enterprise. Communication is important because it removes the uncertainty and doubts concerning risk management. If risk is to be managed and mitigated, it must first be discussed and effectively communicated to the various stakeholders and personnel throughout the enterprise in ways that are appropriate for their respective roles.

The benefits of open communication on risk include:

- More informed risk decisions by executive management due to an improved understanding of actual exposure and potential business impact
- Greater awareness among all stakeholders of the importance and value of integrating risk management into their daily duties
- Transparency to external stakeholders regarding both the actual levels of risk facing the enterprise and the risk management processes in use

The consequences of poor communication on risk include:

- A false sense of confidence at all levels of the enterprise and unintentional acceptance due to ignorance of risk that exceeds the enterprise's risk appetite
- Lack of direction or strategic planning to mandate risk management efforts
- Unbalanced communication of risk to external stakeholders, potentially leading to incorrect and negative perceptions by third parties such as clients, investors and regulators
- The perception that the enterprise is trying to hide risk from stakeholders

Establishing clear lines of communication for risk reporting is an important element of risk management. **Figure 2.12** provides a description of the type of I&T-related information that should be shared and discussed.

Figure 2.12—Risk Communication

Type	Description
Expectations from risk management	Risk strategy, policies, procedures, awareness training and continuous reinforcement of principles. This is essential communication regarding the enterprises overall strategy toward I&T risk. • Drives all subsequent efforts on risk management • Sets the overall expectations about the risk management program
Current risk management capability	• Allows for monitoring of the state of risk management in the enterprise • Is a key indicator for good risk management • Has predictive value for how well the enterprise is managing risk and reducing exposure

Figure 2.12—Risk Communication *(cont.)*	
Type	Description
Status	Includes the actual status with regard to I&T-related risk, including information such as: • The risk profile of the enterprise (i.e., the overall portfolio of [identified] risk to which the enterprise is exposed) • Key risk indicators (KRIs) to support management reporting on risk • Event/loss data • The root cause of loss events • Options to mitigate risk (including cost and benefits)
Source: ISACA, *CRISC Review Manual, 6th Edition*, USA, 2015, figure 1.6, *www.isaca.org/bookstore/crisc-exam-resources/crr6ed*	

The involvement of stakeholders in the risk management process provide many benefits to the enterprise. **Figure 2.13** depicts some of the core benefits derived from active involvement by both internal and external participant groups.

Figure 2.13—Stakeholder Communication About Risk	
Role	Benefits
Boards and executive management	An improved understanding of I&T risk management roles and responsibilities of how I&T-related risk applies to strategy objectives and of how it can be better used to reduce risk incurred in strategic moves.
Enterprise risk managers	Increased assistance managing I&T-related risk following established ERM principles
Operational risk managers	An increased understanding of links between operations and I&T-related risk, as well as improved identification of key operational losses and development of key risk indicators (KRIs)
IT management	Improved identification, management and communication of I&T-related risk to business decision makers
IT service managers	An improved understanding of operational I&T-related risks—an important component of an overall I&T risk management framework
Business continuity managers	Improved alignment of enterprise risk management as risk is a central component of continuity management responsibility
IT security managers	Better positioning of security risk in relation to other I&T-related risk
CFOs	An improved understanding of I&T-related risk and its significance in investment and portfolio management
Enterprise governance officers	More informed monitoring and reviewing of I&T governance roles and responsibilities
Business managers	Improved understanding of management of I&T-related risk toward alignment of all types of business risk
IT auditors	More detailed analysis of risk, improving audit plans and reports

Figure 2.13—Stakeholder Communication (about Risk)

Role	Benefits
Regulators	More informed assessment of an enterprise's approach to I&T risk management
External auditors	Improved view of I&T-related risk levels when assessing the quality of an enterprise's internal control
Insurers	Support in establishing adequate insurance coverage and establishing agreement on I&T risk levels
Rating agencies	A reference for assessing and objectively rating an enterprise's treatment of I&T-related risk in collaboration with insurers

2.5.2 Risk Policy

Risk management requires that policies be part of an overall governance and management framework, providing a (hierarchical) structure into which all policies should nest and provide support to the underlying principles.

As part of including risk management norms or conditions into the enterprise policy framework, the following items should also be described in risk policies:

- Scope and authority—tie to risk appetite or tolerance statements
- Roles and responsibilities of the stakeholders
- The consequences of failing to comply with the policy
- The means for handling exceptions
- The manner in which compliance with the policy will be checked and measured

Policies should be aligned with the enterprise risk appetite. Policies are a key component of the enterprise system of internal control, whose purpose it is to ensure that an enterprise meets its stated objectives. As part of risk governance activities, the enterprise risk appetite is defined, and this risk appetite should be reflected in the policies. This is not meant to suggest that risk appetite or risk tolerance statements be embedded into policy documents, rather, that the policies need to be aligned with the risk-taking culture of the enterprise. Policies need to be re-validated and updated at regular intervals to ensure relevance to business requirements and practices.

Policies provide detailed guidance on how to put principles into practice and how they will influence decision making. Not all relevant policies are written and owned by the IT, information security, information privacy, or risk function. Different types of risk policies are presented in **figure 2.14**.

Figure 2.14—Risk Policy Types

Policies	Description
Core IT risk policy	Defines, at strategic, tactical and operational levels, how the risk of an enterprise needs to be governed and managed pursuant to its business objectives. This policy translates enterprise governance into risk governance principles and policy and elaborates risk management activities.
Information security policy	Sets behavioral guidelines in protecting corporate information and the associated systems and infrastructure. The business requirements regarding security and storage are more dynamic than IT risk management, so, for effectiveness, their governance needs to be handled separately from the governance of IT risk. However, for operational efficiency, it is necessary to keep the information security policy in sync with the IT risk policy.

Figure 2.14—Risk Policy Types (cont.)	
Policies	Description
Crisis management policy	As with IT security, network management and data security, IT crisis management is one of the operational level policies that needs to be considered for complete IT risk management. It sets the guidelines on how to act in situations of crisis and details the sequence in which to deal with each of the identified (key) areas of risk.
Third-party IT service delivery management policy	Sets guidelines for managing risk related to third-party services. It sets out a framework of expectations in behavior and security precautions taken by third-party service providers to manage the risk related to the service provision.
Business continuity policy	Contains management commitment and view on: • Business impact analysis (BIA) • Business contingency plans with trusted recovery • Recovery requirements for critical systems • Defined thresholds and triggers for contingencies • How to handle escalation of incidents • Disaster recovery plan (DRP) • Training and testing
Program/project management policy	Deals with managing risk linked to projects and programs. It details management position and expectation regarding program and project management. Moreover, it handles accountability, goals and objectives regarding performance, budget, risk analysis, reporting and mitigating adverse events during the execution of programs and projects.
Human resources (HR) policies	Detail what employees can expect from the enterprise and what the enterprise expects from employees. They provide detailed acceptable and unacceptable behavior by employees, and, in doing so, manage the risk that is linked to human behavior.
Fraud risk policy	Is concerned with protecting the enterprise brand, reputation and assets from loss and/or damage, resulting from incidents of fraud and/or misconduct. The policy provides guidance to all employees on reporting any suspicious activity and ways to handle sensitive information and evidence. It helps to raise an anti-fraud culture and raise awareness of the risk.
Compliance policy	Explains the assessment process regarding compliance with regulatory, contractual and internal requirements. It lists roles and responsibilities for the different activities in the process and provides guidance on metrics to be used to measure compliance.
Ethics policy	Defines the essentials of how people within an enterprise will interact with each other, as well as how they will interact with any customers or clients they serve.
Quality management policy	Details management vision on the quality objectives of the enterprise, the acceptable level of quality and the duties of specific departments to ensure quality.
Service management policy	Provides direction and guidance to ensure the effective management and implementation of all information technology services to meet the business and customer requirements, within a framework of performance measurement. It also deals with management of risk related to IT services. Detailed guidance on service management and the optimization of risk related to services is included in the ITIL V3 framework.
Change management policy	Communicates management intent that changes to the enterprise information technology be managed and implemented in a way that minimizes risk and impact to the stakeholders. The policy contains information on the assets in the scope and the established standard change management process.

Figure 2.14—Risk Policy Types (cont.)	
Policies	Description
Delegation of authority policy	Details: • The authority that the board strictly retains for itself • The general principles of delegation of authority • A schedule of the delegation of authority (including clear boundaries) • A clear definition of the organizational structures to which the board delegates its authority
Whistle-blower policy	Should: • Encourage employees to raise concerns and questions • Provide avenues for employees to raise concerns in full confidence • Ensure employees will receive a response to raised concerns and be able to escalate a concern if they are not satisfied with the response • Reassure the employees that they are protected when they raise issues and should not be afraid of reprisals
Internal control policy	The purpose is to: • Communicate management internal control objectives • Establish standards for the design and operation of the enterprise system of internal controls to reduce the expose to all risk faced by the enterprise
Intellectual property (IP) policy	The purpose is to ensure that all risk related to the use, ownership, sale and distribution of the outputs of IT-related creative endeavors by employees of the enterprise, e.g., software development, is detailed in an appropriate way, from the start of any endeavor.
Data privacy policy	A statement or document that discloses the ways that a party gathers, uses, discloses and manages personal data. Personal information can be anything that can be used to identify an individual, including but not limited to name, address, date of birth, marital status, contact information, ID issue and expiry date, financial records, credit history, medical history, travel destination, and intentions to acquire goods and services. The policy defines how an enterprise collects, stores and releases the personal information that it collects. The policy informs the client of the specific information that is collected and whether it is kept confidential, shared with partners, or sold to other firms and enterprises. Furthermore, the policy ensures compliance with relevant legislation related to data protection.
Source: ISACA, *COBIT® 5 for Risk*, USA, 2013, figure16, *www.isaca.org/bookstore/cobit-5/wcb5rk*	

2.5.3 Risk Scope

The selection of items included in the risk activities are generally based on understanding the full risk universe and then selecting the specific part of the enterprise to which the risk activities will be applied. This is often called risk scoping.

Risk management requires that the scope of the risk landscape, or risk universe, is set and the criteria against which the identified risk will be assessed, or evaluated are defined. Risk management starts with understanding the enterprise and how it is influenced by the environment, or context, in which it operates. This is particularly true of enterprises that operate in a single sector of the economy, such as financial services, manufacturing or healthcare, because there is a heavy dependency on many of the same supply chains.

The scope should be determined within the context of the enterprise objectives. Defining an initial, preliminary scope for risk management activities can be done using a high-level evaluation of the overall I&T-related risk that the enterprise faces. The outcome of the risk scoping activity is used to focus and prioritize more-detailed risk management activities, and:

- Allows identification of the potential high-impact risk areas throughout the enterprise.
- Provides an overview of major risk factors to which the enterprise is subject, whether or not it has the ability to influence those factors.
- Gathers data on any overarching compliance, regulatory, privacy or other obligations (e.g., GDPR, HIPAA, or country-specific regulations) or contractual obligations that commit the enterprise to specific risk management activities.
- Provides first indications of major risk scenarios, which is an important input to the scenario-building phase of the more-detailed risk analysis activities to be performed at a later stage.

The enterprise risk scoping activity may need to be repeated on a periodic basis; this can be a simple annual confirmation of earlier results if no major changes occurred in any of the risk factors. If major changes (e.g., mergers, new markets) occur to the enterprise, the scoping activity should be refreshed. In stable environments, a yearly update or confirmation of the preliminary scope is recommended. Periodically evaluate risk activities to ensure that the most important assets and services are in scope. Some enterprises start with high-value assets that support the most critical business lines, processes or products, or critical services, and then expand the scope as the risk management capability matures.

Data to collect in the scoping activity include:

- The units or subunits, business processes or services, geographic locations that will be subject to risk management activities
- Impact criteria, e.g., potential consequences of realized risk, and the risk appetite and risk tolerance statements of the enterprise
- Current scoring, severity ratings, or other risk measurement or metrics criteria that is used across the enterprise
- Expected depth and breadth of the risk management activities
- The defined areas that will be subject to reporting and analysis requirements
- The current risk profile of the enterprise, if one exists
- Risk and control self-assessments that may have been completed
- Audit or compliance priorities

An enterprise I&T-related risk scoping exercise should involve all major stakeholders of the enterprise.

2.5.4 Risk Management Workflow

I&T risk management is a cyclical process that includes the:

- **Context of risk management**—where risk is positioned in the context of the enterprise mission, strategy and objectives, and where value-added activities are considered as part of the overall risk management process.
- **Identification of I&T-related risk**—includes identifying assets subject to risk, common risk factor and areas of concern, and the process of identifying and documenting risk. The risk identification effort should result in the listing and documentation of risk.
- **Assessment of I&T-related risk**—the effort to assess and prioritize risk, including the development of risk scenarios.

- **Analysis of I&T-related risk**—includes qualitative assessment or quantitative analysis to estimate the frequency and impact of the risk scenarios and business impact, taking into account the risk factors.
- **Response and mitigation of I&T-related risk**—seeks and implements cost-effective ways to address the risk that is identified, assessed and analyzed. This step should be performed in cooperation with the relevant owners.
- **Monitoring, reporting and communicating of I&T-related risk**—controls, risk management efforts and the current risk state are monitored, and the results are reported back to senior management. The process repeats as the risk environment changes, which may occur as a result of internal or external factors.

Figure 2.15 shows the risk management workflow steps. The steps in the diagram are not necessarily performed sequentially. Each enterprise should develop a workflow that supports the most efficient and effective means to perform these steps.

Figure 2.15—Risk Management Workflow

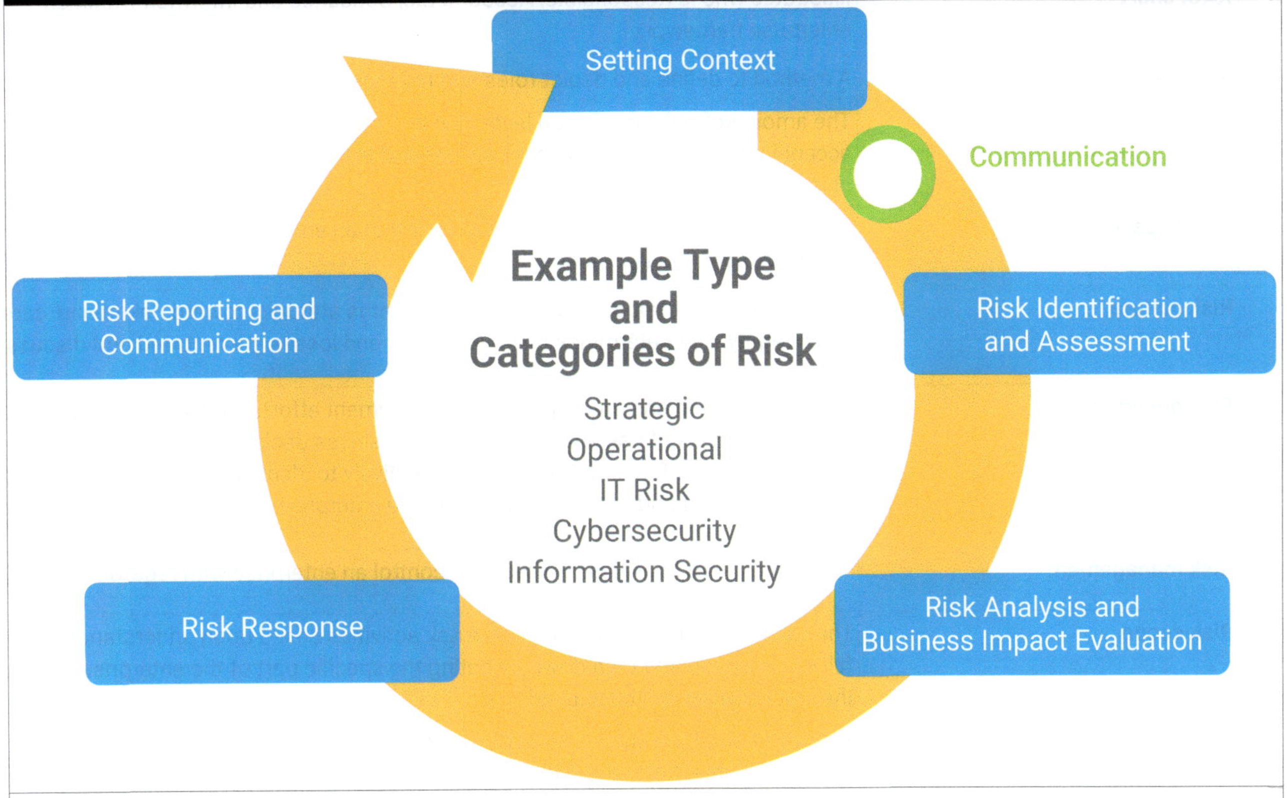

Source: Adapted from ISACA, *Getting Started With Risk Management*, USA, 2018, figure 2, *www.isaca.org/bookstore/bookstore-wht_papers-digital/whpgsr*

2.6 Summary of Terminology

It is important to recognize and understand I&T-related risk terminology. The following terms were introduced in this chapter (**figure 2.16**).

Figure 2.16—Chapter 2 Terminology	
Term	Description
Control objective	A statement of the desired result or purpose to be achieved by implementing control procedures in a particular process
Governance	Ensures that stakeholder needs, conditions and options are evaluated to determine balanced, agreed on enterprise objectives to be achieved; setting direction through prioritization and decision making; and monitoring performance and compliance against agreed-on direction and objectives
I&T risk governance and management	The implementation of a risk strategy that reflects the culture, appetite and tolerance levels of enterprise management, considers technology and budgets and addresses the requirements of regulation and compliance
RACI chart	Illustrates who is Responsible, Accountable, Consulted and Informed within an enterprise framework
RACI model	A method to define and depict roles and responsibilities
Risk appetite	The amount of risk, on a broad level, that an enterprise or other entity is willing to accept in pursuit of its mission (or vision) and the achievement of business objectives
Risk capacity	The objective magnitude or amount of loss that an enterprise can tolerate without risking its continued existence
Risk culture	The set of shared values and beliefs that governs attitudes toward risk-taking, care and integrity, and determines how openly risk and losses are reported and discussed
Risk governance	Sets the direction and strategy of risk management efforts, defines risk culture and acceptable levels of risk, makes risk-aware business decisions and ensures that the risk management function is operating effectively to identify, manage, monitor and report on current and potential risk facing the enterprise
Risk management	The coordinated activities to direct and control an enterprise with regard to risk
Risk scope	The selection of items included in the risk activities based upon understanding the full risk universe and then down-selecting the specific part of the enterprise to which the risk activities will be applied
Risk statement	A description of the current conditions that may lead to the loss; and a description of the loss. Source: Software Engineering Institute (SEI)
Risk tolerance	The acceptable level of variation that management is willing to allow for any particular risk as the enterprise pursues its objectives
Risk universe	Encompasses the overall risk environment, defines the areas risk management activities will address and provides a structure for I&T-related risk management
Stakeholder	Anyone who has a responsibility for, an expectation from or some other interest in the enterprise

Chapter 2 Knowledge Check

Review questions are provided as a means to support the content presented within this study guide and serve as a gauge or assessment of knowledge of I&T-related risk topics. One question is provided for each topic.

For individuals intending to earn the ISACA IT Risk Fundamentals Certificate, these questions are written to depict the type of questions that may appear on the exam. These questions will not specifically appear on the exam, but similar ones may on the exam.

REVIEW QUESTIONS

1. Which of the following approaches to risk governance could result in an enterprise taking risk that unintentionally exposes other parts of the enterprise?

   A. Establishing a risk governance function to oversee the operations of risk management activities.
   B. Enforcing a departmental approach to risk where each department manages risk independently of other departments.
   C. Making risk decisions only after evaluating the full range of opportunities and consequences of each decision and its impact on the enterprise.

2. The effective governance and management of I&T-related risk requires that risk responses are implemented and prioritized:

   A. According to the ease of developing new controls over considering existing controls.
   B. Based on a cost/benefit analysis or where there can be the greatest impact.
   C. Independent of the enterprise-stated risk appetite and risk tolerance.

3. The amount of risk that an enterprise is willing to accept to achieve its business objectives is commonly known as its:

   A. Risk capacity
   B. Risk tolerance
   C. Risk appetite

4. A risk aware culture:

   A. Ensures that acceptable levels of risk are understood and maintained.
   B. Restricts a discussion of risk to only those responsible for managing risk.
   C. Allows business units to voice their complaint when other business units are not meeting expectations.

5. Risk scoping is used to focus risk management activities on:

   A. The full risk universe that an enterprise is subject to.
   B. Potential high-impact risk areas throughout the enterprise.
   C. Only risk that the enterprise has an ability to influence.

Answers on page 68

Chapter 2 ANSWER KEY

Review Questions

1. A. As part of establishing and maintaining a common view of risk, the risk governance function must oversee the operations of the risk management team.
B. Taking a departmental approach to risk could lead to unacceptable consequences. There must be an understanding that risk in one department or system may pose an unacceptable risk to another department or system requires the integration of risk management into the enterprise.
C. In order to make risk aware decisions, the risk governance function must consider the full range of opportunities and consequences of each risk related decision and its potential impact on the enterprise.

2. A. As part of establishing and maintaining a common view of risk, the risk governance function must oversee the operations of the risk management team.
B. An effective risk strategy should include a proper balance between cost and benefits. Therefore, risk responses should be implemented on the basis of cost/benefit analysis, analysis of alternatives and prioritization of risk that has the greatest potential impact on enterprise objectives.
C. I&T-related risk should be prioritized and addressed in line with risk appetite and risk tolerance.

3. A. Risk capacity is the amount of loss that an enterprise can tolerate without risking its continued existence. Risk capacity differs from risk appetite, which generally reflects a board or management decision regarding how much risk is desirable.
B. Risk tolerance is the acceptable level of variation that management is willing to allow for any particular risk as the enterprise pursues its objectives, i.e., the acceptable deviation from the level set by the risk appetite and business objectives.
C. Risk appetite is the amount of risk an enterprise or other entity is willing to accept in pursuit of its mission (or vision) and the achievement of business objectives.

4. **A. A risk aware culture ensures acceptable levels of risk are understood and maintained.**
B. A risk aware culture promotes an open discussion of risk.
C. A risk aware culture should avoid blame, because it inhibits relevant and efficient communication and fails to foster collaboration throughout the enterprise.

5. A. Although risk scoping requires a full understanding of the full risk universe that an enterprise is subject to, it represents selecting or focusing on the specific risk areas to which the risk activities will be applied.
B. The outcome of a risk scoping activity is used to focus and prioritize more detailed risk management activities on potential high-impact risk areas throughout the enterprise.
C. Risk scoping provides an overview of major risk factors to which the enterprise is subject, whether or not it has the ability to influence those factors.

Chapter 3:

Risk Identification

Learning Objectives 70

Risk Identification

3.1 Asset Types 71
3.2 Asset Classification (Criticality and Sensitivity) 72
3.3 Asset Valuation 74
3.4 Information Asset Valuation 75
3.5 Threats 76
3.6 Vulnerabilities 81
3.7 Likelihood 86
3.8 Risk Awareness 88
3.9 I&T-related Risk 88
3.10 Risk Scenarios 95
3.11 Summary of Terminology 102

Knowledge Check 105

Learning Objectives

Risk identification is the process for determining and documenting the risk an enterprise faces. The identification of risk is important because only risk that is identified can be assessed and subjected to appropriate responses. In this chapter, asset, threat and vulnerability types are described. Major IT components and the areas of concern that can lead to risk are presented. Risk scenario approaches are provided.

Learning objectives include the following:

- Categorize enterprise assets and how they are valued.
- Describe the factors that can put enterprise assets at risk.
- Explain the different types of threats and vulnerabilities that exist.
- Identify IT areas of concern that can lead to I&T-related risk.
- Describe the risk identification process.
- Summarize how to apply risk identification methods.
- Define the types and benefits of risk scenarios.
- Describe how to develop a risk scenario.

Risk Identification

The identification of risk depends on the successful identification of assets, threats to those assets and the vulnerabilities that the assets contain.

An asset is something of either tangible or intangible value that is worth protecting. An asset is anything of value to the enterprise in the delivery of its mission or business strategy that can be affected by an event that can lead to business or mission impact.

3.1 Asset Types

Enterprise asset types include:

- People
- Information
- Business processes
- Infrastructure
- Finances
- Reputation

3.1.1 People

People are assets that include employees, contractors, staffing providers and third parties. Many enterprises are vulnerable to the loss of a key employee who may be a single point of knowledge and the only person with knowledge in a certain area or specific expertise. Failure by management to identify key employees and ensure that they are supported through cross-training and incentive programs are unfortunately common. Whether a loss occurs as a result of retirement, illness or recruitment by another enterprise, it may leave the enterprise in a precarious and vulnerable position.

3.1.2 Information

Information assets are essential to the enterprise business and exist in many forms. They can be printed or written on paper, stored electronically, transmitted by post or by using electronic means, shown on films, or spoken in conversation. Information should be protected against disclosure to unauthorized users (confidentiality), improper modification (integrity), and non-access when required (availability). Information may be sensitive, critical or both; sensitive information must be protected from disclosure or modification, while critical information must be protected from destruction or loss. The systems that host, process or transmit information (data) must ensure that information is protected at all times, in all forms and in all locations.

3.1.3 Business Processes

A business process is an interrelated set of cross-functional activities or events that result in the delivery of a specific product or service to a customer and can be an intangible asset. Business processes are controlled by policies, procedures, practices and structures that create value to the enterprise and provide reasonable assurance that a business process will achieve its objectives. An inefficient or ineffective business process may make an enterprise less competitive in the market and lead to financial, market (customer), and reputational loss.

3.1.4 Infrastructure

Infrastructure assets include the physical infrastructure (e.g., facilities and, equipment) and IT infrastructure (e.g., computing hardware, network infrastructure and middleware). IT architecture components include information and applications. New and outdated technologies pose a risk to an enterprise. When new technology emerges, the enterprise needs to consider the:

- Impact of adopting the technology (support, reliability, ease of integration)
- Risk associated with operating the new technology (e.g., security, reliability)
- Consequences of not adopting the new technology (e.g., obsolescence and lagging behind competitors)
- Business benefits of the new technology (e.g., support for new business initiatives, effectiveness and efficiency gains)

With older technology, equipment that is no longer supported or past its mean time between failure (MTBF) may be particularly vulnerable. Lack of patching and updating of systems and applications may leave them vulnerable to malware or misuse, and older systems may require expertise that is not readily available to maintain (potentially increasing key-person dependency).

3.1.5 Finances

Financial assets are those that typically show up on an enterprise balance sheet and include items such as cash, investments or accounts receivable. They receive their value from a contractual claim. Financial assets are subject to many types of risk, including market (e.g., currency, interest rate or commodity), credit (e.g., cash flow, regulatory or callable loans) and operational (e.g., inadequate systems or controls, employee errors or system failures) risk. Nearly every type of risk can have an impact on the financial assets of the enterprise.

3.1.6 Reputation

Reputation is an intangible asset that is difficult to quantify. It represents the value an enterprise has derived from its past actions, be that positive or negative in nature. The impact of various events and decisions often have an impact on reputation. A shared understanding of I&T-related failures, compromises, mistakes or events can impact enterprise objectives and result in the loss of direct costs (e.g., financial), or indirect (e.g., customer sensitive) information resulting in reputational damage. Significant reputational damage or lowered expectations on the part of stakeholders can also result when senior management is thought to be accountable, but fails to take corrective action, or does not adequately represent the corrective action to constituents. The compliance record of an enterprise can also significantly—either positively or negatively—affect its reputation in the community and marketplace.

3.2 Asset Classification (Criticality and Sensitivity)

Asset classification is required to determine the relative sensitivity and criticality of IT assets, sometimes referred to collectively as business value.

- Asset criticality is measured by the impact on the enterprise because of the loss of an asset (i.e., how important the asset is to the business).
- Asset sensitivity is based on the potential damage to the enterprise because of unauthorized disclosure.

The number of information classification levels should be kept to a minimum. Classifications should be simple, such as designations by differing degrees for sensitivity and criticality.

The first step in the classification process is to ensure that the I&T asset inventory is complete and that the location of each asset is identified. This is a necessary step in the risk identification process.

All relevant assets should be accounted for by the enterprise. This may be financial or nonfinancial assets. COBIT 2019 states that an enterprise should "maintain an up-to-date, accurate record of all I&T assets that are required to deliver services and that are owned or controlled by the enterprise with an expectation of future benefits (including resources with economic value, such as hardware or software)."[16] An asset inventory (or asset register) is used to record all relevant assets. An I&T asset inventory differs from enterprise to enterprise but typically includes:

- Owner
- Designated custodian
- Specific identification of the asset
- Relative value to the enterprise
- Loss implications and recovery priority
- Location (physical or logical)
- Security/risk classification
- Asset group (where the asset forms part of a larger IT system)
- Type of information the asset stores or processes.

Common methods to build the initial inventory include consulting the purchasing system, reviewing contracts and reviewing the software currently installed.

Not all assets are equally important; many are absolutely critical to business operations, while others are conveniences. As a result, it is important to determine the importance of assets in the context of enterprise activities so that priority may be given to protecting the most important assets first and addressing less significant assets as time and budget allow.

Some assets may be prioritized as critical where others may not be as critical or may only be critical at certain times of the business cycle. COBIT 2019 states that an enterprise should "identify assets that are critical in providing service capability and maximize their reliability and availability to support business needs."[17] It takes skill, experience and a thorough understanding of business or mission importance to understand the difference between a critical asset and a noncritical asset.

Critical assets can include many types of assets. One example is intellectual property. Intellectual property is a class of information that is treated with special care because it may represent the future earnings potential of the enterprise. Trademarks, copyrights, patents, trade secrets and research that leads to a new product, are examples of intellectual property (see **figure 3.1**). Failure to protect intellectual property may result in the loss of competitive advantage.

Figure 3.1—Intellectual Property Examples

Term	Description
Trademark	A sound, color, logo, saying or other distinctive symbol that is closely associated with a certain product or company. Some trademarks are eligible for registration.
Copyright	Protection of any work that is capture in a tangible form (e.g., written works, recordings, images, software, music, sculpture, dance, etc.)

[16] ISACA, *COBIT 2019 Framework: Governance and Management Objectives*, USA, 2018
[17] *Ibid.*

Figure 3.1—Intellectual Property Examples *(cont.)*

Term	Description
Patent	Protection of research and ideas that led to the development of a new, unique and useful product to prevent the unauthorized duplication of the patented item.
Trade secret	A formula, process, design, practice or other form of secret business information that provides a competitive advantage to the organization that possesses the information.

Source: ISACA, *CRISC Review Manual, 6th Edition*, USA, 2015, figure 1.10, *www.isaca.org/bookstore/crisc-exam-resources/crr6ed*

Other examples of critical assets can include important financial data and information and proprietary processes and products. It is up to each enterprise to determine those specific assets that are most critical to the achievement of business goals and objectives.

3.3 Asset Valuation

Asset value is the value of an asset to both the business and to competitors. An asset may be valued according to what another person would pay for it, or by its measure of value to the enterprise. Asset value is usually done by assigning a quantitative (monetary) value. The process of asset valuation consists of relating all values in a common financial form. Asset valuation is straightforward for some assets, but not for all. For example, hardware can be easily valued based on replacement costs. The value of information, in some cases, is the cost of recreating or restoring it or it may be based on the contribution to generating revenues. In other cases, the value is related to the consequential costs and possible regulatory sanctions stemming from the exposure of confidential information or the loss of trade secrets.

The impact or consequences of a breach of personally identifiable information (PII) can be regulatory sanctions; in addition, the individuals suffering identity theft losses may file lawsuits for damages and class-action lawsuits on behalf of thousands of victims may arise. Another consequence is possible reputational damage, often resulting in loss of share value. Clearly, in this case, the valuation cannot be based on the intrinsic value of the information, which may be low or zero. Rather, valuation must be based on the total range of potential losses and other impacts. Effective valuation protects the enterprise from paying more in protection (e.g., insurance) than the net worth of the asset.

Many enterprises use a quantitative approach that assigns a monetary value, which becomes difficult when the value influences or drives intangibles such as confidence, morale or market perception. For example, if an enterprise, region or product is associated with poor quality, environmental negligence or fraudulent activity, a high-quality product may be perceived as substandard due to this market perception. This negative perception may persist for many years before the enterprise is able to recover.

Contributing factors to calculating asset value include:

- Financial penalties for legal noncompliance
- Impact on business processes
- Damage to reputation
- Additional costs for repair/replacement
- Effect on third parties and business partners
- Injury to staff or other personnel

- Violations of privacy
- Breach of contracts
- Loss of competitive advantage
- Legal costs

3.4 Information Asset Valuation

When viewed from the perspective of how I&T assets are used within the enterprise, the assets have value because of the business or mission purpose they serve. An I&T asset, by itself, may be easily replaceable, such as server hardware, or highly susceptible to vulnerabilities, such as software. However, without the business or mission context, it is not possible to fully understand the criticality of I&T assets.

An enterprise may find it difficult to value information assets and as a result not have an accurate list of their information assets. It is often difficult to place an exact value on assets such as personally identifiable information (PII) or trade secrets, although a high degree of accuracy is not necessary.

Often, information asset valuation is best based on loss scenarios. Information can be recorded into a matrix with each loss scenario to make valuation more manageable and understandable (see **figure 3.2**).

Figure 3.2—Loss Scenario Matrix

Scenario	Type of Data	Size of Loss	Reputation Loss	Lawsuit Loss	Fines/Reg Loss	Market Loss	Expected Loss Per Year	Notes
Hacker steals data, publicly blackmails company.	Customer data	1K records 10K records	USD$1M USD$20M	USD$1M USD$10M	USD$1M USD$35M	USD$1M USD$5M	USD$10M	Regulatory loss of ability to make acquisitions for 1 year
Employee steals data, sells data to competitors.	Strategic plan	3-year plan	Minimal	Minimal	Minimal	USD$20M	USD$2M	Competitor duplicates new products, brings them to market faster.
Contractor steals data, sells data to hackers.	Employee data	10K records	USD$5M	USD$10M	Minimal	Minimal	USD $200,000	
Backup files and data are found in garbage, makes front-page news.	Customer data	10M records	USD$20M	USD$20M	USD$10M	USD$5M	USD $200,000	

Source: ISACA, *CISM Review Manual, 15th Edition*, USA, 2016, figure 2.6, *www.isaca.org/bookstore/cism-exam-resources/cm15ed*

The precision of the valuation is not as critical as having an approach to prioritize efforts and linking assets to business processes. The value of an IT asset is intrinsically linked to the business value it provides. Values within the same order of magnitude as the actual loss (should it occur) are sufficient for planning purposes. Media reports contain many well-documented loss scenarios and loss amounts with which to base a valuation.

3.5 Threats

The risk identification process seeks to improve confidence that the enterprise recognizes and understands any risk with the potential to jeopardize its objectives. As defined in Section 1.1, a threat is anything that is capable of acting in a manner that can result in loss or harm to an enterprise asset. Threats are aimed at exploiting enterprise vulnerabilities and are initiated by a threat agent.

A threat agent is a method or thing used to exploit a vulnerability. A threat agent is often referred to as a threat actor, which is any person, thing or entity that carries out a threat and is responsible for a threat event. An event during which a threat actor acts against an asset in a manner that has the potential to directly result in harm is known as a threat event. Examples of I&T-related threat events include:

- Improper disclosure of information
- Improper modification or use of data
- Interruption of a system or project
- Internal or external theft

Threat actors can be internal or external, and they can be human or nonhuman.

- Internal actors are within the enterprise (e.g., staff, contractors).
- External actors include outsiders, competitors, regulators, hackers and the market.

Not every type of threat requires an actor (e.g., failures or natural causes). If a threat doesn't exist then there is no risk. Similarly, properly protected assets that are not vulnerable to threats being issued present no risk. For example, if a virus has been written to exploit a vulnerability on a system, the virus can only have an impact if the system has not been patched to eliminate the vulnerability. After the patch has been applied, the virus poses no threat to the system. **Figure 3.3** illustrates how threat agents attack assets via vulnerabilities.

Figure 3.3—Risk Factors

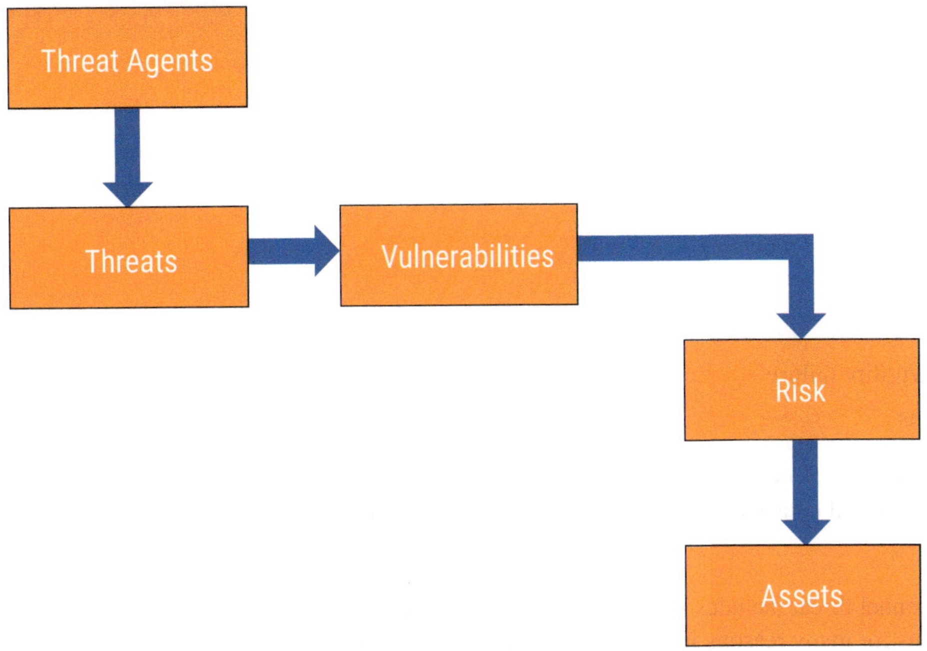

Source: ISACA, *CRISC Review Manual, 6th Edition*, USA, 2015, figure 1.9, *www.isaca.org/bookstore/crisc-exam-resources/crr6ed*

Knowledge of potential threats and the motivations, strategy and techniques of those who perpetrate threats is an important element of risk management. An enterprise needs to know its own weaknesses, strengths and vulnerabilities and build proper protections into each business process, each IT system and all operational procedures.

3.5.1 Threat Types

The threat landscape is always changing. Threats can be external (including advanced persistent threats) or internal. They may also be intentional or unintentional. Threats can also be emerging and brought on by the introduction of new technology. Threats always exist and are typically beyond the direct control of the enterprise. For that reason, it is important to identify the various types of threats that apply or that may be used to compromise systems or otherwise affect an enterprise.

External Threats

External threats to IT systems can originate from anywhere and may take a number of forms, including:

- Espionage
- Theft
- Sabotage
- Terrorism
- Criminal acts
- Software errors
- Hardware flaws

- Mechanical failures
- Lost assets
- Data corruption
- Facility flaws (freezing pipe/pipe burst)
- Fire
- Supply chain interruption
- Industrial accidents
- Disease (epidemic or pandemic)
- Seismic activity
- Flooding
- Power surge/utility failure
- Severe storms

Natural events, such as a flood, storm, earthquake or tornado, are unpredictable and may be extremely damaging. The use of governmental data and weather monitoring services may identify the threats associated with natural events.

An external personnel threat includes a hacker, a criminal, nation state, or hacktivist that is skilled and determined to break into systems for many reasons including for military or economic purposes.

Some breaches are the result of targets of opportunity and not determined attacks. Many enterprises are breached because they were discovered to be easy targets and threat agents took advantage of their vulnerabilities.

Advanced Persistent Threats (APTs)

The term advanced persistent threat refers to advanced, highly skilled attackers who are determined (persistent) in their attempts to exploit systems and networks. The increased skills available to the hacking community and the effectiveness of the tools they possess make the risk of compromise much more significant. APTs may be sponsored by governments, organized crime or competitors.

APTs pose a significant risk to an enterprise. The National Institute of Standards and Technology (NIST) defines an APT as:

> *An adversary that possesses sophisticated levels of expertise and significant resources which allow it to create opportunities to achieve its objectives using multiple attack vectors (e.g., cyber, physical and deception). These objectives typically include establishing and extending footholds within the IT infrastructure of the targeted organizations for purposes of exfiltrating information, undermining or impeding critical aspects of a mission, program or organization; or positioning itself to carry out these objectives in the future. The advanced persistent threat: (i) pursues its objectives repeatedly over an extended period of time; (ii) adapts to defenders' efforts to resist it; and (iii) is determined to maintain the level of interaction needed to execute its objectives.*[18]

Typical APT attacks occur as follows:

- **Initial compromise**—Attackers use social engineering and spear phishing via email, using zero-day viruses. They may plant malware on a website that the victimized employees are likely to visit.
- **Establish foothold**—Attackers may plant remote administration software in the victim's network and/or create network back doors and tunnels that allow stealth access to network infrastructure.

[18] National Institute of Standards and Technology, Special Publication 800-39, *Managing Information Security Risk,* 2011

- **Escalate privileges**—APTs use exploits and password cracking to acquire administrator privileges over the victim's computer and possibly expand it to Windows domain administrator accounts.
- **Internal reconnaissance**—Attackers collect information on surrounding infrastructure, trust relationships and Windows domain structure.
- **Move laterally**—They expand control to other workstations, servers and infrastructure elements and perform data harvesting on them.
- **Maintain presence**—APTs ensure continued control over access channels and credentials acquired in previous steps.
- **Complete mission**—Attackers exfiltrate stolen data from the victim's network.

Figure 3.4 shows the typical sources of an APT. Due to the required sophistication, expertise, time and costs involved, these efforts are normally mounted only against high-value targets.

Figure 3.4—Typical APT Sources

Threat	What They Seek	Business Impact
Intelligence agencies	Political, defense or commercial trade secrets	Loss of trade secrets or commercial, competitive advantage
Criminal groups	Money transfers, extortion opportunities, personal identity information or any secrets for potential onward sale	Financial loss, large-scale customer data breach or loss of trade secrets
Terrorist groups	Production of widespread terror through death, destruction or disruption of services	Loss of production and services, stock market irregularities, and potential risk to human life
Activist groups	Confidential information or disruption of services	Major data breach or loss of service
Armed forces	Intelligence or positioning to support future attacks on critical national infrastructure	Serious damage to facilities in the event of a military conflict

Source: ISACA, *Advanced Persistent Threats: How to Manage the Risk to Your Business*, USA, 2013, figure 2, page 29

Internal Threats

In most enterprises, employees are considered to be the most important asset. However, an employee can become discontented or unhappy if they are inadequately trained, treated poorly or not given enough time to do their jobs properly. Disillusionment and resentment can lead to a higher risk of errors, negligence and more conscious actions, such as theft. Key personnel also may be drawn to another enterprise and leave serious gaps in the knowledge and skills needed to operate systems effectively.

Employees are the cause of a significant number of business impacts, which can be intentional and unintentional. A disgruntled employee may intentionally compromise systems or release data that expose the enterprise to legal or reputational risk. Employees may be convinced, bribed or threatened to disclose trade secrets for ideological or economic reasons. Many employees have a level of access to systems and data that far exceeds their actual job requirements, which can be exploited in an attack. The solution to the employee problem, therefore, lies at least in part in the application of need-to-know and least privilege, but it is an imperfect solution. Any system has trusted insiders, and one of them choosing to violate trust is difficult to either predict or prevent.

The typical malicious insider is a current or former employee, contractor or other business partner who has or had authorized access to the enterprise network, system or data and intentionally intercepted (exfiltrated), interrupted, modified or fabricated data on the enterprise's IT systems. The first step in addressing personnel threats is to start with the hiring process and to review the qualifications and attitude of prospective employees. Employment candidates may have submitted incorrect information on job applications and claimed education, certification or experience that they did not actually possess.

At the time of hiring, the employee should be required to sign a nondisclosure agreement and be advised of the ethics and policies of the enterprise, and a review of references and performance of background checks may be worthwhile where permitted by law.

Throughout employment, employees should be reminded of enterprise policies and their responsibilities through awareness sessions and regular management reviews. One of the best employee-based controls is to interact with employees to understand any frustrations, complaints or issues that they may be facing and to seek to resolve those issues. During times of strike, layoffs, mergers, relocation and reorganization, an employee is more likely to be a risk. An employee who has been recently demoted or bypassed for a promotion is also a risk.

At the end of employment, an employee should return all enterprise assets, including identification badges, equipment (e.g., laptops, mobile phones, and access cards) and uniforms so that unauthorized access cannot be gained in the future. In addition, systems, network and facility access should be removed immediately prior to the employee's departure to minimize the potential for crimes of opportunity.

Emerging Threats

Innovations in technology are important to all enterprises. Each emerging technology offers different IT solutions, with its own risk and reward. Indications of emerging threats can include:

- Unusual activity on a system
- Repeated alarms
- Slow system or network performance
- New or excessive activity in logs

In many cases, an IT system that has been compromised may have evidence of a threat in their logs well in advance of the actual compromise due to emerging technology, but the evidence is either not noticed or acted on. Lack of effective monitoring, when combined with a threat, is a combination that can lead to a breach.

Most technologies are built with an emphasis on function and purpose without due consideration for the adequate protection against threats. As a result, new technology tends to be a source of new vulnerabilities and may even itself be a threat agent within an IT system.

3.5.2 Threat Intelligence

Threat intelligence is organized, analyzed and refined information about potential threats provided by service providers and some computer emergency response teams (CERTs). The primary purpose of threat intelligence is to help an enterprise understand common and severe external threats, such as the zero-day threats, advanced persistent threats (APTs) and exploits. The emphasis is on the attacks that are most likely to affect the enterprise IT environment. Threat intelligence is based on the collection of information using external and internal sources and includes in-depth information about specific threats that help the enterprise to protect itself from the attacks.

Examples of external sources include open-source intelligence (OSINT), social-media intelligence information from ISACA; indicators of compromise (IoC) provided by an external entity or intelligence gathered from the deep and dark web (e.g., enterprise information or credentials are being offered for sale). The purpose of threat intelligence is to research and analyze trends and technical developments to provide an understanding of potential threat events and related threat actors.

3.5.3 Threat Assessment

A threat assessment/analysis is an evaluation of the type, scope and nature of events or actions that can result in adverse consequences; identification of the threats that exist against enterprise assets. Threat assessment is an active process in which an enterprise seeks to identify any attempt to create adverse effects and understand the motivation of threat actors. Because intent is the key factor, threat assessment generally excludes natural events, but may include accidental threat actors. Depending on the observed action(s), an enterprise may be able to determine what the threat actor is trying to do, and thus leverage the understanding of intent to identify additional vulnerabilities. Enterprises can then apply that knowledge in risk treatment decisions.[19]

IT threats to an enterprise can evolve from a number of places including the:

- Implementation of new technologies
- Granting of broader network and application access to partners and customers
- Advanced capabilities of attackers

These threats warrant a periodic assessment of the threat landscape an enterprise faces. This activity is particularly important for an enterprise that is either too small or resource-constrained to adopt a continuous assessment approach to threat management.

A threat assessment should be performed at least annually by evaluating changes in the technical and operating environments of the enterprise, particularly where external entities are granted access to enterprise resources.

Internal factors that represent areas where the level of threat may increase or new threats may emerge include:

- New business units
- New or upgraded technology
- Changes to products and services
- Changes in roles and responsibilities

As new threats or changes in threat levels are identified and prioritized in terms of impact, the ability of existing controls to mitigate risk associated with these threats should be evaluated. Threat sources can include technical/cyber, human, facility-based, natural and environmental, and pandemic events.

The range of possible threats must be evaluated to determine if they are viable; the likelihood they will materialize; and their potential impact to systems, operations, personnel or facilities.

3.6 Vulnerabilities

Vulnerabilities are control conditions that are deemed to be deficient relative to requirements of the threat levels being faced. A vulnerability represents a weakness in the design, implementation, operation or internal control of a process that could expose the system to adverse threats from threat events. Vulnerabilities are weaknesses, gaps or holes that provide an opportunity for a threat or create consequences that may impact the enterprise.

Many I&T-related vulnerabilities are conditions that exist in IT systems and must be identified so that they can be addressed. The purpose of vulnerability identification is to find the problems before they are found by an adversary and exploited, which is why an enterprise should conduct regular vulnerability assessments and penetration tests to identify, validate and classify its vulnerabilities. Where vulnerabilities exist, there is a potential for risk.

[19] National Institute of Standards and Technology, Special Publication 800-39, *Managing Information Security Risk,* 2011

Enterprises need to identify and assess vulnerabilities to determine the threat and potential impact and to determine the best course of action in addressing each vulnerability. Vulnerabilities can be identified by information provided by software vendors (e.g., through the release of patches and updates) and by utilizing processes and tools that identify known vulnerabilities in the enterprise's specific environment. The two most common techniques to identify technical vulnerabilities are vulnerability scanning and penetration testing.

3.6.1 Vulnerability Types

There are many types of vulnerabilities that can exist within IT systems. These include vulnerabilities associated with:

- Networks
- Physical access
- Applications and web-facing services
- Utilities
- Supply chain
- Processes
- Equipment
- Cloud computing services
- Big data
- Cybersecurity

Networks

Network vulnerabilities are often related to misconfiguration of equipment, poor architecture or traffic interception. Misconfiguration is a common problem with network equipment that is not properly installed, operated or maintained. Any open services are a potential attack vector (a path or route used by the adversary to gain access to the target (asset)) that can be exploited by an attacker, so network equipment should be hardened by disabling any unneeded services, ports or protocols.

Traditionally, networked systems have been limited to devices whose primary purpose was to provide computing power, either for direct processing of data or to regulate the flow of data within the network. However, as the cost of networking technology drops in terms of dollars, power and physical size, the ability to transmit and receive data is being incorporated into a growing number of devices whose primary purposes are not of a data processing or regulatory nature, such as home appliances and automobiles. These devices create new vulnerabilities for the network. The resulting Internet of Things is emerging as both a tremendous opportunity for increasing convenience and a vast new target for threat agents.

Physical Access

A significant number of all incidents relate to physical theft or loss of equipment or data. However, physical security goes far beyond theft. Threat agents who are able to gain physical access to systems have the potential to bypass nearly every other type of control.

With access to server rooms, network cabling, information systems equipment and buildings, an attacker can circumvent passwords, install skimmers to intercept data communications and take logical ownership of systems or devices. Because numerous incidents are related to misuse of systems by insiders who may already have an advantage in terms of gaining physical access, the need for strong physical security is clear and growing.

Applications and Web-facing Services

Applications in general, web applications in particular, are among the most common vulnerability (entry) points currently used by attackers. Many applications are written to support business function without due regard to the security requirements of the applications and may be subject to the following common vulnerabilities, among others:

- Buffer overflows
- Logic flaws
- Injection attacks
- Bugs
- Incorrect control over user access

Applications may also be vulnerable due to poor architecture. Applications that process payment card data or other sensitive information or store those data in an insecure location, such as in a demilitarized zone (DMZ), may come under repeat or even continuous attack, increasing the likelihood that an attacker will find a vulnerability to exploit.

Utilities

IT systems rely on controlled environmental conditions, including clean and steady power and controls over humidity and temperature. An enterprise should be prepared for power failure or other environmental conditions in order to avert conditions that may lead to system failure. Having an uninterruptible power supply (UPS), backup generators and surge protectors can protect equipment from damage or failure, but these systems require more than an initial investment. For example, a UPS must be validated to ensure that it has adequate power to run critical systems until a backup generator can come online, and then be tested periodically, while generators must be checked for fuel and mechanical function.

Supply Chain

Many enterprises rely on products, raw materials and supplies that originate from various locations around the world, and any interruption in the supply chain may affect their ability to function. For example, a shortage in supply of fuel to an airport would impact all flight operations. Reliance on a supply chain should be documented even if it is understood that the risk is one that is accepted by senior management.

Processes

Maintaining operational integrity often requires procedures spanning a variety of topics, including:

- Incident management
- Identity management
- Change control
- Patch management
- Project planning

These processes must be defined and deployed in a consistent manner across the enterprise. Without them, or if they are deployed haphazardly, the enterprise may be vulnerable to risk of inconsistent management and results, lack of governance and reporting, and failure to ensure compliance with regulations.

Equipment

Equipment creates a vulnerability as it ages, as it becomes less efficient, effective, and able to support business functions. Equipment is often provided at the time of production with a Mean Time Between Failures (MTBF) rating that indicates its anticipated life span and when it should be scheduled for removal or replacement.

Cloud Computing Services

Cloud computing offers many business advantages. However, the outsourcing of data processing does not remove the liability of the outsourcing enterprise to ensure proper data protection. Also, while larger data centers that are established to serve hundreds or thousands of customers are typically better protected than stand-alone operations, the ability of the outsourcing enterprise to see what goes on inside the host enterprise its data center may be very limited. When one considers that the cloud data centers are large, visible and tempting targets for the best-funded and most experienced threat agents, it is clear that cloud computing services are vulnerable and at risk. The decisions of whether to leverage cloud services, which systems should be transferred and which might be better retained within the control of the enterprise should be made by senior management.

Big Data

Advances in the capability to perform analysis of data from various sources of structured and unstructured data allow enterprises to make better business decisions and increase competitive advantage. This change in analytics capabilities dealing with big data can introduce technical and operational risk, and enterprises should understand that risk can be incurred either through adoption or nonadoption of these capabilities.

The risk of adopting or not adopting big data analytics includes:[20]

Technical and operational risk that considers that certain data elements may be governed by regulatory or contractual requirements and that data elements may need to be centralized in one place (or at least be accessible centrally) so that the data can be analyzed. In some cases, this centralization can compound technical risk.

For example:

- *Amplified technical impact—If an unauthorized user were to gain access to centralized repositories, it puts the entirety of those data in jeopardy rather than a subset of the data.*
- *Privacy (data collection)—Analytics techniques can impact privacy; for example, individuals whose data are being analyzed may feel that revealed information about them is overly intrusive*
- *Privacy (re-identification)—Likewise, when data are aggregated, semianonymous information or information that is not individually identifiable information might become non-anonymous or identifiable in the process.*

Cybersecurity

Vulnerabilities can occur in many forms and at different architectural levels. **Figure 3.5** provides a list of common types of cybersecurity vulnerabilities.

[20] ISACA, *Generating Value from Big Data Analytics*, USA, 2014, *https://www.isaca.org/bookstore/bookstore-wht_papers-digital/whpgv*

Figure 3.5—Cybersecurity Vulnerabilities

Type of Vulnerability	Cause	Cybersecurity Examples
Technical	Errors in design, implementation, placement or configuration	• Coding errors • Inadequate passwords • Open network ports • Lack of monitoring
Process	Errors in operation	• Failure to monitor logs • Failure to patch software
Organizational	Errors in management, decision, planning or from ignorance	• Lack of policies • Lack of awareness • Failure to implement controls
Emergent	Interactions between, or changes in, environments	• Cross-organizational failures • Interoperability errors • Implementing new technology

Source: ISACA, *Cybersecurity Fundamentals Study Guide, 2nd Edition*, USA, 2017

It is important to analyze vulnerabilities in the context of how they are exploited, and vulnerabilities and exploits need to be considered in vulnerability assessments. Vulnerabilities and exploits can be identified in many ways. At a technical level, automated tools (both proprietary and open source) can be used to identify common vulnerabilities in computer and network implementations and configurations. Other vulnerability analysis tools include open source and proprietary sources.

3.6.2 Vulnerability Assessment and Penetration Testing

A vulnerability assessment/analysis is a process of identifying and classifying vulnerabilities. A vulnerability assessment provides a careful examination of a target environment to discover any potential points of compromise or weakness. Vulnerabilities that may be identified by an assessment include:

- Network vulnerabilities
- Poor physical access controls (e.g., buildings, offices)
- Insecure applications
- Poorly designed or implemented web-facing services
- Disruption to utilities (e.g., power, telecommunications)
- Unreliable supply chain
- Untrained personnel (human resources)
- Inefficient processes (e.g., change control, incident handling)
- Poorly maintained or old equipment

A vulnerability assessment may be a manual process or use automated tools. Automated tools have the ability to filter large amounts of data and can be used to:

- Examine logs
- Compile and analyze data from multiple sources (e.g., a security incident and event management [SIEM] tool)
- Examine the functions of a program and run test files or data against a tool such as a firewall or application

Where content is not easily quantified and requires judgment— including reviews of business processes, physical security and source code—a manual test is better (although automated tools for reviewing code continue to improve).

Vulnerability assessments may contain data that is not accurate, particularly false positives that indicate a vulnerability where none exists. To validate the results of a vulnerability assessment, the enterprise may conduct a penetration test against a potential vulnerability or attack vector.

Penetration testing includes identifying existing vulnerabilities and then using known exploit methods to:

- Confirm exposures
- Assess the level of effectiveness and quality of existing controls
- Identify how specific vulnerabilities expose IT resources and assets
- Ensure compliance

Penetration testing simulates actual attacks and must be planned carefully. Failure to do so may result in ineffective results, negative impact on or damage to the enterprise's IT infrastructure, potential liability or criminal prosecution.

Penetration testing requires specialized knowledge of vulnerabilities, exploits, IT technology and the use of testing tools. Any penetration tests should be carefully planned to mitigate the risk of causing a service outage, and the results require careful interpretation and elimination of false positives. Penetration testing can be covert (i.e., the general IT staff do not know the testing is going to take place), so that the reactions of the enterprise to detect and respond are also tested.

Penetration testing uses the same sort of tools as those used by a real adversary, which can help to establish the extent to which an identified vulnerability is a true weakness. Penetration tests may be conducted by internal or external teams, and rules can range from full knowledge of the infrastructure to a zero-knowledge tests in which the testing team has no knowledge of the infrastructure being attacked. An expert penetration testing team will be creative and attempt several types of tests to ensure that as many attack vectors as possible have been tested, generating a report that can be used in the process of risk identification.

3.7 Likelihood

Likelihood is the probability of something happening. It is the measure of the probability of which an event may occur, which depends on whether there is a potential source for the event (threat) and the extent to which the particular type of event can affect its target (vulnerability), taking into account any controls or countermeasures that the enterprise has put in place to reduce its vulnerability. In the context of risk identification, likelihood is used to calculate the risk that an enterprise faces based on the number of events that may occur within a given time period (often an annual basis).

Specific factors that can affect likelihood include:

- **Volatility**—Unpredictability, also referred to as dynamic range; the degree to which conditions vary from one moment to another, making projections difficult.
- **Velocity**—Speed of onset, a measure of how much prior warning and preparation time an enterprise may have between the event's occurrence and impact, which itself can be split into speed of reaction and speed of recovery.
- **Proximity**—The time from the event occurring and the impact on the enterprise.
- **Interdependency**—The degree to which materialization of two or more types of risk might impact the enterprise differently, depending on whether the events occur simultaneously or consecutively.
- **Motivation**—In cases involving an active/sentient threat, the extent to which the perpetrator of the threat wants to succeed, which may result in a higher chance of success.
- **Skill**—The ability brought to bear by the perpetrator of an active/sentient threat relative to other perpetrators.
- **Visibility**—The extent to which a vulnerability is known, which can make it a more likely target of attack.

The risk faced by an enterprise consists of some combination of known and unknown threats, directed against systems that have some combination of known and unknown vulnerabilities. A vulnerability assessment that identifies no vulnerabilities is not equal to the system being invulnerable in the absolute sense. It means only that the types of vulnerabilities that the assessment was intended to detect were not detected. Failure to detect a vulnerability may be the result of its absence, or it may be a false negative arising from misconfiguration of a tool or improper performance of a manual review. In the case of a zero-knowledge penetration test that fails to identify opportunities to exploit a system, it may be that the team was unlucky or lacked imagination, which may not be true of an outside attacker.

Even if no known vulnerabilities exist within the system, the system may still remain vulnerable to unknown vulnerabilities. The likelihood of an attack is often a component of external factors, such as the motivation and skill of the attacker. **Figure 3.6** shows how all of these factors influence risk.

Figure 3.6—Factors Influencing Risk

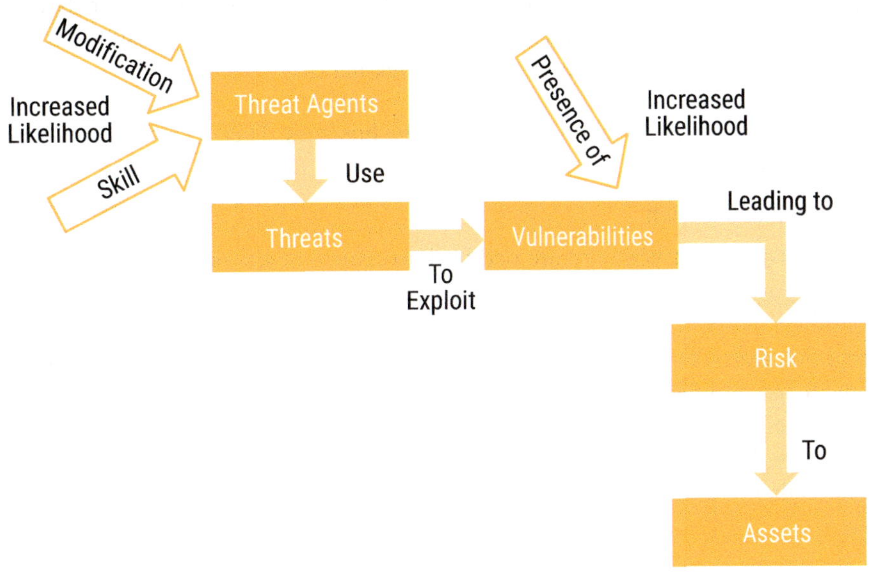

Source: ISACA, *CRISC Review Manual, 6th Edition*, USA, 2015, figure 1.13, *www.isaca.org/bookstore/crisc-exam-resources/crr6ed*

Given the combination of unknown threat and unknown vulnerability, it is difficult to estimate the likelihood of a successful attack. Vulnerability assessments and penetration tests provide valuable information on which to partially estimate this likelihood, because:

- Although the presence of a vulnerability does not guarantee a corresponding threat, the all-hours nature of I&T and the rapid speed of processing makes it much more likely that an I&T system will come under an assortment of attacks in a short time than would be true of a physical system.
- A vulnerability known to an assessment tool is also knowable to threat agents, all but the most elite of whom tend to build their attacks to target common vulnerabilities.
- The presence of one or more known vulnerabilities—unless these have been previously identified and the risk is accepted by the enterprise for good reason—suggests a weakness in the overall security program.

In some cases, where clear, statistically sound data are available, likelihood may appear to be a simple matter of mathematical probability, but there may still be many variables and uncertainty. This is true with situations such as weather events or natural disasters. However, sometimes accurate data are simply not available. Some factors create situations where the likelihood of certain threats is more or less prevalent for a given enterprise. For example, a connection to the Internet will predispose a system to port scanning. Typically, qualitative rankings such as High, Medium, Low or Certain, Very Likely, Unlikely, Impossible, can be used to rank and prioritize threats stemming from human activity. Estimates of probability can be accurately defined without statistically significant data. Regardless, when using qualitative rankings the most important step is to rigorously define the meaning of each category and use definitions consistently throughout the assessment process.

3.8 Risk Awareness

Risk awareness is a powerful tool in creating the culture, forming ethics and influencing the behavior of the members of an enterprise. The staff and operational teams of an enterprise are often the first to be aware of any problems or abnormal activities.

Through awareness programs, it is possible to develop a team approach to risk management that enables every member of an enterprise to identify and report on risk and to work to defend systems and networks from attacks. Each member of the team can help identify vulnerabilities, suspicious activity and possible attacks. This may enable a faster response and better containment of a risk when an attack happens.

Risk awareness acknowledges that risk is an integral part of the business. This does not imply that all risk is to be avoided or eliminated, but rather that:

- Risk is well understood and known.
- I&T-related risk issues are identifiable and are tied back to critical business processes.
- The enterprise recognizes and uses the means to manage risk.

A risk awareness program creates an understanding of risk, risk factors and the various types of risk that an enterprise face. An awareness program should be tailored to the needs of the individual groups within an enterprise and deliver content suitable for that group. A risk awareness program should not disclose vulnerabilities or ongoing investigations except where the problem has already been addressed. Using examples and descriptions of the types of attacks and compromises that other enterprises have experienced can reinforce the need for diligence and caution when addressing risk.

3.9 I&T-related Risk

Risk identification seeks to:

- **Identify common risk factors**—Make sure that interrelated events are grouped by type. Common risk factors can be sourced from a risk taxonomy or a control catalog. A risk taxonomy provides a scheme for classifying sources and categories of risk and provides a common language for discussing and communicating risk to stakeholders.
- **Identify areas of concern**—Management and staff often have concerns related to tasks and activities that may expose the enterprise, or make the enterprise more susceptible to certain types of risk. This is a good step to engage the stakeholders to make sure a thorough identification of risk occurs.

Identifying risk requires a combination of imagination and analysis. Risk is most likely to be identified when it takes the form of something that can already be envisioned. For this reason, it is beneficial to know the types of I&T-related business risk (not exhaustive) in **figure 3.7**.

Figure 3.7—I&T-related Business Risk Types

Type	Description
Access risk	The risk that information may be divulged or made available to recipients without authorized access by the information owner, reflecting a loss of confidentiality
Availability risk	The risk that service may be lost or data are not accessible when needed
Infrastructure risk	The risk that the I&T infrastructure and systems may be unable to effectively support the current and future needs of the business in an efficient, cost-effective and well-controlled fashion (includes hardware, networks, software, people and processes)
Integrity risk	The risk that data may be unreliable due to incompleteness or accuracy
Investment or expense risk	The risk that the I&T investment fails to provide value commensurate with its cost or is otherwise excessive or wasteful, including the overall I&T investment portfolio
Project ownership risk	The risk of I&T projects failing to meet objectives through lack of accountability and commitment
Relevance risk	The risk that the right information may not get to the right recipients at the right time to allow the right action to be taken or the right decisions to be made
Schedule risk	The risk of I&T projects taking longer than expected

Source: ISACA, *CRISC Review Manual, 6th Edition*, USA, 2015, figure 1.15, *www.isaca.org/bookstore/crisc-exam-resources/crr6ed*

3.9.1 IT Components and Areas of Concern

To identify and assess I&T-related risk, a general knowledge of IT systems and applications is needed. This knowledge is invaluable for anyone who works with or interacts with IT staff and will help to identify potential threats, vulnerabilities or impacts on the business. The primary IT components that follow are briefly described, along with potential areas of concern or risk.

Hardware

IT systems and business processes rely on hardware—the equipment and devices that process, store and transmit data. Hardware includes many devices, such as:

- Central processing units (CPUs)
- Motherboards
- Random access memory (RAM)
- Read-only memory (ROM)
- Networking components (switches, routers, hubs, etc.)
- Firewalls and gateways
- Keyboards
- Monitors
- Printers
- Smart and cell phones

- Laptops and tablets

Areas of concern associated with hardware include:

- Obsolescence
- Poor maintenance
- Misconfiguration
- Lack of documentation
- Loss or theft
- Data loss due to insecure disposal
- Sniffing (capturing traffic)
- Physical access
- Failure
- Use without authorization

Software

Software manages data, interfaces between systems, provides a user interface to hardware, and processes transactions, and includes:

- Applications
- Operating systems (OSs)
- Utilities
- Drivers
- Middleware
- Application program interfaces (APIs)
- Database management systems (DBMS)
- Network operating systems

Areas of concern associated with software include:

- Logic flaws or semantic errors
- Bugs (semantic errors)
- Lack of patching
- Lack of access control
- Disclosure of sensitive information
- Unauthorized modification of information
- Loss of source code
- Lack of version control
- Lack of input and output validation

Operating Systems

The operating system (OS) is the core software that allows the user to interface with hardware and manages all system operations. The OS manages access to system resources and controls the behavior of system components.

Areas of concern associated with the OS include:

- Unpatched vulnerabilities
- Poorly written code (buffer overflows, etc.)
- Complexity
- Misconfiguration
- Weak access controls
- Lack of interoperability
- Uncontrolled changes

Applications

Applications are the face of the information system and are the mechanism by which most users can access information, perform transactions and use system features.

Areas of concern associated with applications include:

- Poor or no data validation
- Exposure of sensitive data (i.e., lack of encryption/obfuscation)
- Improper modification of data
- Logic flaws (i.e., logic errors)
- Software bugs (i.e., coding errors)
- Lack of logs
- Lack of version control
- Loss of source code
- Weak or lack of access control
- Lack of operability with other software
- Back doors
- Poor coding practices

Software Utilities

Software utilities help to manage, analyze, configure and maintain I&T resources. A driver is used to control the various devices connected or used by an I&T system.

Areas of concern associated with utilities and drivers include:

- Use of outdated drivers
- Unavailability of drivers
- Unpatched drivers
- Use of insecure components (older encryption algorithms)
- Unpatched vulnerabilities

Environmental Systems

Environmental systems include power and heating, ventilation and air conditioning (HVAC) systems that support IT operations.

Areas of concern associated with environmental systems include:

- Power interruptions
  - Loss of power (e.g. surge, spikes, sags, brownouts, faults)
  - Generators (e.g,. insufficient capacity, poor maintenance)
  - Batteries (e.g., poorly maintained, outdated)
- HVAC
  - Overheating
  - Humidity problems (e.g., corrosion and condensation (high humidity), static (low humidity)
  - Clogged filters
  - Lack of maintenance
- Water
  - Loss of water (needed for cooling systems)
- Health and safety issues
- Secure operational areas
  - Restricted access to server rooms and wiring closets
  - Secure access to power supplies, generators, elevator shafts

Platforms

IT platforms vary by enterprise. Less complex enterprises may have all of their technology residing on a single platform such as the mainframe, while other enterprises utilize a variety of platforms to capture, store and process information. An enterprise IT infrastructure location may be:

- A single, centralized location
- Decentralized, in multiple locations

IT platforms may be managed by its own staff or outsourced to a service provider located within the enterprise or at the provider's facility.

Areas of concern:

- Some platforms are more secure than others, such as a mainframe, while others are more vulnerable, such as a web application or a kiosk operating in a public area.
- A system deployed into a vulnerable environment or a legacy system may not have sufficient native controls.
- A combination of different technologies can often introduce new risk and change a secure system or platform into one that has new vulnerabilities.
- An unhardened platform may be subject to vulnerabilities.

Networks

Networks are systems of interconnected computers and the communication equipment used to connect them. Networks may range in size from a small personal area network to a global area network that links devices together worldwide. A network is made up of many devices including:

- Cabling
- Repeaters
- Switches
- Routers
- Firewalls
- Gateways
- Wireless access points

Most modern networks are digital, where the communications are sent via digital signals such as bits or pulses of light. Networks are an important part of I&T risk management because they are often targets or channels used to attack systems or applications. The network itself is often essential to business operations, and many business processes rely on the availability of the network.

Networks are used for many purposes, including:

- Transferring data between individuals
- Transferring data between applications
- Controlling and monitoring of remote equipment (supervisory control and data acquisition [SCADA] networks)
- Backing up data (storage area networks [SANs])
- Enabling communication between devices (Bluetooth)

Areas of concern include:

- Improper network configuration
- Inadequate network equipment protection
- Unsuitable levels of redundancy
- Unavailability of suitable bandwidth
- Lack of the use of proper encryption for transmission of sensitive data
- Lack of the use of certificates to support PKI
- Damage to cabling and network equipment
- Lack of proper documentation of network architecture
- Unpatched systems

3.9.2 Risk Identification Overview

When the enterprise fails to identify a risk, it is left out of the strategic planning process used by senior management to promote value creation. The risk identification process seeks to improve confidence that the enterprise recognizes and understands any risk with the potential to jeopardize enterprise objectives.

Risk can be differentiated by its state of risk (inherent, current and residual). These risk states are described in Section 5.9.

3.9.3 Risk Identification Sources

Gathering information and having a thorough knowledge of the enterprise and its internal and external environments are very important elements in identifying risk.

Risk identification can occur in formal contexts (e.g., during brainstorming sessions or workshops) or informal settings (e.g., incidental discussion of issues in meetings or during office conversations). A brainstorming session usually starts with a list of items that keep participants up at night, including cyberthreats or other areas of concern. Often, issues that keep people awake contribute to risk—rather than contribute to the risk itself. For example, staff may worry about unpatched systems and often miscategorize them as risk.

Historical information about the enterprise or similar enterprises is useful since the information can lead to reasonable predictions about current and evolving issues that have not yet been faced by the enterprise. However, identifying what may happen is rarely sufficient. The fact that there are many ways that an event can occur makes it important to identify all reasonably possible and significant causes and scenarios.

Methods and tools used to identify risk and its occurrence include:

- Checklists
- Judgments based on experience and records
- Flowcharts
- Brainstorming
- Systems analysis
- Scenario analysis
- Root cause analysis
- Systems engineering techniques

When selecting a risk identification methodology, the following techniques should be considered:

- Team-based brainstorming, where workshops can prove effective in building commitment and making use of different experiences
- Structured techniques, such as flowcharting, system design review, systems analysis, hazard and operability studies, and operational modeling
- What-if and scenario analysis for less clearly defined situations, such as the identification of strategic risk and processes with a more general structure
- Identified internal and external threats mapped to identified and suspected vulnerabilities

There are several sources of information that are available for the identification of risk. These include:

- Historic information
- Systematic data gathering approaches
- Inductive methods

Historical information about the enterprise or similar enterprises is useful since the information can lead to reasonable predictions about current and evolving issues that have not yet been faced by the enterprise. Historical, or evidence-based methods is where data is gathered from internal and external sources and include such things as:

- Audit or incident reports
- Public media (e.g., newspapers, television, etc.)
- Annual reports and press releases

A systematic approach (expert opinion) is where potential risk or points of failure are determined in a systematic manner by examining and questioning a business process. Examples of a systematic approach include:

- Vulnerability assessments
- Review of business continuity and disaster recovery plans
- Interviews and workshops with managers, employees, customers, suppliers and auditors

An inductive method (theoretical analysis) is where a process is examined to determine the possible point of attack or compromise. An example of an inductive method to gathering information is performing penetration testing.

Interviews

Gathering information from staff is a valuable method of gaining insight into the business from those closest to the processes and most likely to understand their fundamental workings. However, a few pitfalls can occur. For example, sometimes staff members may:

- Exaggerate their role, or the role or importance of their team or department in connection with a specific business process.
- Not fully understand the overall business process or the dependencies between their department and other departments.
- Intentionally provide incorrect information.

To improve the odds of an interview producing useful information the following good practices should be followed by an interviewer:

- Know as much as possible about the business process in advance of the interview, which reduces time spent on general explanations of core business functions.
- Obtain and review relevant documentation related to the scope of the risk landscape such as process maps, standard operating procedures, the results of impact assessments and network topologies before the interview.
- Prepare questions and provide them to the interviewee in advance so that he or she can bring any supporting documentation, reports or data that may be necessary.
- Conduct interviews with senior leaders in order to ensure a thorough understanding of the enterprise, including every aspect of each business operation. Senior leaders may include board members, administrators, critical third-party service providers, customers, suppliers and managers.
- Encourage interviewees to be open about challenges they face and risk that concerns them, as well as any potential missed opportunities or problems associated with their current processes, systems and services/products.
- Avoid setting incorrect expectations regarding confidentiality of interview answers. People may worry about the repercussions of discussing flaws or missed opportunities — promise confidentiality only if it will actually be maintained.

One important detail to obtain during an interview is the level of impact that previous incidents have had on the enterprise, including how the incident was handled, results of post-incident review and root cause analysis, and current status of any noted remediation activities from prior incidents, including whether the recommendations from the previous incident were addressed and resolved.

3.10 Risk Scenarios

A risk scenario is a tangible and assessable representation of risk.

The development of risk scenarios provides a way to:

- Conceptualize risk that can aid in the process of risk identification.
- Document risk in relation to business objectives or operations impacted by events, making them useful as the basis for quantitative risk assessment.

The development of risk scenarios is based on describing a potential risk event and documenting the factors and areas that may be affected by the risk event. Each scenario should be related to a business objective or impact.

Risk events can include:

- System failure
- Loss of key personnel
- Theft
- Network outages
- Power failures
- Natural disasters
- Other situations that could affect business operations and mission

The key to developing effective scenarios is to focus on real and relevant potential risk events such as a:

- Radical change in the market for an enterprise's products
- Change in government or leadership
- Supply chain failure

One of the challenges for I&T risk management is to identify the important and relevant risk among all that can possibly go wrong with IT or in relation to IT, given the pervasive presence of IT and the business's dependence on it. One of the techniques to overcome this challenge is the development and use of risk scenarios. It is a core approach to bring realism, insight, enterprisewide engagement, improved analysis and structure to the complex matter of I&T-related risk. After these scenarios are developed, they are used during the risk analysis, process where frequency and business impacts are estimated.

3.10.1 Risk Scenario Approaches

Risk scenarios can be developed from a top-down perspective driven by business goals or from a bottom-up perspective originating from hypothetical scenarios.

Top-down Approach

A top-down approach to scenario development is based on understanding business goals and how a risk event could affect the achievement of those goals. Mission strategy and business objectives form the basis for identifying and analyzing risk that is plausible and relevant to desired outcomes. If impact criteria are well aligned with the real value drivers of the enterprise, relevant risk scenarios can be developed.

The top-down approach is suited to general risk management of the enterprise because it looks at I&T- and non-I&T-related events. A benefit of this approach is that because it is more general, it is easier to achieve management buy-in even if management usually is not interested in IT. The top-down approach also deals with the goals that senior managers have already identified as important to them.

Bottom-up Approach

The bottom-up approach to developing risk scenarios is based on describing risk events that are specific to individual enterprise situations, typically hypothetical situations envisioned by the people performing the job functions in specific processes.

Beginning with assets, systems or applications deemed important to the enterprise, a list of threats or generic loss scenarios is compiled. The resulting list is then used to define a set of concrete, customized scenarios that are applied to the enterprise context. The bottom-up approach is commonly used in cyberthreat and vulnerability assessments; however, it may limit visibility or obfuscate business impact, if its results are not considered in conjunction with the top-down approach. One downside of bottom-up scenario development is that it may be more difficult to maintain management interest in highly specialized technical scenarios.

The approaches are complementary and should be used simultaneously (see **figure 3.8**).

Figure 3.8—I&T-related Risk Scenario Approaches

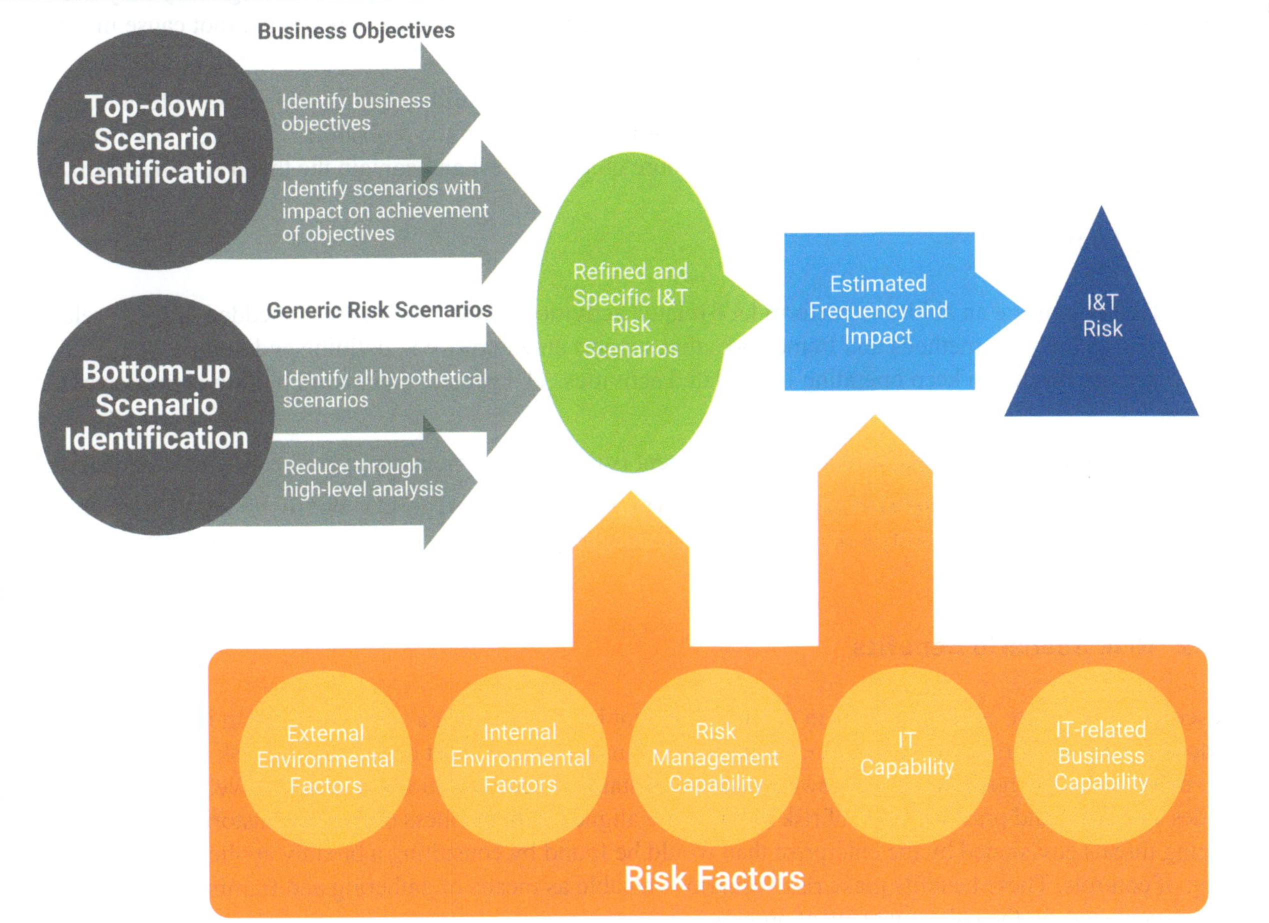

Source: ISACA, *Risk IT Framework, 2nd Edition*, USA, 2020, figure 6.1, *www.isaca.org/bookstore/bookstore-risk-digital/ritf2*

This is where a taxonomy of risk (defined earlier) may be useful. The path from a threat or area of concern to a risk requires that the statement of risk be decomposed into components that are actionable. A risk taxonomy provides a common language for discussing and communicating risk to stakeholders. Risk scenarios must be relevant and linked to real business or mission risk.

After the set of risk scenarios is defined, it can be used for risk analysis (covered in Chapter 4), where frequency and impact of the scenario are assessed. An important component of this assessment are risk factors. Risk factors are those factors that influence the frequency and/or business or mission impact of risk scenarios; they can be of different natures, and can be classified into:

- Contextual factors
- Capability factors

Contextual Factors

Contextual factors can be internal or external to the enterprise with the main difference being the degree of control that an enterprise has over them.

- Internal contextual factors are, to a large extent, under the control of the enterprise, although they may not always be easy to change. For example, poor user awareness training practices are often a root cause in a risk that is realized and results in an incident.
- External contextual factors are, to a large extent, outside the control of the enterprise. For example, a mature risk management approach will spend less time on performing analysis on the probability of a threat occurring and more time on developing capabilities that would more quickly detect and contain the threat if it materializes.

Capability Factors

Capacity factors indicate an ability to perform I&T-related activities. These themes are embedded in many related ISACA tools, techniques, methods and frameworks that support an enterprise in defining and improving the IT and related processes needed to keep operating I&T-related activities. The general themes are built to help answer these questions:

- **I&T risk management capabilities**—To what extent is the enterprise mature in performing risk management?
- **I&T-related business or mission capabilities (or value management)**—How closely do the I&T capabilities support and enable the enterprise objectives while managing the risk that could prevent the realization of the objectives?

3.10.2 Risk Scenario Benefits

Risk scenarios facilitate communication in risk management by constructing a narrative that can inspire people to take action. The use of risk scenarios can enhance the risk management effort by helping the risk team to understand and explain risk to the business process owners and other stakeholders. Additionally, a well-developed scenario provides a realistic and practical view of risk that is more aligned with business objectives, historical events and emerging threats envisioned by the enterprise than would be found by consulting a broadly applicable standard or catalog of controls. These benefits make risk scenarios valuable as means of gathering and framing information used in subsequent steps in the risk management process.

3.10.3 I&T-related Risk Scenario Development

An I&T risk scenario is a description of an I&T-related event that can lead to a business impact, when and if it should occur. Sometimes, this type of activity is called a business impact assessment (BIA) and is done as part of the business continuity planning phase. For risk scenarios to be complete and usable for risk management and decision analysis purposes, they should contain the components, shown in **figure 3.9**.

Figure 3.9—I&T-related Risk Scenario Development Structure

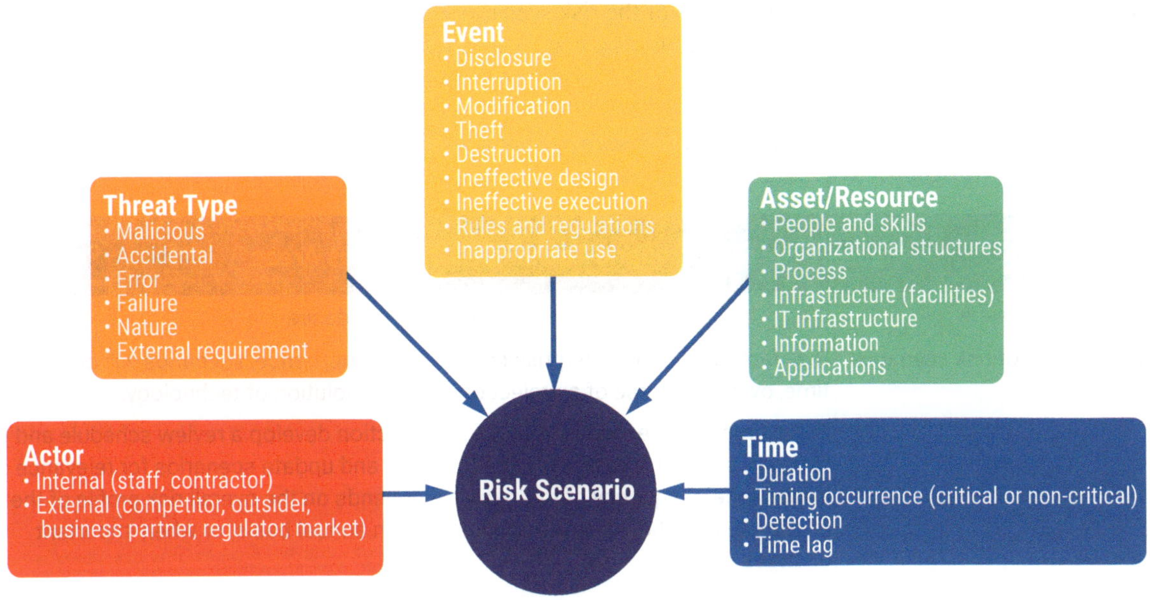

Source: ISACA, *COBIT® 5 for Risk*, USA, 2013, figure 36, *www.isaca.org/bookstore/cobit-5/wcb5rk*

- **Actor**—Any person, thing or entity that acts or carries out a threat. An actor can be Internal or external.
- **Threat type**—The nature of the threat may be malicious, accidental, process failure, naturally occurring (force majeure), business cycle or something else that would impact the ability of the enterprise to meet its objectives.
- **Event**—The impact or outcome may be the disclosure of information, interruption of a system, unintended modification or change, theft, destruction, etc. The term event also includes ineffective design (of systems, processes, etc.), ineffective execution of processes (e.g., change management procedures, acquisition procedures, project prioritization processes), regulation (impact of) and inappropriate use or cost of cleanup or remediation from the scenario.
- **Asset/Resource**—As defined earlier, an asset is anything of value to the enterprise in the delivery of its mission or business strategy that can be affected by the condition and lead to business or mission impact. A resource (IT) is anything that helps to achieve I&T goals. Assets and resources can be identical (e.g., IT hardware is an important resource because all IT applications use it, and is an asset because it has a certain value to the enterprise). I&T assets/resources include:
    - People (e.g., employees, contractors, staffing providers, third parties)
    - IT processes and business processes
    - Physical infrastructure (e.g., facilities, equipment)
    - IT infrastructure (e.g., computing hardware, network infrastructure, middleware)
    - Other enterprise architecture components (e.g., information, applications)
- **Timing**—May be relevant to some scenarios and can be described as follows:
    - Point of occurrence (Does the event occur at a critical moment?)
    - Duration of the event (extended outage of a service or data center)
    - Time lag between the event and the impact. (Is there an immediate consequence [e.g., network failure, immediate downtime], or a delayed impact [e.g., obsolete IT architecture with accumulated high costs over a time span of several years]?)

The risk scenario structure differentiates between loss events (events generating the negative impact), vulnerabilities or vulnerability events (events contributing to the impact or frequency of loss events occurring), and threat events (circumstances or events brought about by a threat actor that can trigger loss events). It is important to accurately describe and understand the different components of the risk scenario so appropriate actions may be taken. This is difficult to do if you have one large list of conditions that may occur rather than a list of relevant risk that has been analyzed and prioritized by business impact.

Some key issues relating to the development of a risk scenario are addressed in **figure 3.10**.

Figure 3.10—Risk Scenario Technique Main Focus Areas

Focus/Issue	Summary Guidance
Maintain currency of risk scenarios and risk factors.	Risk factors and the enterprise change over time; hence, scenarios will change over time, over the course of a project or over the evolution of technology. For example, it is essential that the risk function develop a review schedule and the CIO works with the business lines to review and update scenarios for relevance and importance. Frequency of this exercise depends on the overall risk profile of the enterprise and should be done at least on an annual basis, or when important changes occur.
Use generic risk scenarios as a starting point and build more detail where and when required.	One technique of keeping the number of scenarios manageable is to propagate a standard set of generic scenarios through the enterprise and develop more detailed and relevant scenarios when required and warranted by the risk profile only at lower (entity) levels. The assumptions made when grouping or generalizing should be well understood by all and adequately documented because they may hide certain scenarios or be confusing when looking at risk response. For example, if 'insider threat' is not well defined within a scenario, it may not be clear whether this threat includes privileged and non-privileged insiders. The differences between these aspects of a scenario can be critical when one is trying to understand the frequency and impact of events, as well as mitigation opportunities.
Number of scenarios should be representative and reflect business reality and complexity.	Risk management helps to deal with the enormous complexity of today's IT environments by prioritizing potential action according to its value in reducing risk. Risk management is about reducing complexity, not generating it; hence, another plea for working with a manageable number of risk scenarios. However, the retained number of scenarios still needs to accurately reflect business reality and complexity.
Risk taxonomy should reflect business reality and complexity.	There should be a sufficient number of risk scenario scales reflecting the complexity of the enterprise and the extent of exposures to which the enterprise is subject. Potential scales might be a 'low, medium, high' ranking or a numeric scale that scores risk importance from 0 to 5. Scales should be aligned throughout the enterprise to ensure consistent scoring.

Figure 3.10—Risk Scenario Technique Main Focus Areas (cont.)

Focus/Issue	Summary Guidance
Use generic risk scenario structure to simplify risk reporting.	Similarly, for risk reporting purposes, entities should not report on all specific and detailed scenarios, but could do so by using the generic risk structure. For example, an entity may have taken generic scenario 15 (project quality), translated it into five scenarios for its major projects, subsequently conducted a risk analysis for each of the scenarios, then aggregated or summarized the results and reported back using the generic scenario header 'project quality'.
Ensure adequate people and skills requirements for developing relevant risk scenarios.	Developing a manageable and relevant set of risk scenarios requires: • Expertise and experience, to not overlook relevant scenarios and not be drawn into highly unrealistic or irrelevant scenarios. While the avoidance of scenarios that are unrealistic or irrelevant is important in properly utilizing limited resources, some attention should be paid to situations that are highly infrequent and unpredictable, but which could have a cataclysmic impact on the enterprise. • A thorough understanding of the environment. This includes the IT environment (e.g., infrastructure, applications, dependencies between applications, infrastructure components), the overall business environment, and an understanding of how and which IT environments support the business environment to understand the business impact. • The intervention and common views of all parties involved—senior management, which has the decision power; business management, which has the best view on business impact; IT, which has the understanding of what can go wrong with IT; and risk management, which can moderate and structure the debate amongst the other parties. • The process of developing scenarios usually benefits from a brainstorming/workshop approach, where a high-level assessment is usually required to reduce the number of scenarios to a manageable, but relevant and representative, number.
Use the risk scenario building process to obtain buy-in.	Scenario analysis is not just an analytical exercise involving risk analysts. A significant additional benefit of scenario analysis is achieving organizational buy-in from enterprise entities and business lines, risk management, IT, finance, compliance and other parties. Gaining this buy-in is the reason why scenario analysis should be a carefully facilitated process.
Involve first line of defense in the scenario building process.	In addition to coordinating with management, it is recommended that selected members of the staff who are familiar with the detailed operations be included in discussions, where appropriate. Staff whose daily work is in the detailed operations are often more familiar with vulnerabilities in technology and processes that can be exploited.
Do not focus only on rare and extreme scenarios.	When developing scenarios, one should not focus only on worst-case events because they rarely materialize, whereas less-severe incidents happen more often.

Figure 3.10—Risk Scenario Technique Main Focus Areas (cont.)

Focus/Issue	Summary Guidance
Deduce complex scenarios from simple scenarios by showing impact and dependencies.	Simple scenarios, once developed, should be further fine-tuned into more complex scenarios, showing cascading and/or coincidental impacts and reflecting dependencies. For example: • A scenario of having a major hardware failure can be combined with the scenario of failed DRP. • A scenario of major software failure can trigger database corruption and, in combination with poor data management backups, can lead to serious consequences, or at least consequences of a different magnitude than a software failure alone. • A scenario of a major external event can lead to a scenario of internal apathy.
Consider systemic and contagious risk.	Attention should be paid to systemic and/or contagious risk scenarios: • **Systemic**—Something happens with an important business partner, affecting a large group of enterprises within an area or industry. An example would be a nationwide air traffic control system that goes down for an extended period of time, e.g., six hours, affecting air traffic on a very large scale. • **Contagious**—Events that happen at several of the enterprise's business partners within a very short time frame. An example would be a clearinghouse that can be fully prepared for any sort of emergency by having very sophisticated disaster recovery measures in place, but when a catastrophe happens, finds that no transactions are sent by its providers and hence is temporarily out of business.
Use scenario building to increase awareness for risk detection.	Use development also helps to address the issue of detectability, moving away from a situation where an enterprise 'does not know what it does not know'. The collaborative approach for scenario development assists in identifying risk to which the enterprise, until then, would not have realized it was subject to (and hence would never have thought of putting in place any countermeasures). After the full set of risk items is identified during scenario generation, risk analysis assesses frequency and impact of the scenarios. Questions to be asked include: • Will the enterprise ever detect that the risk scenario has materialized? • Will the enterprise notice something has gone wrong so it can react appropriately? Generating scenarios and creatively thinking of what can go wrong will automatically raise and, hopefully, cause response to, the question of detectability. Detectability of scenarios includes two steps: visibility and recognition. The enterprise must be in a position that it can observe anything going wrong, and it needs the capability to recognize an observed event as something wrong.

Source: ISACA, *COBIT® 5 for Risk*, USA, figure 37, *www.isaca.org/bookstore/cobit-5/wcb5rk*

3.11 Summary of Terminology

It is important to recognize and understand I&T-related risk terminology. The following terms were introduced in this chapter.

Figure 3.11—Chapter 3 Terminology

Term	Definition
Access risk	The risk that information may be divulged or made available to recipients without authorized access by the information owner, reflecting a loss of confidentiality
Advanced persistent threat (APT)	An adversary that possesses sophisticated levels of expertise and significant resources which allow it to create opportunities to achieve its objectives using multiple attack vectors (NIST SP800-61)
Asset	Something of either tangible or intangible value that is worth protecting
Asset inventory	A register used to record all relevant assets
Asset value	The value of an asset to both the business and to competitors
Attack vector	A path or route used by the adversary to gain access to the target (asset)
Availability risk	The risk that service may be lost or data are not accessible when needed
Business process	An interrelated set of cross-functional activities or events that result in the delivery of a specific product or service to a customer
Infrastructure risk	The risk that I&T infrastructure and systems may be unable to effectively support the current and future needs of the business in an efficient, cost-effective and well-controlled fashion
Integrity risk	The risk that data may be unavailable due to incompleteness or inaccuracy
Investment (or expense) risk	The risk that I&T investment fails to provide value commensurate with its cost or is otherwise excessive or wasteful, including the overall I&T investment portfolio
Project ownership risk	The risk that I&T projects fail to meet objectives through lack of accountability and commitment
Relevance risk	The risk that the right information may not get to the right recipients at the right time to allow the right action to be taken or the right decisions to be made
Resource (IT)	Any enterprise asset that helps to achieve I&T goals
Risk awareness program	A program that creates an understanding of risk, risk factors and the various types of risk that an enterprise faces
Risk identification	Risk identification is the process for determining and documenting the risk an enterprise faces
Risk scenario	The tangible and assessable representation of risk
Risk taxonomy	A scheme for classifying sources and categories of risk that provides a common language for discussing and communicating risk to stakeholders
Schedule risk	The risk that I&T projects take longer than expected
Threat actor	Any person, thing or entity that acts or carries out a threat and is responsible for a threat event
Threat assessment/analysis	An evaluation of the type, scope and nature of events or actions that can result in adverse consequences; identification of the threats that exist against enterprise assets
Threat event	Any event during which a threat actor acts against an asset in a manner that has the potential to directly result in harm
Vulnerability assessment/analysis	A process of identifying and classifying vulnerabilities

Page intentionally left blank

Chapter 3 Knowledge Check

Review questions are provided as a means to support the content presented within this study guide and serve as a gauge or assessment of knowledge of I&T-related risk topics. One question is provided for each topic.

For individuals intending to earn the ISACA IT Risk Fundamentals Certificate, these questions are written to depict the type of questions that may appear on the exam. These questions will not specifically appear on the exam, but similar ones may appear.

REVIEW QUESTIONS

1. When establishing a process for the valuation of IT assets, it is **MOST** important to:

   A. Map IT assets to business processes.
   B. Assemble a complete inventory of all IT assets.
   C. Assign both qualitative and quantitative values to IT assets.

2. Which of the statements pertaining to threat actors is **TRUE**?

   A. Every threat requires a threat actor.
   B. Threat actors refer exclusively to humans.
   C. Threat actors include competitors.

3. A vulnerability assessment:

   A. Identifies how specific vulnerabilities expose IT assets.
   B. Only renders data where a vulnerability exists.
   C. Discovers potential points of compromise or weakness.

4. An inability to provide the correct I&T-related information to the correct recipients, at the right time, to allow the right actions to be taken is known as:

   A. Access risk
   B. Relevance risk
   C. Availability risk

5. The use of risk scenarios is **MOST** effective when they:

   A. Exclusively utilize all actual past risk events that an enterprise has experienced.
   B. Are developed independently of business objectives and impacts to the enterprise.
   C. Only focus on real and relevant potential risk events that an enterprise may encounter.

Answers on page 106

Chapter 3 ANSWER KEY

Review Questions

1. **A. The value of an IT asset is intrinsically linked to the business value it provides.**
   B. An enterprise may find it difficult to value IT assets and as a result may not have an accurate list. Having a complete list is helpful, but not as important as linking to business processes.
   C. Assign both qualitative and quantitative values to IT assets.

2. A. Not every type of threat requires an actor (e.g., failures or natural causes).
   B. Threat actors can be internal or external, and they can be human or nonhuman.
   C. External threat actors include competitors.

3. A. Identifying existing vulnerabilities and then using known exploit methods to identify how specific vulnerabilities expose IT resources and assets is associated with penetration testing.
   B. Vulnerability assessments may contain data that is not accurate, particularly false positives that indicate a vulnerability where none exists.
   C. A vulnerability assessment provides a careful examination of a target environment to discover any potential points of compromise or weakness.

4. A. Access risk is the risk that information may be divulged or made available to recipients without authorized access by the information owner, reflecting a loss of confidentiality.
   B. Relevance risk is the risk that the right information may not get to the right recipients, at the right time, to allow the right action to be taken or the right decisions to be made.
   C. Availability risk is the risk that service may be lost or data are not accessible when needed.

5. A. Although past risk events may be useful, they should only be considered in the development of risk scenarios if they focus on current, real and relevant potential risk events.
   B. Each risk scenario should be related to a business objective or impact.
   C. The key to developing effective scenarios is to focus on real and relevant potential risk events.

Chapter 4:

Risk Assessment and Analysis

Learning Objectives 108

Risk Assessment and Analysis

4.1 Risk Assessment Processes 109
4.2 Risk Scenario Evaluation 110
4.3 Risk Analysis Process, Approaches and Methods 113
4.4 Risk Ranking, Prioritization and Aggregation 121
4.5 Risk Documentation 125
4.6 Control Assessment 130
4.7 Summary of Terminology 134

Chapter 4 Knowledge Check 137

Learning Objectives

After risk is identified, the next step is to assess, analyze and evaluate risk. This step includes an evaluation of risk scenarios. This chapter discusses risk analysis approaches and provides examples. The use of risk maps, risk aggregation and a risk register are also discussed. Creating risk documentation is another task in this step that is reviewed in this chapter. Finally, the assessment of controls is explained.

Learning objectives include the following:

- Explain the risk assessment process.
- Describe frequency and magnitude and how they apply to a risk scenario.
- Explain the risk analysis process and available approaches.
- Apply risk analysis methods and techniques.
- Explain how to rank and prioritize risk.
- Describe risk aggregation and it applies to risk maps.
- Summarize how to document risk (risk register).
- Explain how to assess the current state of controls.
- Define risk and control ownership.

Risk Assessment and Analysis

4.1 Risk Assessment Processes

4.1.1 Risk Assessment

Risk assessment is the process used to identify and evaluate risk and its potential effects.

The purpose of an I&T-related risk assessment is to build an initial view of the overall I&T-related risk for the enterprise by looking at the components of the risk universe at a high level. The assessment enables those responsible for risk governance to:

- Identify potential high-risk areas
- Gain an overview of major risk factors
- Detect the most critical risk scenarios that should be examined in greater detail at a later stage

A risk assessment should involve all major stakeholders of the enterprise and should be facilitated by a knowledgeable and experienced risk professional to guarantee impartiality and consistency throughout the enterprise.

Meaningful I&T-related risk assessments and risk-based decisions require I&T-related risk to be expressed in unambiguous and clear, business or mission-relevant terms, such as financial, revenue, or meeting desired strategic outcomes. To increase the effectiveness of the risk management function, IT and the rest of the business need to establish a mutual understanding of identifying the risk that needs to be managed and why. All stakeholders must have the ability to understand and express how adverse events may affect business or mission objectives. This means that:

- A shared understanding of I&T-related failures, compromises, mistakes or events can impact enterprise objectives and result in the loss of direct costs (e.g., financial), or indirect (e.g., customer sensitive) information resulting in reputational damage.
- Losses to the enterprise from I&T-related events can affect the ability for an enterprise to deliver its key services and products. This is true even when the enterprise relies on IT suppliers to provide goods and resources that are integral to its strategic objectives.

To remain relevant, an I&T-related risk assessment must be regularly repeated. If no major changes have occurred in any of the risk factors, a simple annual confirmation of earlier results is sufficient. Major changes in an enterprise environment, such as mergers and new markets, necessitate a new assessment. An annual update or confirmation of the assessment is recommended for stable environments.

Risk assessment is slightly broader than risk analysis and includes the activities of:

- Ranking or prioritizing risk according to defined enterprise risk thresholds (based on tolerances)
- Grouping like risk types together for mitigation action
- Documenting existing controls that provide mitigation for similar risk types

4.1.2 Risk Analysis

Risk analysis is the process by which frequency and magnitude of I&T-related risk scenarios are estimated. As part of the evaluation of risk, an analysis of the individual scenarios is necessary to determine the probabilities of a particular event, taking into account frequency and impact (magnitude) of the risk scenarios. Before beginning the analysis, the data gathered must be validated for accuracy and completeness. There are many ways to conduct risk analyses, including qualitative, quantitative and semi-quantitative methods. After the risk scenarios are analyzed, the collected data are used to help select risk response options (discussed in Chapter 5).

4.1.3 Risk Evaluation

Risk evaluation is the process of comparing the estimated risk against given risk criteria to determine the significance of the risk. Risk identified by the high-level risk assessment must be evaluated by comparing the results of the risk analysis against established criteria for acceptability, impact, likelihood and the need for further treatment. Deciding whether risk treatment is required is usually based on operational, technical, financial, regulatory, legal, social or environmental criteria, or combinations of criteria. The criteria should be in line with the scope and qualitative analysis of the enterprise's internal policies and procedures and must support its goals and objectives. After this evaluation has been performed, the output is a prioritized list of risk, presented in business terms.

4.2 Risk Scenario Evaluation

During risk identification, risk scenarios are developed and used to identify and describe potential risk events. These scenarios are useful to communicate with the business and gather input data required to understand the potential or probable impact of the risk event if it were to occur.

The impact of a risk event can be difficult to estimate with any degree of accuracy without a structured methodology because there are many factors that affect the outcome of an event. If the event is detected quickly and appropriate measures are taken to contain the incident, then the impact may be minimized and the recovery process may be fairly rapid. However, if the enterprise is unable to detect the incident promptly, the same incident could cause severe damage and result in much higher recovery costs.

As previously described, risk analysis is the process used to:

- Estimate the frequency and magnitude of a given risk scenario.
- Identify and evaluate risk, its potential impact on the enterprise, and the likelihood (probability) that a particular event will occur.

Risk analysis makes it possible to more clearly communicate impact in terms of lost productivity and other specific measures of value, which is useful for many reasons:

- Using a quantitative value of loss (or gain), based in the language of currency, time, productivity units or other measurable values, is easier to communicate to everyone.
- Defining every consequence that is, or is not acceptable in dozens or more different areas of business or mission functions, using only qualitative labels (low, high, catastrophic) and differing scales of measurement does not allow for confident or justified decision-making about risk.
- Quantifying the potential loss or other negative impact associated with risk provides a basis for deciding how to respond to risk that is out of tolerance with acceptable levels and where a traditional controls-based mitigation approach may not be applicable.

All I&T assets are not equal, and the budget needed to respond to risk should be commensurate with the value or criticality of the asset in the delivery of the business and mission objectives.

4.2.1 Frequency Analysis

A frequency analysis can determine how often a particular risk scenario might be expected to occur during a specified period of time. The first step in a frequency analysis is to identify the analysis method or methods, for example, deciding whether the estimates will be based on historical data, models, professional judgment or a combination of methods. Whether an established scientific or statistical protocol will be followed must also be decided. The choice of method will reflect the accuracy needed, cost, available data, the level of expertise on the team and the method's acceptability to stakeholders.

When validating the results of a frequency analysis, it is important to ensure that the:

- Scope is appropriate for the analysis's stated objectives.
- Analysis can be reproduced by personnel other than the original analyst(s).
- Analysis is not sensitive to the formatting of data or results.
- Estimation process assumptions and uncertainties have been acknowledged and documented.
- Critical assumptions have been reviewed to determine credibility.
- Appropriate models, methods and data have been fully documented and explained.

Estimations that are based on related historical data and estimations based on derived models should be distinguished. In the event of little or no available relevant historical data, methods such as fault-tree or event-tree analysis or other mathematical or econometric models may be used.

Expert experience and judgment may also serve as a basis for estimates. Frequency estimates are most often derived from a combination of these different methods. This usually generates an expected range of frequencies with an estimate of uncertainty, rather than a single number.

4.2.2 Impact Criteria

Risk management is an enterprise activity that benefits from a standardized, structured approach that can be applied to the entire enterprise without substantial modification or customization. It is possible to identify risk on a system-by-system or project-by-project basis, but the result of such an approach creates the risk of false assurance by having neither consistency nor interoperability among the risk methods, techniques, or processes that are implemented. Without a structured approach, risk may be measured differently in different parts of the enterprise, creating confusion and resulting in the managing of an individual risk rather than risk management across the enterprise.

One analysis technique that is useful is the development of enterprise-specific impact criteria. Impact criteria gives risk meaning and helps the enterprise to set specific risk appetites or risk tolerances. Criteria may be qualitative in nature or quantitative. One reason for developing impact criteria with defined quantitative ranges (thresholds) is that the criterion can act as an input to or a double-check of the risk appetite and risk tolerance statements. Impact criteria applies to the enterprise, not a specific I&T asset, and reflect the areas that are most relevant to the business or mission objectives.

A good general starter set of impact criteria should, at a minimum, include financial, productivity, business interruption or system availability tolerances, tangible losses (e.g. property, equipment, etc.), physical security, life, health, and safety, fines and legal penalties. As the impact criteria becomes refined over time, distinguishing the types of risk that would result in immediate direct costs versus future loss of revenue or liabilities to the enterprise may be useful to management.

An example of the development of impact criteria is provided in **figure 4.1**.

Figure 4.1—Impact Criteria

Impact Area	Low	Moderate	High
Reputation	• Reputation is minimally affected; little or no effort or expense is required to recover. Impact limited to internal/few customers.	• Reputation is damaged, and some effort and expense is required to recover. Impact limited to local to specific market area.	• Reputation is irrevocably destroyed or damaged. All geographic market areas affected.
Core Customer Loss	• Less than 1% reduction in customers for 1 to 30 day(s) due to loss of confidence.	• 1% to 5% reduction in customers for 1 to 30 day(s) due to loss of confidence.	• More than 5% reduction in customers for 1 to 30 day(s) due to loss of confidence.
Financial	• Fines less than $50,000 are levied. • Nonfrivolous lawsuit or lawsuits less than $250,000 are filed against the enterprise, or frivolous lawsuit(s) are filed against the enterprise.	• Fines between $50,000 and $100,000 are levied. • Nonfrivolous lawsuit greater than $250,000 but less than $500,000 are filed against the enterprise.	• Fines greater than $100,000 are levied. • Nonfrivolous lawsuit or lawsuits greater than $500,000 are filed against the enterprise.
Productivity/Staff hours	• Staff work hours are increased by less than 5% for 1 to 30 day(s). • Less than 25% of staff out for 1 week or less.	• Staff work hours are increased between 3% and 7% for 30 to 60 day(s). • More than 25% of staff out for 1 to 3 weeks.	• Staff work hours are increased by greater than 8% for greater than 60 days. • More than 25% of staff out for more than 3 weeks.

Source: Derived from Software Engineering Institute, Carnegie Mellon University, *http://resources.sei.cmu.edu/library/asset-view.cfm?AssetID=8419*

Many enterprises use their own developed scales to describe and estimate impact. There is benefit in using the same metrics groups for frequency and impact across the entire (extended) enterprise to allow better understanding of risk and easier comparisons across the value chains.

4.2.3 Business Impact Analysis

Business impact is the net effect, positive or negative, on the achievement of business objectives. A business impact analysis (BIA) is the process to determine the impact of losing the support of any resource.

A business impact analysis:

- Determines the impact of losing the support of any resource to an enterprise.
- Establishes the escalation of that loss over time.
- Identifies the minimum resources needed to recover.

- Prioritizes the recovery of processes and the supporting system.

It involves evaluating the criticality and sensitivity of I&T assets and estimating the impact of various scenarios on anything affected by the activity.

The impact of the consequence on the needs, issues and concerns of the stakeholders must be considered and may be positive or negative in nature. Impact is often measured by:

- Income loss
- Unexpected expense
- Legal issues (regulatory compliance or contractual)
- Interdependent processes
- Impact on an enterprise's reputation or public confidence

Measuring impact in financial terms allows dollars to function as the unit of measurement. This provides a common metric for comparing dissimilar conditions and a compelling motivation for decision-makers to take action.

A final consideration when estimating impact and obtaining reliable and accepted estimations is to involve all stakeholders in scenario-analysis exercises. Separate assessments, followed by group discussion to achieve consensus, and workshops are ways to include stakeholders and ensure estimations are reliable.

4.3 Risk Analysis Process, Approaches and Methods

4.3.1 Risk Analysis Process

Risk analysis is used to:

- Estimate the frequency and magnitude of a given risk scenario.
- Identify and evaluate risk, its potential impact on the enterprise, and the likelihood (probability) that a particular event will occur.

More specifically, risk analysis involves the:

- Thorough examination of the risk sources (threats and vulnerabilities) determined during risk identification
- Extent to which I&T-related assets have exposure to potential threats and the effect on likelihood
- Potential negative consequences (impact)
- Likelihood that those consequences may occur and the factors that affect them
- Assessment of any existing controls or processes that tend to minimize negative risk or enhance positive outcomes (these controls may derive from a wider set of standards, controls or good practices selected according to an applicability statement [i.e., the application of controls identified in the risk register] and may also come from previous risk treatment activities)

The level of risk can be estimated in various ways, including using statistical analysis and calculations combining impact and likelihood.

Any formulas and methods for combining impact and likelihood must be consistent with the criteria defined when establishing the risk management context. This is because an event may have multiple impacts (consequences) and affect different objectives; therefore, impact and likelihood need to be combined to calculate the level of risk. If no reliable or statistically reliable and relevant past data are available (e.g., incident data kept for an incident database), other estimates based on such things as impacts affecting other enterprises may be made as long as they are appropriately communicated and approved by the decision makers.

There are many good sources of data to support risk analysis, and there are many sources where data can be obtained including:

- Data from risk events that have caused or may cause impacts

- Past experience or historical data and records (e.g., financial records, incident reporting, investigations, problem reporting)
- Internal department I&T-related risk data, such as from business, legal, audit, compliance and IT department
- Reliable practices, international standards, guidelines and benchmarks
- Market research on other enterprises and industry peer analysis
- Regulatory requirements and data
- IT trends
- Experiments and prototypes
- Economic, engineering or other models
- Specialist and expert advice
- Product liability information

Risk analysis may vary in detail according to the risk, the purpose of the analysis, and the required protection level of the relevant information, data and resources.

4.3.2 Risk Analysis Approaches

Several risk analysis approaches exist. Some attributes of the enterprise that determine which approach to use are culture, resources, skills and knowledge, environment and risk appetite.

Risk can be discussed in quantitative (using numbers) or qualitative (using descriptive words) terms, and the specific definitions of risk sometimes vary from source to source. The fundamental nature of risk is uncertainty. This means that the uncertainty of risk being realized and resulting in loss or damage may or may not occur and is generally discussed related to risk using terms like probability, likelihood, volatility, or frequency. Another part of the uncertainty is what the loss or damage would mean for the enterprise if that risk materializes and is generally discussed using terms such as impact, magnitude or consequence.

Several risk analysis approaches exist, including:

- Qualitative (high-level)
- Quantitative (detailed)
- Hybrid

Each of these approaches tend to be used for different purposes. For example, a:

- Qualitative approach is most effectively used to identify like or unlike characteristics for grouping purposes, and may assist in efficiencies in applying controls or mitigation techniques to respond to risk that would be effective against common risk types. A qualitative approach is not meant to be a measurement method. A qualitative risk assessment approach is usually applied when only limited or low-quality information is available.
- Quantitative approach is used to provide the required rigor and accuracy for the selected high-risk areas.
- Hybrid approach is used to provide an intermediary level between the conceptual evaluation of a qualitative approach and the numerical evaluation of a quantitative approach.

Qualitative Approach

A qualitative risk analysis approach is based on expert opinion, judgement, intuition and experience. The frequency and the impact are estimated using qualitative labels, such as High, Medium, or Low. Many enterprises use a numerical qualitative measurement scale by arbitrarily assigning the risk rating scale to numbers 1 (High), 2 (Medium) or 3 (Low) to rank-stack a list of risk. Using a numeric scale like this to plot identified risk on a chart is also an example of a qualitative risk analysis. These labels can vary depending on the circumstances and different environments. A problem with assigning risk a qualitative label is that it makes it difficult to distinguish or differentiate between risk that has been grouped together. That is, there is no way to know which high risk is higher than another high risk in the same bucket. Alternatively, there is no way to know if putting together a group of "low" risk is equivalent to one or more medium or one high risk. The assignment of qualitative values relies heavily on experience and expert knowledge, but such reliance does not make qualitative risk assessment less effective than quantitative risk assessment. However, qualitative approaches do not support risk aggregation in a meaningful way when attempting to look at risk across the enterprise.

Some types of risk can be difficult for beginners to calculate in purely numeric terms at first, and controlling for the unknown variables in a quantitative process can require so many assumptions as to render the apparently precise results relatively unhelpful. In contrast, although qualitative approaches are not meant to be a measurement method, the relative values offered by a qualitative process can typically be used to order response actions in terms of perceived importance. When the perception is based on a broad enough sample of stakeholders, the resulting course of action is likely to be acceptable to those stakeholders.

A qualitative approach is usually based on scenarios or descriptions of situations that either have occurred or may occur and assist an enterprise with decision-making about the uncertainty of a risk scenario materializing. The intention of these scenarios is to elicit feedback from multiple stakeholders (e.g., departments, customers, management). Communicating with all affected stakeholders is a good way to eliminate unlikely assumptions and determine a level of risk that reflects a reasonable consensus of feedback from all potentially affected groups.

Scenarios under a qualitative approach may be based on threats, vulnerabilities, assets/impact or some combination of these factors.

- A threat-based approach examines a risk event on the basis of threat agents and seeks to identify potential methods of attack. From this information, it can be inferred which vulnerabilities will be exploited by the attacker along with the intent and skill of the attacker and the potential damage to the assets affected.

This scenario approach is especially beneficial when examining the emergence of new threats and determining the risk related to advanced persistent threats (APTs), whose capabilities and available time make waiting for suitable vulnerabilities more feasible than is true of conventional attackers.

- A vulnerability-based approach takes the opposite approach. It examines the enterprise's known vulnerabilities and then attempts to anticipate threats that could exploit those vulnerabilities, projecting from these the consequences and magnitude of impact. Vulnerability-based scenarios are especially valuable after completing vulnerability assessments, and their findings can be further assessed by carrying out penetration testing to determine whether the anticipated threats are feasible in the context of the enterprise and its systems.
- An asset/impact approach is based on the identification of critical and sensitive assets and the potential ways that these could be damaged—typically by attacking their confidentiality, integrity and availability.

The results of a qualitative approach are typically presented in the form of a table that compares the likelihood of a risk event with its impact to the enterprise, where the confluence of the two factors generates the relative level of the risk. For instance, a risk that is highly likely and has a high level of impact would be identified as an area of immediate concern, whereas a risk of lower likelihood or a lower level of exposure would represent a lower level of priority for risk response. A common approach to qualitative analysis can be accomplished by using a 5-by-5 matrix, as shown in **figure 4.2**.

Figure 4.2—Qualitative Approach

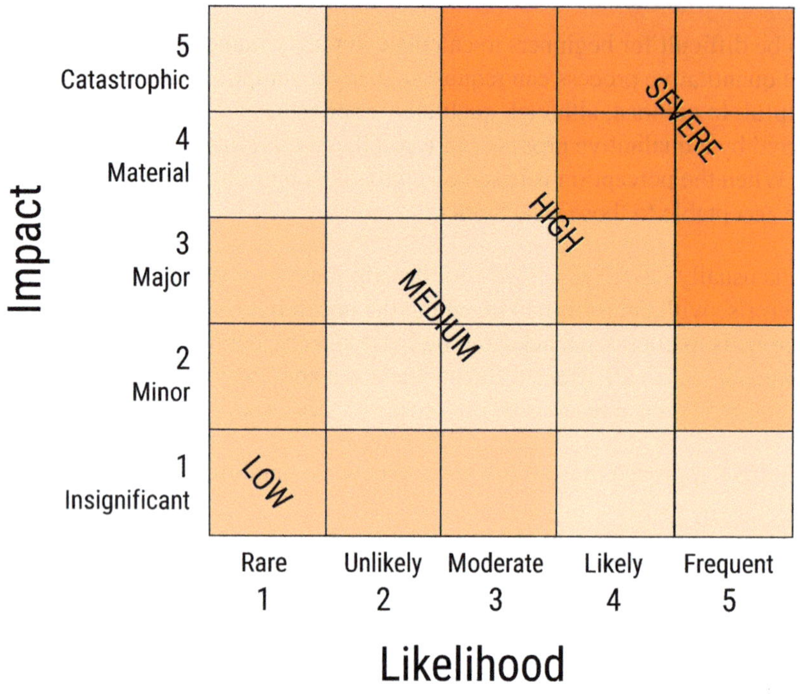

Source: ISACA, *CISM Review Manual, 15th Edition*, USA, 2016, figure 2.17, *https://www.isaca.org/bookstore/cism-exam-resources/cm15ed*

Qualitative analysis may be used:

- As an initial assessment to identify risk that will be the subject of further, detailed analysis
- Where nontangible "soft" aspects of risk are to be considered (e.g., reputation, culture, image)
- Where there is a lack of adequate information and numerical data or resources necessary for a statistically acceptable quantitative approach

Qualitative analysis generally cost much less than quantitative analysis and usually results in a better understanding of business unit dependencies and interactions. Qualitative analysis depends on the human factor; it is more consensus-based, and participants do not invest a lot of time trying to calculate precise financial numbers for risk valuation, impacts or investments in controls.

When applying subjective information to analyzing risk, the following challenges must be considered:

- Subjectivity or bias in data collected
- Overemphasis on minor events
- Does not provide useful data for cost/benefit analysis
- Ranking levels may not be meaningful to data providers

A qualitative approach is best where only limited or low-quality information is available.

The disadvantages of qualitative methods include a high degree of subjectivity, differences in human judgment and the lack of a standardized approach, which can introduce ambiguities into the results. However, a qualitative analysis approach is usually less complex, and therefore less expensive than a quantitative analysis approach. It is also better suited to considering hard-to-quantify risk, such as enterprise reputation or the value of human life.

Operationally Critical Threat Asset and Vulnerability Evaluation® (OCTAVE®)[21]

OCTAVE is a qualitative risk analysis approach used to assist an enterprise in understanding, assessing and addressing information security risk from the perspective of the enterprise. The OCTAVE methodology is process-driven and used to identify, prioritize and manage information security risk. It is intended to help an enterprise:[22]

- Develop qualitative risk evaluation criteria based on operational risk tolerances.
- Identify assets that are critical to the mission of the enterprise.
- Identify vulnerabilities and threats to the critical assets.
- Determine and evaluate potential consequences to the enterprise if threats are realized.
- Initiate corrective actions to mitigate risk and create practice-based protection strategy.

OCTAVE focuses on critical assets and the risk to those assets using a comprehensive, systematic, context-driven and self-directed evaluation approach. It can help an enterprise to maintain a proactive security posture and apply the enterprise point of view to information security risk management activities.

Quantitative Approach

A quantitative risk analysis approach is the calculation of the risk's likelihood and impact using numerical and statistical techniques. It incorporates financial data, percentages and ratios to approximate the magnitude of impact in financial terms. It is particularly suitable for cost-benefit analysis because risk that can be mapped to monetary values can easily and directly be compared to the costs of various risk responses. Unfortunately, the cost associated with a particular risk can be very difficult to quantify, especially if it includes subjective elements such as reputation and employee morale. Many events used in quantitative assessment are also unpredictable.

The numerical values that are assigned to impact and likelihood are derived from a variety of sources. The quality of the entire analysis depends on the accuracy of the assigned values and the validity of the statistical models used. Impact can be determined by evaluating and processing the various results of an event or by extrapolation from experimental studies or past data and may be expressed in various terms of:

- Monetary
- Technical
- Operational
- Human impact criteria

The essence of quantitative risk assessment is to derive the frequency and impact of risk scenarios, based on measurement, statistical methods and data.

A quantitative analysis approach is data-driven. This method allows for:

- Classification and counting of data
- Construction of statistical models that explain what is being observed
- Generalization of findings to a larger population and direct comparison between different sets of data and observations

[21] Carnegie Mellon Software Engineering Institute, *Operationally Critical Threat Asset and Vulnerability Evaluation® (OCTAVE®) Framework*, version 1.0, 1999, *https://resources.sei.cmu.edu/asset_files/TechnicalReport/1999_005_001_16769.pdf*

[22] *Ibid.*

- Production of statistically reliable results
- Discovery of genuine phenomena versus chance occurrences

Because quantitative risk analysis is based on formal, empirical data, it is more consistent and objective in nature than qualitative analysis. This also means that reliable results depend on reliable data concerning past and comparable risk events. Such data can be very difficult to obtain, limiting the application of a quantitative analysis.

Quantitative analysis is limited when dealing with considerations that are difficult or impossible to quantify—for example, the value of human life, cost of terrorist attacks or similar events and loss of reputation.

Quantitative Approach Uses and Examples

Quantitative approaches are used in calculating annual loss expectancy and value at risk.

Annual Loss Expectancy

Quantitative risk assessments attempt to arrive at a numerical value, usually expressed in financial terms. The most common form is either single loss expectancy (SLE) or ALE.

SLE is the product of the asset value (AV) multiplied by the exposure factor (EF): SLE = AV × EF. EF is the probability that an event will occur and its likely magnitude, and equals the percentage of asset loss caused by the identified threat. The result is that the greater the value, coupled with a greater probability and greater magnitude, the greater the potential risk of loss.

ALE adds the annualized rate of occurrence (ARO) to the equation with the result that multiple occurrences will result in greater potential losses. ALE is usually expressed as: ALE = SLE × ARO.

ALE is the annual expected financial loss to an asset, resulting from one specific threat.

ARO is the number of times a threat on a single asset is estimated to occur. The higher the risk associated with the threat, the higher the ARO. For example, if insurance data suggest that a serious fire is likely to occur once in 25 years, then the annualized rate of occurrence is $1/25 = 0.04$.

EF represents the percentage of loss that a realized threat could have on a specific asset when the specific threat matches up with a specific vulnerability. Said another way, EF is the proportion of an asset's value that is likely to be destroyed by a particular risk, expressed as a percentage.

Value at Risk

Value at risk (VaR) estimates the probability of losses based on the statistical analysis of historical price trends and volatilities. Banks, security firms and companies that are involved in trading energy and other commodities commonly use the VaR method. VaR is a computation based on historical data of the probability distribution of loss for a given period of time at a certainty factor typically of 95 percent or 99 percent. The probability distribution is arrived at using Monte Carlo simulations typically run through thousands of iterations with random variables based on historical information.

Earnings at Risk

Earnings at risk (EaR) measures potential net income changes in the event of an adverse change in interest rates. Cash flows or earnings are used.

Cost-benefit Analysis

A cost/benefit analysis (also discussed in Section 5.5) of recommended risk controls often incorporates the results of quantitative analysis. The mathematical nature of quantitative analysis, however, does not eliminate all subjectivity from the method. Likelihood, impact and asset value figures may result from speculation and represent factors difficult to quantify. Thus, a margin of error must be allowed in the results of a quantitative analysis.

Hybrid Approach

A hybrid risk analysis approach is sometimes used as a way to apply a quantitative measure (numerical range) to a subjective categorization of risk. A hybrid analysis does not contain the same mathematical vigor and amounts of data as quantitative risk assessment analysis, but instead maps estimated numerical ranges to qualitative labels.

Practical Guidance on Choosing Methods

The different methods—quantitative and qualitative—have some common limitations:

- No method is fully objective, and the results of the assessments and analysis may be subject to personal bias, knowledge and skills of the assessor, and available data used in the evaluation.
- Quantitative approaches are subject to creating over-confidence in complex models based on insufficient data.
- Qualitative approaches have a high level of subjectivity, great variance in human judgment and lack a standardized approach. Qualitative-only evaluations are also subject to unreliable results because of the over-simplified nature of using an ordinal or taxonomy-based measurement scale.

The selection of qualitative or quantitative risk analysis methods depends on many factors:

- The potential user need for highly accurate data or adequate qualitative approach
- Availability and quality of the data related to I&T-related risk
- Time available for risk analysis
- Level of comfort and expertise of those experts who are giving input

Statistical data may be available in different quantities and quality, ranging on a continuous scale from almost nonexistent to widely available. At the higher end of the scale (i.e., when a wide choice of statistical data is available), a quantitative method may be preferred; at the other end of the scale, with very little, incomplete or poor data, a qualitative approach may be the only available solution. Hybrid methods may be applied to situations in between both extremes described.

4.3.3 Risk Analysis Methods (Techniques)

A variety of risk analysis methods are available, and some are more complex than others. The choice of a methodology, unless mandated by management or a regulatory body, should be based on the best fit for the enterprise. No single best method exists; however, the results must meet the goals and objectives of the enterprise in identifying the relative risk rating of assets and processes critical to the business. It is also essential to identify as much significant risk as possible. An approach to achieving this is to develop risk scenarios (see Section 3.10).

A consistent risk analysis method should be used whenever the goal is to produce results that can be compared over time. However, an enterprise need not rely exclusively on one (or even several) methods. Each method has certain advantages and possible weaknesses, and the enterprise should choose a method appropriate for their specific needs. Common risk analysis methods include:

- **Bayesian analysis**—A Bayesian analysis is a method of statistical inference that uses prior distribution data to determine the probability of a result. This technique's effectiveness and accuracy rely on the accuracy of the prior distribution data.
- **Bow tie analysis**—A bow tie analysis provides a diagram to communicate risk assessment results by displaying links among possible causes, controls and consequences. The cause of the event is depicted in the middle of the diagram (the "knot" of the bow tie) and triggers, controls, mitigation strategies and consequences branch off of the "knot."
- **Brainstorming/structured interview**—The structured interview and brainstorming model gathers a large group of types of potential risk or ideas to be ranked by a team. The initial interview or brainstorming may be completed using prompts or interviews with an individual or small group.
- **Business impact analysis**—Business impact analysis (BIA) is a process to determine the impact of losing the support of any resource. In addition to identifying initial impact, a comprehensive BIA seeks to establish the escalation of loss over time. The goal of BIA is to provide reliable data on the basis of which senior management can make the appropriate decision (also see Risk Scenario Evaluation)
- **Cause and consequence analysis**—A cause and consequence analysis combine techniques of a fault tree analysis and an event tree analysis and allows for time delays to be considered.
- **Cause and effect analysis**—A cause-and-effect analysis looks at the factors that contributed to a certain effect and groups the causes into categories (using brainstorming), which are then displayed using a diagram, typically a tree structure or a fishbone diagram.
- **Checklists**—A checklist is a list of potential or typical threats or other considerations that should be of interest to the enterprise, whose items can be checked off one at a time as they are completed. Previously developed lists, codes or standards can be used when employing this method.
- **Delphi method**—The Delphi method uses expert opinion, which is often received using two or more rounds of questionnaires. After each round of questioning, the results are summarized and communicated to the experts by a facilitator. This collaborative technique is often used to build a consensus among the experts.
- **Event tree analysis**—An event tree analysis is a forward-looking, bottom-up model that uses inductive reasoning to assess the probability of different events resulting in possible outcomes.
- **Fault tree analysis**—A fault tree analysis starts with an event and examines possible means for the event to occur (top down) and displays these results in a logical tree diagram. This diagram can be used to generate ways to reduce or eliminate potential causes of the event.
- **Hazard analysis and critical control points (HACCP)**—Originally developed for the food safety industry, HACCP is a system for proactively preventing risk and assuring quality, reliability and safety of processes. The system monitors specific characteristics, which should fall within defined limits
- **Hazard and operability studies (HAZOP)**—HAZOP is a structured means of identifying and evaluating potential risk by looking at possible deviations from existing processes.
- **Human reliability analysis (HRA)**—HRA examines the effect of human error on systems and their performance.
- **Layers of protection analysis (LOPA)**—LOPA is a semi-quantitative risk analysis technique that uses aspects of HAZOP data to determine risk associated with risk events. It also looks at controls and their effectiveness.
- **Markov analysis**—A Markov analysis is used to analyze systems that can exist in multiple states. The Markov model assumes that future events are independent of past events.
- **Monte Carlo analysis**—Monte Carlo analysis is a powerful method for combining qualitative and quantitative approaches. It involves working on the basis of a normal deterministic simulation model, but iteratively evaluating the model using sets of random numbers as inputs. While deterministic models will provide the expected value, Monte Carlo simulation will give the value as a probability distribution based on the quality of the information provided.

- **Preliminary hazard analysis**—Preliminary hazard analysis looks at what threats or hazards may harm an enterprise's activities, facilities or systems. The result is a list of potential risk.
- **Reliability-centered maintenance**—Reliability-centered maintenance analyzes the functions and potential failures of a specific asset, particularly a physical asset such as equipment.
- **Root cause analysis**—Root cause analysis is a process of diagnosis to establish the origins of events, which can be used for learning from consequences, typically from errors and problems. Root cause analysis is further explained in Section 6.2.2.
- **Scenario analysis**—Scenario analysis examines possible future scenarios that were identified during risk identification, looking for risk associated with the scenario should it occur.
- **Sneak circuit analysis**—A sneak circuit analysis is used to identify design errors or sneak conditions such as latent hardware, software or integrated conditions that are often undetected by system tests and may result in improper operations, loss of availability, program delays or injury to personnel.
- **Structured "what if" technique (SWIFT)**—A structured "what if" technique uses structured brainstorming to identify risk, typically within a facilitated workshop. It uses prompts and guide words and is typically used with another risk analysis and evaluation technique.

The enterprise's culture, resources, skills and knowledge of I&T risk management, environment, risk appetite, and its existing approach to risk will determine which methods are chosen and how they are used.

4.4 Risk Ranking, Prioritization and Aggregation

I&T-related risk is most often measured by the impact of an IT-related problem on the business services that the IT system supports. Calculations or assessments of I&T-related impact must consider the dependencies of the other systems, departments, business partners and users on the affected IT system.

After risk has been determined using qualitative, quantitative or a hybrid method, the results should be placed in an order that can be used to direct the risk response effort (risk response is covered in Chapter 5).

Risk ranking is derived from a combination of all the components of risk including the:

- Recognition of the threats and the characteristics and capabilities of a threat source
- Severity of a vulnerability
- Likelihood of attack success when considering effectiveness of controls
- Impact to the enterprise of a successful attack

Taken together, these indicate the level of risk associated with a threat.

4.4.1 Risk Map

A very common and intuitive technique to present risk is in a two-dimensional diagram known as a risk map. A risk map is a (graphic) tool for ranking and displaying risk by defined ranges for frequency and impact (magnitude).

A risk map should be an expression of risk that has been evaluated using well-defined and non-ambiguous impact criteria. Initial maps or an aggregation of risk types may be useful to develop trends or common profiles for which risk response activities could be made more efficient but may not always be the right technique for management decision making.

A generic risk map is shown in **figure 4.3.** The map is helpful in providing a quick prioritization triage exercise, but may not give management enough information to take a decision on appropriate action.

Figure 4.3—Generic Risk Map

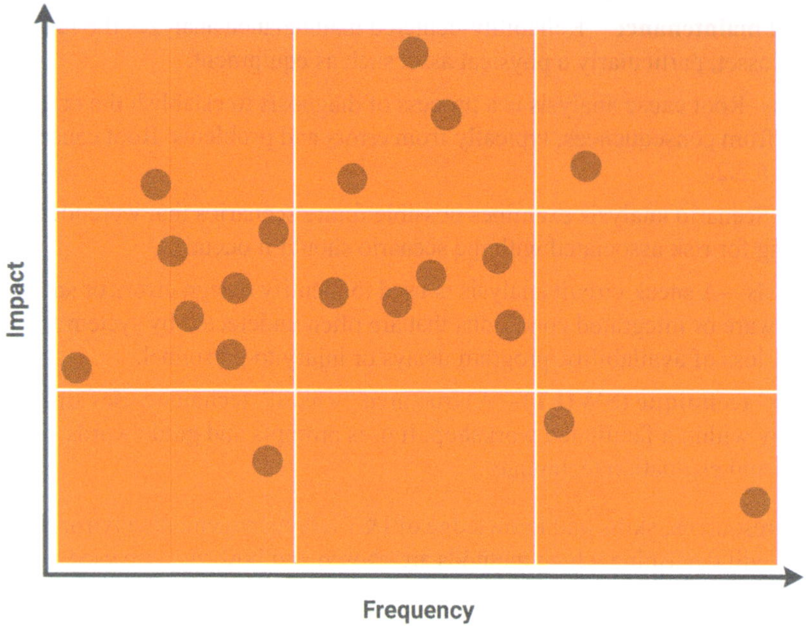

Source: ISACA, *Risk IT Practitioner Guide, 2nd Edition*, USA, 2020, figure 3.9, *https://www.isaca.org/bookstore/bookstore-risk-digital/ritpg2*

A risk map becomes more useful when it is combined with the different zones of risk appetite (the amount of risk an enterprise is willing to accept). Different risk appetite bands of significance can be defined and illustrated in a risk map along with identified risk using colored zones (see **figure 4.4**).

Figure 4.4—Risk Map with Risk Appetite Example

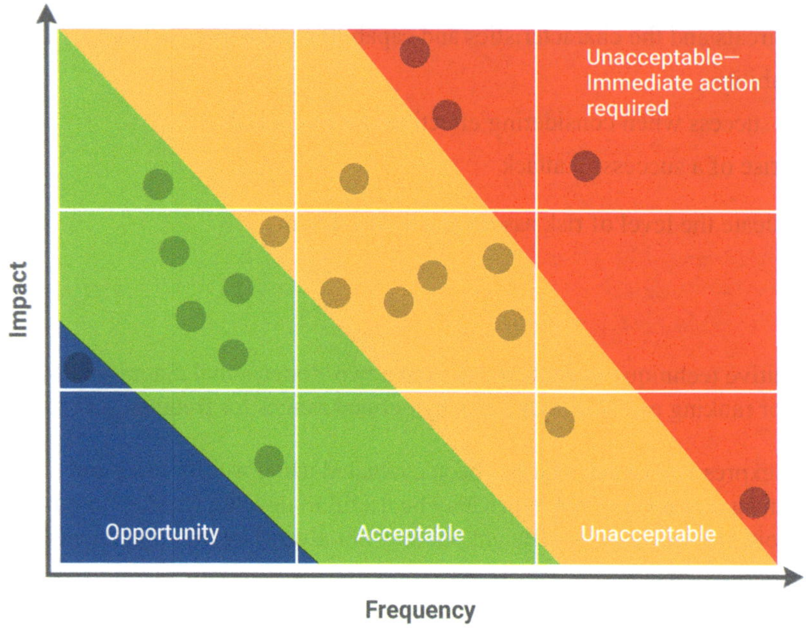

Source: ISACA, *Risk IT Practitioner Guide, 2nd Edition*, USA, 2020, figure 4.3, *https://www.isaca.org/bookstore/bookstore-risk-digital/ritpg2*

- **Red**—Indicates unacceptable risk, greatly exceeding the normal risk appetite. This should trigger an immediate response.
- **Yellow**—Indicates risk that is unacceptable, falling above normal risk appetite. The enterprise may require mitigation or response within a certain time period at this level.
- **Green**—Indicates risk at the normal, acceptable level. At this level, no special action is required other than maintaining current controls or other responses.
- **Blue**—Indicates very low risk. Cost-saving opportunities may be found by decreasing degree of control or where opportunities exist for assuming more risk.

There is value in using a risk map if the underlying measurement criteria and impact scales are well-defined and the language is well-understood by the enterprise. As the risk management process and risk decision-making matures, there is often a divergence away from calculating the probability of a risk occurring and increased focus on the financial impact the realized risk could have on the enterprise.

4.4.2 Risk Aggregation

Risk aggregation is the process of integrating risk assessments at an enterprise level to obtain a complete view on the overall risk for the enterprise. It involves combining individual risk for the purpose of reporting or treatment (**see figure 4.5**), or to obtain an integrated risk profile or risk score.

Figure 4.5—Aggregated Risk Map

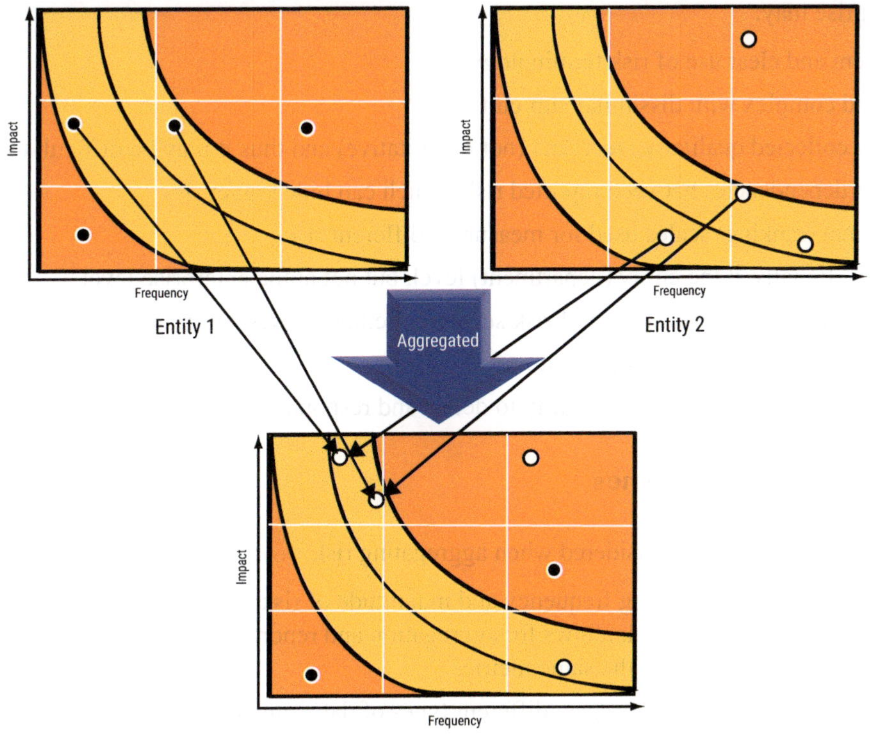

Decisions regarding I&T risk management are more beneficial to the enterprise if risk is managed from the perspective of end-to-end aggregated risk. An aggregated view of risk supports a complete and thorough review of risk appetite and risk tolerance, and always surpasses—in terms of enterprise benefit—relatively isolated recognition and/or treatment of risk. While a single event may constitute an acceptable risk, if it is a frequent occurrence, the aggregate risk may not be acceptable.

I&T-related risk is often grouped together by risk type, similarity of risk response or specific control treatment. This allows senior management to assess the impact of risk decisions on the entire enterprise, across multiple business lines, countries, partners and customers. For example, if an enterprise access management approach generates repeated audit findings or control deficiencies across different business or mission areas, then an enterprise initiative in access management may resolve the issue.

The financial impact of risk is often aggregated, for executive or board-reporting purposes, into ranges of monetary loss that can be expected if certain types of risk are realized. Many enterprises maintain a set of impact criteria and risk tolerances expressed in financial terms.

Aggregation allows risk that span across an entire enterprise to become visible and leads to better informed management decision making on risk responses. Risk, when aggregated at an enterprise level, may be so far out of the range of tolerance that immediate action or widespread responses are required. Risk aggregation is the main driver for developing and refining risk impact criteria that reflects the specific and common scales of measurement needed to truly manage I&T-related risk commensurate with other enterprise risk. Maturing the risk management functions and processes to the level of capability that allows more certainty in decision-making creates greater value for the enterprise rather than just managing a single risk. Informed decision-making is truly the value of a mature risk management process.

However, difficulties can be encountered when gathering and grouping risk to provide an aggregated view. For example, the enterprise may:

- Lack a consistent and clear use of risk terminology
- Be too large and complex with dissimilar sub-cultures
- Have primarily collected qualitative risk data (not quantitative) and thus it may be difficult to aggregate
- Have unknown dependencies between reported risk, which can hide bigger risk
- Have used ordinal (ranking) scales used for measuring different risk
- Scale risk proportionally at the entity (department) level, but not at the enterprise level
- Lack a standardization or consistent use of risk scenario methodologies and frameworks
- Have an immature process management system
- Not understand gaps in the enterprise's ability to detect and respond to threats

4.4.3 Risk Aggregation Guidelines

The following guidelines should be considered when aggregating risk:

- Standardize the method for assessing frequency and magnitude of risk scenarios across the enterprise. Using the same terminology for describing risk allows for aggregation and reporting based on terms of business impact for the reason that entities are utilizing the same metrics.
- Only aggregate like data. Do not aggregate different types of data; only data and numbers that are consistent and meaningful should be aggregated.
- Focus on real risk, and avoid focusing on risk that is easy to measure but less relevant. For example, reporting firewall attacks might be a simple matter, but if up-to-date security measures are in place, these attacks probably carry little business impact.
- Do not aggregate risk information to the extent of obscuring actionable details. The root cause of risk must be visible to those responsible for managing them.

- Consider aggregating risk in multiple dimensions. For example, aggregate risk by department, business unit, business process or types of risk. Sometimes a combination of dimensions may be needed to satisfy risk management and business needs.
- Aggregate risk at the enterprise level, where it can be considered in combination with all other risk that the enterprise needs to manage. The enterprise's structure (e.g., geographic split, business units) should be considered to set up a meaningful cascade of risk aggregation without losing sight of any important specific risk.
- Consider dependencies at different levels of the enterprise:
  - First, understand the dependency between event and ultimate business impact. For example, when a server goes down, vendors and customers, as well as different entities within the enterprise, could be impacted.
  - Next, consider dependencies between events not fully represented by a mathematical addition. Events can magnify each other leading to far greater consequences than a single event. For example, a single data center that goes down could be acceptable, while losing a second data center simultaneously might be a catastrophe.

4.5 Risk Documentation

At the conclusion of the I&T-related risk assessment process, the results are compiled into a comprehensive report for senior management. The risk assessment report should:

- Indicate any gaps between the current risk environment and the desired state of I&T-related risk.
- Advise whether these gaps are within acceptable levels.
- Provide some basis on which to judge the severity of the identified issue.

The risk assessment report should document the process used and the result of the risk assessment. Each risk should be documented in a manner that is understandable to management and clearly states the risk levels and priorities.

The risk assessment report may be adjusted according to the needs of the enterprise and the direction of senior management. A typical risk assessment report includes the following sections:

- Objectives of the risk assessment process
- Scope and description of the area subject to assessment
- External context and factors affecting risk
- Internal factors or limitations affecting risk assessment
- Risk assessment criteria
- Risk assessment (analysis) methodology used
- Resources and references used
- Identification of risk, threats and vulnerabilities
- Assumptions used in the risk assessment
- Potential of unknown factors affecting assessment
- Results of risk assessment
- Recommendations and conclusions

The risk assessment should be performed in a consistent manner that supports future risk assessment efforts and would provide predictable results. All risk should be noted in the report, including issues that may already have been addressed, in order to provide an accurate picture of risk to senior management.

An enterprise assesses I&T-related risk because IT risk is a form of business risk, not because it is a nuisance to the IT staff. The use of terminology that is specific to IT or may be misinterpreted by management should be avoided. Many terms and acronyms commonly used in IT have different meaning to other disciplines in the enterprise, which may result in the misunderstanding of the problem and the proposed solutions. A risk assessment report should be clear, concise and accurate and free from terminology that could be misunderstood or that may be subject to misinterpretation.

4.5.1 Addressing Bypassed Risk

All I&T-related risk should be evaluated or intentionally bypassed. Some I&T-related risk events apply only to enterprises that meet particular criteria. For example, not all regions are subject to the same natural disasters. Likewise, the risk of losing credit card data applies only to those enterprises that store or process credit card data. When an assumption is made to not include a particular risk in an assessment, any risk that was intentionally bypassed should be included in the report rather than missed in the risk assessment process. In general, this occurs during the risk identification process, but as a deeper level of investigation and evaluation of risk is conducted, new types of risk may surface while others that were previously overlooked are found to be relevant. For this reason, each documented risk should be reevaluated to ensure that it was identified and assessed accurately based on the current risk landscape.

4.5.2 Risk Register

A list of risk that have been identified, analyzed and prioritized is called a risk register. A risk register is the list of potential adverse events that have been identified and analyzed to understand the potential impact should the risk be realized. The risk register is not a list of control deficiencies or missing software patches from a server. If there is no uncertainty, i.e., the control deficiency is a process or procedural issue, not necessarily a risk. The risk register can be seen as an extension of the risk map, providing detailed information on each identified risk, including:

- Risk ID
- Risk owner
- Details of the risk scenario
- Enterprise or business unit
- Date of risk identification
- Source of risk (if known)
- Risk owner/point of contact
- Risk title
- Risk statement (e.g. a statement describing insiders taking advantage of credentials to exfiltrate data)
- Heat (map)
- Score (qualitative)
- Information on detailed analysis results or scores (quantitative)
- Detailed information on risk response
- Current risk response status
- Information on controls (if applicable)
- Primary risk category
- Secondary risk category (if using)
- Remediation or disposition status
- Current status date
- Follow-up date
- Comments

An enterprise maintains a risk register in order to consolidate and track all information about risk into one central repository. The risk register allows senior management and the managers of each department to obtain the status of the risk management process from a single source, which in turn makes it possible to better manage and report on risk and coordinate risk response activities. At any given time, the risk register should document the entire risk universe of the enterprise. Often when an enterprise decides to purchase a commercial tool for managing risk there is an out-of-the box risk register template provided that can be customized for the unique needs of the enterprise.

A risk register must be kept up to date and its content periodically reviewed both to add new risk and remove risk that may no longer be relevant to the enterprise. The risk register should contain all risk that has been detected by various parts and activities of the enterprise including risk identified in:

- Audits
- Vulnerability assessments
- Penetration tests
- Incident reports
- Process reviews
- Management input
- Risk scenario creation
- Security assessments.

This allows management to refer to one place to gain insight into the:

- Outstanding risk issues
- Status of risk mitigation efforts
- Emergence of newly identified and documented risk.

An IT risk register is a repository of the key attributes of potential and known IT risk issues. Attributes may include name, description, owner, expected/actual frequency, potential/actual magnitude, potential/actual business impact, disposition.

An example of a risk register is shown in **figures 4.6** and **4.7**.

Figure 4.6—Risk Register Part 1

Part I—Summary Data						
Risk statement						
Risk owner						
Date of last risk assessment						
Due date for update of risk assessment						
Risk category	☐STRATEGIC (IT Benefit/Value Enablement)	☐PROJECT DELIVERY (IT Program and Project Delivery)	☐OPERATIONAL (IT Operations and Service Delivery)			
Risk classification (copied from risk analysis results)	☐LOW	☐MEDIUM	☐HIGH	☐VERY HIGH		
Risk response	☐ACCEPT	☐TRANSFER	☐MITIGATE	☐AVOID		
Part II—Risk Description						
Title						
High-level scenario (from list of sample high-level scenarios)						
Detailed scenario description—Scenario components	Actor					
	Threat Type					
	Event					
	Asset/Resource					
	Timing					
Other scenario information						
Part III—Risk Analysis Results						
Frequency of scenario (number of times per year)	0	1	2	3	4	5
	N ≤ 0.01 ☐	0.01 < N ≤ 0.1 ☐	0.1 < N ≤ 1 ☐	1 < N ≤ 10 ☐	10 < N ≤ 100 ☐	100 < N ☐
Comments on frequency						
Impact of scenario on business	0	1	2	3	4	5
1. Productivity	Revenue Loss Over One Year					
Impact rating	I ≤ 0.1% ☐	0.1% < I ≤ 1% ☐	1% < I ≤ 3% ☐	3% < I ≤ 5% ☐	5% < I ≤ 10% ☐	10% < I ☐
Detailed description of impact						
2. Cost of response	Expenses Associated With Managing the Loss Event					
Impact rating	I ≤ 10k$ ☐	10K$ < I ≤ 100K$ ☐	100K$ < I ≤ 1M$ ☐	1M$% < I ≤ 10M$ ☐	10M$ < I ≤ 100M$ ☐	100M$ < I ☐
Detailed description of impact						
3. Competitive advantage	Drop-in Customer Satisfaction Ratings					
Impact rating	I ≤ 0.5 ☐	0.5 < I ≤ 1 ☐	1 < I ≤ 1.5 ☐	1.5 < I ≤ 2 ☐	2 < I ≤2.5 ☐	2.5 < I ☐
Detailed description of impact						
4. Legal	Regulatory Compliance—Fines					
Impact rating	None ☐	< 1M$ ☐	< 10M$ ☐	< 100M$ ☐	< 1B$ ☐	> 1B$ ☐
Detailed description of impact						
Overall impact rating (average of four impact ratings)						
Overall rating of risk (obtained by combining frequency and impact ratings on risk map)	☐LOW	☐MEDIUM	☐HIGH	☐VERY HIGH		

Source: ISACA, *COBIT® 5 for Risk*, USA, 2013, figure 62, *https://www.isaca.org/bookstore/cobit-5/wcb5rk*

Figure 4.7—Risk Register Part 2

Part III—Risk Response				
Risk response for this risk	☐ACCEPT	☐TRANSFER	☐MITIGATE	☐AVOID
Justification				
Detailed description of response (NOT in case of ACCEPT)	Response Action		Completed	Action Plan
	1.		☐	☐
	2.		☐	☐
	3.		☐	☐
	4.		☐	☐
	5.		☐	☐
	6.		☐	☐
Overall status of risk action plan				
Major issues with risk action plan				
Overall status of completed responses				
Major issues with completed responses				
Part IV—Risk Indicators				
Key risk indicators for this risk	1. 2. 3. 4.			

Source: ISACA, *COBIT® 5 for Risk*, USA, 2013, figure 62, *https://www.isaca.org/bookstore/cobit-5/wcb5rk*

4.5.3 Risk Owner

The term risk owner is one that tends to cause confusion within enterprises, as it is contextual in nature. A risk owner is defined as the person in whom the enterprise has invested the authority and accountability for making risk-based decisions and who owns the loss associated with a realized risk scenario.

From a governance aspect, senior management (e.g., CEO, president, founder) is the risk owner as they are the one ultimately accountable for answering as why risk were responded to, for the entirety of the enterprise.

From a management (e.g., directors, vice presidents, managers) perspective, these are the individuals who have the authority, be held accountable, and the responsibility for making decisions relating to risk, as a part of routine operations. Additional confusion arises when we talk about risk associated with IT, as most within an enterprise will attempt to place the accountability and responsibility for IT-related risk on the IT department. While IT will serve as custodians/stewards of those systems to support business operations, the risk ownership falls to the individual within the business who requires and consumes those services in order to provide their business functions.

The risk owner may, or may not be responsible for the implementation of risk treatment.

Risk ownership should be established up front before there is a crisis or loss event. Ideally, ownership should be assigned to those best situated to keep an eye on the risk and take full responsibility for the enterprise's performance.

It is important for the groups and individuals who own parts of the risk process to understand their roles, responsibility and accountability for risk management. Clearly defining ownership, ensuring agreement about that ownership and documenting who owns various parts of the risk process are integral to clear risk management.

4.6 Control Assessment

When assessing risk, the current control environment must be evaluated. Controls are implemented to reduce or maintain risk at acceptable levels; however, controls may be poorly maintained, unsuitable for the risk that they are meant to control or incorrectly configured.

Controls should be regularly reviewed to:

- Determine and ensure their effectiveness and identify weaknesses.
- Verify the correct balance between technical, managerial (administrative) and physical or operational control types.

A control weakness is a deficiency in the design or operation of a control procedure. Control weaknesses can potentially result in risk relevant to the area of activity not being reduced to an acceptable level (relevant risk threatens achievement of the objectives relevant to the area of activity being examined). Control weaknesses can be material when the design or operation of one or more control procedures does not reduce to a relatively low level the risk that misstatements caused by illegal acts or irregularities may occur and not be detected by the related control procedures.

Implementation of a technical control such as a firewall, requires training for the staff who manages or operates it, correct procedures for its configuration, assignment of responsibilities for its monitoring, and schedules for regular testing. If these coinciding controls are not in place, stakeholders may develop a false sense of security, resulting in:

- Unidentified vulnerabilities
- An ineffective use of resources
- Greater risk than anticipated or intended

Controls are implemented for a number of reasons and are generally categorized by their intent (type), described **in figure 4.8**.

Figure 4.8—Control Intent

Category	Description
Preventive	Inhibit attempts to violate security policy. Encryption, blocking emails, user authentication, such as a strong password policy and two-factor authentication and firewalls that block all traffic on ports that are known to be associated with malicious tools are examples of preventive controls.
Detective	Provide warnings of violations or attempted violations of security policy. Audit trails, intrusion detection systems, (IDS), and checksums are examples of detective controls.
Corrective	Remediate errors, omissions, unauthorized uses and intrusions when detected. Data backups, error correction and automated failover are examples of corrective controls.
Compensating	An alternate form of a control that corrects a deficiency or weakness in the control structure of the enterprise. This may be considered when an entity cannot meet a stated requirement due to legitimate technical or business constraints but can create a comparably acceptable level of risk by other means. Placing unsecured systems on isolated network segments with strong perimeter security and adding third-party challenge-response mechanisms to devices that do not support individual log-in accounts are examples of compensating controls.

Source: ISACA, *CRISC Review Manual, 6th Edition*, USA, 2015, figure 2.3, *https://www.isaca.org/bookstore/crisc-exam-resources/crr6ed*

A preventive control is an internal control that is designed to avoid undesirable events, errors and other occurrences that an enterprise has determined could have a negative material effect on a process or end product.

Fundamentally, the purpose of a preventative control is to try and to keep something from happening. For example, to protect the enterprise from a successful attack.

Examples of preventive controls (in addition to those provided in **figure 4.8**) include:

- A strong password policy
- Two-factor authentication
- Blocking emails
- Firewalls that blocks all traffic on ports that are known to be associated with malicious tools

A detective control is a control designed to detect and report when errors, omissions and unauthorized uses or entries occur. A detective control does not stop unauthorized uses or entries from occurring, but it indicates that a threat event has happened or is happening. Not everything can be blocked in the moment. However, by detecting a threat event, the enterprise can respond more promptly and limit any potential impact.

For example, an enterprise typically implements strong incident response capabilities and plans. When an active penetration of the enterprise network is detected, resources can be mobilized to address the threat.

A corrective control is a control designed to correct errors, omissions and unauthorized uses and intrusions, once they are detected.

If a threat event occurs, a corrective control's purpose is to help an enterprise recover from the effects of an attack. For example, if unauthorized access has been gained to a specific enterprise computer, a procedure is initiated to protect the rest of the network.

A compensating control is an internal control that reduces the risk of an existing or potential control weakness resulting in errors and omissions.

Compensating controls address the weaknesses in the existing controls through concepts, such as:

- Layered defense
- Increased supervision
- Procedural controls
- Increased audits and logging of system activity
- Administrative alert
- Double-checking input data
- Password change

These measures will work to compensate for the risk that could not be addressed in other ways.

The interaction between the control types and how they affect a threat event is shown on **figure 4.9**.

Figure 4.9—Threat Event Control Interactions

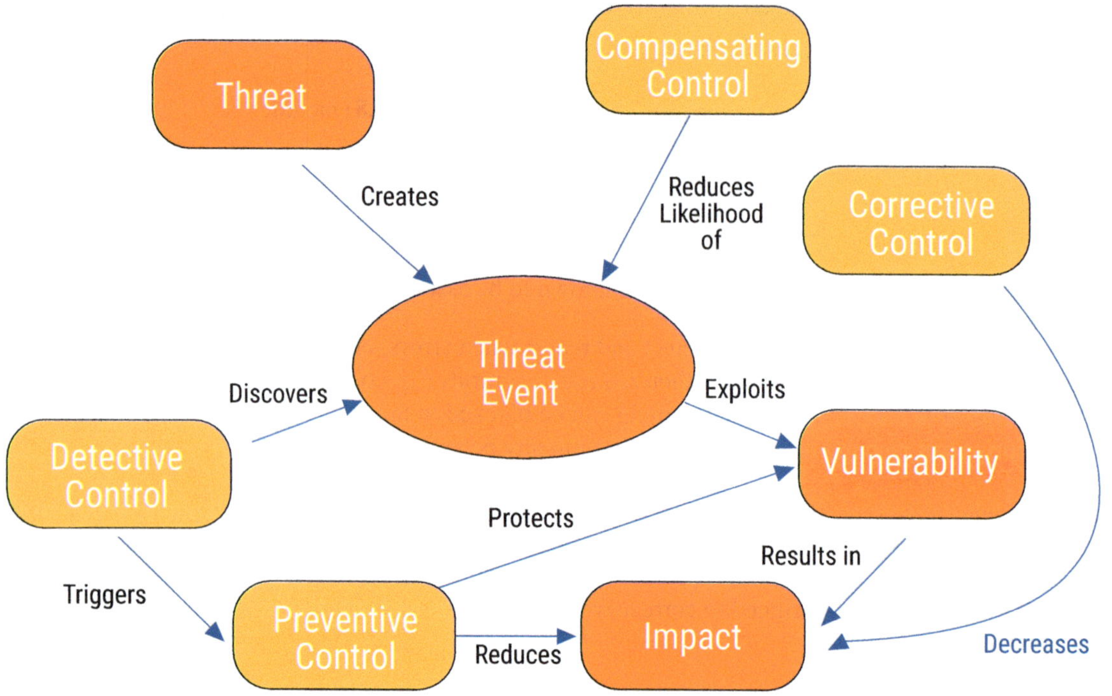

Source: ISACA, *CRISC Review Manual, 6th Edition*, USA, 2015 (adapted), figure 2.4, *https://www.isaca.org/bookstore/crisc-exam-resources/crr6ed*

Assessing the control environment provides an opportunity to evaluate the risk culture and effectiveness of the current risk management program, which can be used to determine both the level of risk currently facing the enterprise and the seriousness of that risk.

In general, risk is more serious when any of the following are true:

- Controls are inadequate
- The wrong controls are being used
- Controls are ignored or bypassed
- Controls are poorly maintained
- Logs or control data are not reviewed
- Controls are not tested
- Changes to the configuration of controls are not managed
- Controls can be physically accessed and altered
- Duties are inadequately segregated
- Lack of timely update

4.6.1 Current State of Controls Sources

The current state of I&T-related risk can be assessed using the reports generated by the controls themselves and the results of control testing activities and incident management programs. A current-state control assessment refers to the condition of the program at a point in time.

Sources that can be used to identify and assess the current state of controls include:

- **Audits**—An audit report often provides a summary assessment of internal controls and recommendations from audits are often related to the improvement of managerial, technical and operational controls
- **Business continuity plans (BCPs)**—A BCP contains controls that reduce the risk of losing critical processes to acceptable levels
- **Capability maturity models**—The use of a capability maturity model provides a comparison of the state of the enterprise's risk management program to an established model of capability maturity, which contains the essential elements of effective processes for one or more disciplines
- **Control tests conducted by the control owner or custodian**—The results of control tests provide an assessment of the technical and nontechnical aspects of the control, such as the rules governing the operation of the control, the procedures used in monitoring and operating the control and the proficiency of the staff responsible for the operation of the control
- **Incident reports**—A thorough review of an incident report can identify threats, vulnerabilities and impact and weak controls
- **IT operations and management evaluation**—Interviewing operations staff and reviewing logs and trouble tickets can provide insight into weak controls and recurring problems within a system.
- **Enterprise architecture assessment**—An enterprise —architecture assessment is useful in demonstrating the links between I&T and enterprise objectives and produce a view of current risk and controls
- **Logs**—Logs contain a record of important events that occur on a system and can identify risk-relevant events such as compliance violations, suspicious behavior, errors, probes or scans and abnormal activity and the presence of weak controls
- **Observation**—Observing a process may help to identify situations in which documented processes and controls are not being followed
- **Self-assessments**—Self-assessment reports can often provide an evaluation of control effectiveness.
- **Third-party assurance reviews**—Third-party reviews often provide an analysis enterprise processes, incidents, logs and the threat environment and can be a valuable source of information about vulnerabilities, control effectiveness and risk
- **User feedback**—System users are an excellent source for gathering information about system shortcomings, including potential vulnerabilities and concerns about controls

4.6.2 Control Self-Assessment

A control self-assessment (CSA) is an assessment of controls made by the staff and management of the unit or units involved. It is a management technique that assures stakeholders, customers and other parties that the internal control system of the enterprise is reliable. It also ensures that employees are aware of the risk to the business, and they conduct periodic, proactive reviews of controls. It is a methodology used to review:

- Key business objectives
- Risk involved in achieving the business objectives
- Internal controls designed to manage business risk in a formal, documented and collaborative process

A control risk self-assessment (CRSA) is a method/process by which management and staff of all levels collectively identify and evaluate risk and controls within their business areas. This may be under the guidance of a facilitator (auditor or risk manager).

Business process should define and assess appropriate controls based on risk to the business processes. The process owners and the personnel who run the processes use their knowledge and understanding of the business function to evaluate the performance of controls against the established control objectives, while considering the risk appetite of the enterprise. Process owners are in an ideal position to define the appropriate controls because they have a greater knowledge of the process objectives.

Benefits of a CSA and CRSA include:

- Early detection of risk
- More effective and improved internal controls
- Development of a sense of ownership of the controls in the employees and process owners and reduction of their resistance to control improvement initiatives
- Increased employee awareness of enterprise objectives, and knowledge of risk and internal controls
- Reduction in control cost

4.6.3 Control Owner

The term control owner, like its counterpart the risk owner, is a term which also often gets confused. IA control owner is a person in whom the enterprise has invested the authority and accountability for making control-related decisions and is responsible to ensure the control is implemented and is operating effectively and efficiently.

The control owner and the risk owner are normally the same individual, as any modifications to or removal of a control will impact the risk being treated leading to the risk exceeding the defined risk appetite. Just as with risk ownership, control ownership falls to those individuals within the business who have the authority to make decisions relating to the controls and whom will be held accountable for how risk is being managed. IT may serve as the custodians/stewards of the controls; however, ultimately it is the business who bears the accountability should that control be ineffective in properly treating risk.

There are instances where the business will not be the control owner, such as the case with technology controls, such as:

- Intrusion detection/prevention systems
- Email filters
- Data loss prevention platforms
- End-point detection

These are typically enterprise wide controls, which are configured and managed by the enterprise's security operations staff.

4.7 Summary of Terminology

It is important to recognize and understand I&T-related risk terminology. The following terms were introduced in this chapter.

Figure 4.10—Chapter 4 Terminology	
Term	Definition
Business impact	The net effect, positive or negative, on the achievement of business objectives
Business impact analysis (BIA)	A process to determine the impact of losing the support of any resource
Compensating control	An internal control that reduces the risk of an existing or potential control weakness resulting in errors and omissions
Control owner	A person in whom the enterprise has invested the authority and accountability for making control-related decisions and is responsible to ensure the control is implemented and is operating effectively and efficiently
Control risk self-assessment	A method/process by which management and staff of all levels collectively identify and evaluate risk and controls with their business areas. This may be under the guidance of a facilitator such as an auditor or risk manager
Control self-assessment	An assessment of controls made by the staff and management of the unit or units involved
Control weakness	A deficiency in the design or operation of a control procedure. Control weaknesses can potentially result in risk relevant to the area of activity not being reduced to an acceptable level (relevant risk threatens achievement of the objectives relevant to the area of activity being examined). Control weaknesses can be material when the design or operation of one or more control procedures does not reduce to a relatively low level the risk that misstatements caused by illegal acts or irregularities may occur and not be detected by the related control procedures.
Corrective control	Designed to correct errors, omissions and unauthorized uses and intrusions, once they are detected
Detective control	Designed to detect and report when errors, omissions and unauthorized uses or entries occur
Frequency analysis	Determines how often a particular risk scenario might be expected to occur during a specified period of time
IT risk register	A repository of the key attributes of potential and known IT risk issues. Attributes may include name, description, owner, expected/actual frequency, potential/actual magnitude, potential/actual business impact, disposition.
Preventive control	An internal control that is used to avoid undesirable events, errors and other occurrences that an enterprise has determined could have a negative material effect on a process or end product
Qualitative risk analysis	Approach based on expert opinion, judgement, intuition and experience
Quantitative risk analysis	Approach based on a calculation of a risk's likelihood and impact using numerical and statistical techniques
Risk aggregation	The process of integrating risk assessments at a corporate level to obtain a complete view on the overall risk for the enterprise
Risk analysis	A process by which frequency and magnitude of IT risk scenarios are estimated
Risk assessment	A process used to identify and evaluate risk and its potential effects
Risk evaluation	The process of comparing the estimated risk against given risk criteria to determine the significance of the risk. [ISO/IEC Guide 73:2002]
Risk map	A (graphic) tool for ranking and displaying risk by defined ranges for frequency and magnitude

Figure 4.10—Chapter 4 Terminology *(cont.)*

Term	Definition
Risk owner	The person in whom the enterprise has invested the authority and accountability for making risk-based decisions and who owns the loss associated with a realized risk scenario
Risk register	A list of risk items that have been identified, analyzed and prioritized

Chapter 4 Knowledge Check

Review questions are provided as a means to support the content presented within this study guide and serve as a gauge or assessment of knowledge of I&T-related risk topics. One question is provided for each topic.

For individuals intending to earn the ISACA IT Risk Fundamentals Certificate, these questions are written to depict the type of questions that may appear on the exam. These questions will not specifically appear on the exam, but similar ones may appear.

REVIEW QUESTIONS

1. Which of the following activities is **MOST** often associated with I&T-related risk analysis?

   A. I&T-related risk scenarios are cataloged.
   B. The frequency and impact of I&T-related risk scenarios are estimated.
   C. IT controls that provide mitigation for similar risk types are documented.

2. A risk scenario utilizes a measure of the rate by which events occur over a certain period of time. This measure is known as:

   A. Magnitude
   B. Frequency
   C. Impact

3. A quantitative risk analysis approach is **MOST** likely to be chosen when:

   A. Financial resources to conduct an analysis are limited.
   B. A cost-benefit analysis is required.
   C. Reputation and employee morale are being quantified.

4. A risk map is **MOST** useful for:

   A. Ranking and displaying risk.
   B. Making risk actions and decisions.
   C. Quantifying risk.

5. A risk register is **MOST** likely to include:

   A. A list of control deficiencies discovered during a penetration test
   B. Missing software patches from a server
   C. A statement describing insiders taking advantage of credentials to exfiltrate data

6. The use of a firewall to block all traffic on ports that are known to be associated with malicious tools is what type of control?

   A. Preventive
   B. Detective
   C. Compensating

Answers on page 138

Chapter 4 ANSWER KEY

Review Questions

1. A. Identifying I&T-related risk and cataloging scenarios is part of the risk assessment process and is not typically done as part of risk analysis.
B. Risk analysis is the process by which frequency and magnitude of I&T-related risk scenarios are estimated. As part of the evaluation of risk, an analysis of the individual scenarios is necessary to determine the probabilities of a particular event, taking into account frequency and impact of the risk scenarios.
C. Documenting existing IT controls that provide mitigation for similar I&T-related risk types is part of the risk assessment process and is not typically done as part of risk analysis.

2. A. Magnitude is a measure of the potential severity of loss or the potential gain from realized events/scenarios.
B. Frequency is a measure of the rate by which events occur over a certain period of time.
C. Impact is a measure of the magnitude of loss resulting from a threat exploiting a vulnerability.

3. A. A qualitative analysis generally costs much less than quantitative analysis.
B. A quantitative approach is particularly suited for cost-benefit analysis, because risk that can be mapped to monetary values can easily and directly be compared to the costs of various risk responses.
C. A qualitative risk analysis approach is better suited when there is hard-to-quantify risk, such as enterprise reputation or the value of human life.

4. **A. A risk map is a (graphic) tool for ranking and displaying risk by defined ranges for frequency and impact (magnitude).**
B. A risk map is helpful in providing a quick prioritization triage exercise, but may not give management enough information to take a decision on appropriate action.
C. A risk map is not a quantification approach, but instead a tool risk for displaying the results of a risk analysis.

5. A. A risk register should not include a list of control deficiencies. A control deficiency is a problem, not a risk.
B. A risk register should not include missing software patches from a server. Missing software patches are a problem, not a risk.
C. A risk register should contain statements of risk such as a statement describing insiders taking advantage of credentials to exfiltrate data.

6. **A. The use of a firewall to block all traffic on ports that are known to be associated with malicious tools is a preventive control. The purpose of a preventative control is to try to keep something from happening; f. For example, to protect the enterprise from a successful attack.**
B. The use of a firewall to block all traffic on ports that are known to be associated with malicious tools is a preventive control. A detective control is a control designed to detect and report when errors, omissions and unauthorized uses or entries occur. For example, a detective control does not stop unauthorized uses or entries from occurring, but it indicates that a threat event has happened or is happening.
C. The use of a firewall to block all traffic on ports that are known to be associated with malicious tools is a preventive control. A compensating control is a control that reduces the risk of an existing or potential control weakness resulting in errors and omissions.

Chapter 5:

Risk Response

Learning Objectives 140

Risk Response

5.1 Risk Response and Strategies 141
5.2 Control Design and Implementation 146
5.3 Incident Management, Business Continuity and Disaster Recovery 148
5.4 Risk States 150
5.5 Risk Response Selection, Prioritization and Communication 153
5.6 Summary of Terminology 158

Chapter 5 Knowledge Check 161

Learning Objectives

After risk has been identified and assessed decisions need to be made about the appropriate risk response. A risk response takes into consideration the constraints placed on the enterprise through budget, time, resources, strategic plans, regulations, customer expectations and other business factors. This chapter describes risk response strategies, control design and implementation and other response approaches. Risk states and response options and prioritization are also discussed.

Learning objectives include the following:

- Explain the risk response process and the importance of alignment with business objectives.
- Illustrate risk response strategies and examples of each.
- Outline control design and implementation and control activities that can reduce risk to acceptable levels.
- Articulate the role that incident management, business continuity and disaster recovery play in mitigating risk.
- Define the characteristics of inherent and residual risk.
- Explain how to select and prioritize risk response alternatives.
- Describe how to document and communicate risk responses.
- Define the elements of a risk response plan.

Risk Response

5.1 Risk Response and Strategies

5.1.1 Purpose and Business Objective Alignment

The purpose of defining a risk response is to bring risk in line with management's acceptable level of risk based on the risk analysis. In other words, a response needs to be defined such that future residual risk (current risk with the risk response defined and implemented) is, as much as possible (usually depending on available budget), within risk tolerance limits. There may also be an exception process that allows some period of time to implement a risk response or for which management may decide to accept any risk, regardless of circumstances. The purpose is not to eliminate or minimize risk at all costs.

The risk assessment report and risk register document the risk identified during the identification and assessment phases of the risk management process. Both the report and the register should indicate the assessed level or priority of each risk. The recommendations in the report are guidelines, and several recommendations may be provided. Management is responsible for evaluating and responding to the recommendations included in the report, first by determining the best response and then developing an action plan and implementation strategy that addresses the risk in a manner consistent with the risk appetite and risk tolerance of the enterprise.

The enterprise exists to meet its mission. Management must always be aware of the drivers for risk management, such as compliance with regulations and the need to support and align the risk response with business priorities and objectives. A risk response that would negatively impact the ability of the enterprise to meet its mission must be considered very carefully. **Figure 5.1** shows the phases in the risk response process.

Figure 5.1—Risk Response Process Phases

Phase	Step	Background
1	Review results of the risk analysis. Determine if the risk level exceeds the risk tolerance level. If yes, go to phase 2. If no, no action is required.	Risk analysis identifies and prioritizes risk levels based on risk scenarios and makes assessments based on the likelihood and magnitude of the risk, taking potential business impact into account. In addition, the risk assessment should provide recommendations for risk response.
2	Select risk response options.	In instances where the risk analysis shows that risk exceeds the defined risk tolerance levels, select the appropriate response by weighing the projected risk vs. the potential cost of implementing and maintaining controls.
3	Prioritize each response option.	Select a risk response implementation strategy according to the priorities for addressing risk, and develop the risk action plan.
4	Implement the risk action plan.	Implement the selected risk response following the risk action plan.

5.1.2 Risk Response Strategies

The goal of risk management is to bring risk to a level that is acceptable or tolerable to the enterprise. Risk response strategies are designed to lead to a situation that as much future residual risk as possible falls within risk appetite limits.

The evaluation of an appropriate risk response is part of the risk management process cycle, not a one-time effort. There are four commonly accepted strategic options for risk response:

- Risk acceptance
- Risk mitigation
- Risk transfer (sharing)
- Risk avoidance

Risk Acceptance

Risk acceptance is a strategy used by an enterprise when:

- Risk is within the enterprise's risk tolerance.
- The cost of mitigating the risk is higher than the potential economic or reputational loss.

Risk acceptance is the decision to accept a risk and is made according to the risk appetite and risk tolerance set by senior management where the enterprise can assume the risk and absorb any losses.

When an enterprise formally accepts risk, it recognizes the implication of everything it has done and fully understands how its operations might be affected if assumptions change. In short, when an enterprise accepts a risk, it removes uncertainty associated with effects of the risk.

Risk acceptance means that no action is taken relative to a particular risk, and the loss is accepted when/if it occurs. This is different from being ignorant of risk. Risk acceptance assumes that the risk is known, i.e., an informed decision has been made by management to accept it.

If an enterprise chooses to adopt a risk acceptance stance, it should carefully consider who can accept the risk—even more so with I&T-related risk. I&T-related risk should be accepted only by business management (and business process owners) in collaboration with and supported by the IT department or IT support function, and acceptance should be communicated to appropriate stakeholders, such as senior management and the board as necessary and dictated by policy. In addition, losses or incidents related to accepted risk should be tracked and communicated over time, and accepted risk should be reassessed periodically for changes in the business landscape, assumptions, or other factors.

Because the goal of risk management is to bring risk within acceptable levels as cost-effectively as possible, risk that falls within the enterprise risk appetite should be accepted. Risk tolerance is used as an exceptional circumstance where the level of risk may exceed the risk acceptance boundary set by senior management, but the decision is made to accept the risk anyway. Risk tolerance is typically a factor when either:

- No controls are available.
- The cost of the controls would outweigh their benefits.

Examples of risk acceptance as a result of risk tolerance follow:

- Projections indicate that a certain project will not deliver the required business functionality by the planned delivery date, but management decides to proceed with the project.

- A particular risk would have catastrophic consequences but is assessed to be extremely rare, and approaches to reduce it are cost-prohibitive. Management may decide to accept this risk.

Self-insurance, or deciding to absorb the potential costs of an incident, is another form of risk acceptance.

Acceptance of risk must be done by someone empowered to act on behalf of the enterprise at a level commensurate with the projected consequences associated with the risk. As mentioned, risk acceptance is not the same as risk ignorance, which refers to both the:

- Failure to identify or acknowledge risk.
- Acceptance of risk without knowing or acknowledging what the risk level really is.

Too often, the acceptance of risk is based on poorly calculated risk levels, and many enterprises have found, in the wake of an incident, that the actual level of risk accepted was far greater than what they had intended to accept. Careful review of actuarial data or the outcomes of similar incidents at other enterprises and their resulting impact may help to better understand and estimate true likely incident costs.

Risk acceptance is not a one-time process. The level of risk and potential impact of an incident can change dramatically as:

- Assets increase or decrease in value
- New threats emerge
- Attackers gain additional skills or motivation
- Vulnerabilities are discovered
- Existing controls become weaker
- The operations team becomes less diligent

An enterprise should monitor their accepted risk to ensure that these continue to be consistent with senior management's level of risk tolerance.

Risk Acceptance Framework

A risk acceptance framework can be a useful tool used to set the criteria for the acceptance of risk and the level at which management acceptance is executed.

A typical risk acceptance framework is shown in **figure 5.2**.

Figure 5.2—Risk Acceptance Framework

Risk Level	Level Required for Acceptance
Low	Risk acceptance possible by local management
Medium	Risk acceptance possible by chief information officer (CIO)
High	Risk acceptance possible by CIO, director or chief information security officer (CISO), depending on potential impact
Severe	Risk acceptance only at board level, depending on potential impact. Risk reduction is mandatory through rigorous controls or monitoring. Management notification process is required.

Source: ISACA, *CISM Review Manual, 15th Edition, USA*, 2016, figure 2.18, *https://www.isaca.org/bookstore/cism-exam-resources/cm15ed*

Risk Mitigation

Risk mitigation is a response to risk used by an enterprise when the management of risk is accomplished through the use of countermeasures and controls.

Risk mitigation means that once risk has been identified and analyzed actions are taken to reduce the frequency and/or impact of a risk. Mitigation refers to the idea of trying to take some kind of action that will affect the risk value. This can be by changing the:

- Threat
- Vulnerability
- Impact to the enterprise

In general, it is not feasible to affect the threat. It is difficult to identify all threat actors, their motives, their location, etc. Threat actors may be deterred from taking action that results in substantial penalties. As such, influencing the threat component is by far the hardest for enterprises to do, even when the impact of a threat is enormous and thus risk management efforts tend to focus on either reducing the vulnerability or reducing the impact to the enterprise.

Various types of controls are available to help achieve risk mitigation (see Section 5.2). Carefully integrating all types of control is how an enterprise composes a complete risk mitigation portfolio. The main control types are:

- Managerial (e.g., policies)
- Technical (e.g., tools such as firewalls and intrusion detection systems [IDSs])
- Operational (e.g., procedures, separation of duties)

Examples of risk mitigation techniques include:

- Strengthening overall risk management practices, such as implementing sufficiently mature risk management processes. This can be assigning responsibility for risk identification and management of risk to those closest to the activities that generate significant risk. This type of activity also assists with raising awareness of risk across the enterprise.
- Embedding risk awareness activities into the regular business workflow, so that they become part of the regular course of daily activities. This allows staff to better understand and recognize risky behaviors before an incident materializes.
- Improving the risk management processes and developing relevant tolerances that cascade from strategy through the entire enterprise.
- Automating, where possible, the triggers or alerts that would identify or indicate when thresholds are out of tolerance.
- Introducing or strengthening controls intended to reduce either the frequency or impact of a realized risk.
- Deploying new managerial, technical, or operational controls that reduce either the likelihood or the impact of an adverse event.
- Installing a new access control system.
- Implementing policies or operational procedures.
- Developing an effective incident response and business continuity plan (BCP) (see Section 5.3).
- Using compensating controls—internal controls that reduce the risk of an existing or potential control weakness resulting in errors and omissions.

Realistic choices for risk mitigation may be determined in part by the scope of the risk or the speed at which an incident can expand. In some cases, multiple controls may be needed in order to reduce risk to an acceptable level.

Acceptance of residual risk should be documented and subject to periodic reevaluation in the same manner as applies to the acceptance of inherent risk.

Awareness Education and Training

Awareness education and training can serve to mitigate enterprise risk in a cost-effective manner. This can generally be achieved by educating an enterprise's staff in required procedures and policy compliance, as well as ensuring that staff can identify and understand the risk that threatens the enterprise. It is critical that the training effectively communicate the risk and its potential impact in order for staff to understand the justification for risk mitigation efforts or potential need for additional controls.

In order for awareness and training programs to be effective, the enterprise's structure and culture as well as the types of communication must be well understood. Periodically changing risk awareness messages and the means of delivery will help maintain a higher level of risk awareness. Procedural controls can be complex, and it is essential to provide training as needed to ensure that staff understand the procedures and can correctly perform the required steps.

Awareness of policies, standards and procedures by all personnel is essential to achieving effective risk management. Employees cannot be expected to comply with policies or standards that they are not aware of or follow procedures they do not understand. The use of questionnaires and testing can help with risk awareness as well as provide metrics on training effectiveness and needs for additional training. Additional training content can come from various sources, including help desk activity, operational errors, security events and audits.

An awareness program for management should highlight the need for management to play a supervisory role. Awareness training for senior management should highlight the liability, need for compliance, due care and due diligence and the need to create the tone and culture of the enterprise through policy and good practice.

Risk Transfer (Sharing)

Risk transfer (sharing) is a strategy used by an enterprise of assigning risk to another enterprise. The assignment of risk is a better way of thinking of this option.

Risk transfer means reducing the impact by transferring or otherwise sharing a portion of the risk. Common techniques include insurance and outsourcing. I&T-related examples include:

- Taking out insurance coverage for I&T-related activities (e.g., disaster recovery) or cyber incidents (e.g., data breach, ransomware)
- Outsourcing part of the I&T activities, or sharing I&T project mitigations with the provider through fixed price arrangements or shared investment arrangements.

Risk transfer does not relieve an enterprise of a risk, but can involve the skills of another party in managing the risk and reduce the financial impact if an adverse event occurs. Risk ownership always stays with the enterprise, even when entering into a risk transfer, risk sharing, or outsourcing arrangement.

Risk transfer does not always result in all of the risk being transferred or shared. For example, an enterprise that sustains a substantial loss may accrue costs beyond what can be reimbursed by insurance, particularly in the form of damage to its brand (reputational risk). An enterprise that exposes large amounts of confidential customer data might be reimbursed for immediate expenses by an insurance policy, but may lose current and future customers and revenue.

The strategy of transferring risk should be reviewed on a regular basis to ensure that it remains appropriate and adequate. For example, an enterprise should ensure that:

- Current insurance amounts are adequate to cover losses and that the enterprise is compliant with the terms and conditions of the coverage.
- Insurance and outsourcing agreements are current and properly maintained. The moment after an incident occurs is the worst time to realize that any agreement has recently expired or that the enterprise has not complied with its terms.

Risk Avoidance

Risk avoidance is a strategy used by an enterprise for systematically avoiding risk.

Risk avoidance means exiting the activities or conditions that give rise to risk. Risk avoidance applies when no other risk response is adequate. This is the case when:

- There is no other cost-effective response that can succeed in reducing the impact of the realized risk below the defined thresholds for loss. That is, no cost-effective responses are available to mitigate the risk via controls that contain its likelihood and magnitude within the risk appetite's defined thresholds.
- The risk cannot be shared or transferred.
- The risk is deemed unacceptable by management.

Some I&T-related examples of risk avoidance include:

- Relocating a data center away from a region with significant natural hazards.
- Declining to engage in a very large project when the business case shows a notable risk of failure.
- Deciding not to use proprietary technology or software from a vendor because it has only recently begun operations or is undergoing bankruptcy.

Risk avoidance is not a decision to make lightly, but it may be the best choice in some instances.

5.2 Control Design and Implementation

Risk mitigation is often accomplished through the use of controls.

In this section, the risk mitigation aspect of controls is presented along with examples.

Controls may be proactive, meaning that they attempt to prevent an incident. Proactive controls are often called safeguards. A safeguard is a practice, procedure or mechanism that reduces risk.

Controls may also be reactive, meaning that they allow the detection, containment and recovery from an incident. Reactive controls are known as countermeasures. A countermeasure is any process that directly reduces a threat or vulnerability.

For example, a sign that warns a person about a dangerous condition is a safeguard, whereas a fire extinguisher or sprinkler system is a countermeasure.

5.2.1 Control Design

Every enterprise has some controls in place, and the risk assessment should document those controls and calculate their effectiveness in mitigating risk. In some cases, the controls may be sufficient, whereas in others, the controls may need adjustment or replacement. An effective control is one that prevents, detects and/or corrects damage resulting from an incident and enables recovery from a risk event.

It is common for an enterprise to have some situations where the controls currently in place are not sufficient to adequately protect the enterprise. In most cases, this requires the adjustment of the current controls or the implementation of new controls. However, it may not be feasible to reduce the risk to an acceptable level by either adjusting or implementing controls due to reasons such as cost, job requirements or availability of controls. An example of this could be found in a small enterprise when an individual is given administrator rights on a system and there is not adequate segregation of duties (SoD). In this case, it may not be feasible to implement a new or enhanced control; some personnel need administrator rights to perform their jobs, and the risk cannot justify the cost of hiring new staff to address SoD deficiencies or issues. Therefore, the risk owner may consider implementing compensating controls to reduce the risk.

5.2.2 Control Matrix

Controls may be grouped into a control matrix consisting of managerial, technical or physical controls. Often operational controls that concern day-to-day operations, functions and activities are included within managerial controls.

An example of a control matrix is shown in **figure 5.3**, that includes examples of different types of controls. Many controls may fit into more than one control category.

Figure 5.3—Control Matrix

	Managerial	Technical	Physical
Compensating	Separation of duties (SoD)	Two-factor authentication	Dual control operations
Corrective	Remove access	Network isolation	Close fire doors
Detective	Audit	Intrusion detection system (IDS)	Motion sensor
Preventive	User registration process	Login screen	Fence

Source: Adapted from ISACA, *CRISC Review Manual, 6th Edition*, USA, 2015, figure 3.3, *https://www.isaca.org/bookstore/crisc-exam-resources/crr6ed*

5.2.3 Control Management

Controls are chosen to reduce risk to acceptable levels, which requires the measurement and monitoring of risk. The metrics used in the course of risk response are significant in that they are generally carried forward to risk and control monitoring and reporting, where these same metrics are often used to measure the effectiveness of controls after they have been implemented. An enterprise typically defines their own metrics and thresholds for control performance, which may be compared to industry standards, benchmarks and good practices. Risk metrics is covered in Section 6.2.

It is important that controls are set up, operated correctly, and maintained, evaluated and reported to management on a regular basis.

Control management procedures include:

- Proper installation
- Creation of policies and procedures to support operations
- Implementation of change management procedures to ensure correct configuration
- Training of staff to monitor, manage and review controls

- Assignment of responsibility for monitoring and investigation (which may be distinct)
- Creation of a schedule for review and reporting

The decision plan to implement a control is based on many factors, including:

- Current risk level
- Applicable laws and regulations
- Ongoing projects
- Strategic plans and management priorities
- Current and projected budgets
- Availability of staff
- Public pressure
- Actions of competitors

Risk response is subject to the strategic direction and technological direction of the enterprise, which can affect both the choice of one control over another and its schedule for deployment. These decisions can be difficult to make and often require some method of comparing control options.

Questions to consider include:

- Will the control be effective?
- Will the control provide a satisfactory ROI (in enterprises where this is a driving concern)?
- Does the enterprise have sufficient skill to implement, configure and maintain the control?
- Is there sufficient budget and time to implement the control?
- How much will the control cost to operate on an annual basis, or what will the impact of the control be on productivity?

5.3 Incident Management, Business Continuity and Disaster Recovery

The risk environment changes as enterprises, technologies and business practices change and threat agents focus on new areas of attack. Systems and applications that were once thought to be secure are often found to be vulnerable at a later time.

Any change made to a risk environment may affect the accuracy and appropriateness of plans associated with business continuity or disaster recovery. For instance, a risk that was previously accepted by management may now require mitigation. As a result, changes in the risk environment may warrant review and revision of these plans.

There are a number of considerations when developing response and recovery plans, including available resources; expected services; and the types, kinds and severity of threats faced by the enterprise. The state of monitoring and detection capabilities must also be known, and the level of risk the enterprise is willing to accept must be determined. An effective strategy for recovery plans strikes the most cost-effective balance among risk management efforts, incident management and response, and business continuity/disaster recovery planning.

5.3.1 Incident Management

An I&T-related incident is an event that causes an operational, developmental and/or strategic business impact. Incident management starts with the preparation and planning that build an incident response plan. An enterprise should prevent incidents where possible but also have the controls in place to detect and respond to an incident when it occurs. The sooner an incident can be detected, the easier it is to contain the incident and minimize the damage or impact caused by the incident. Incident response teams generally consist of employees assigned specific roles during various types of incidents, but external resources may be needed as well.

The primary focus of incident management is to get the enterprise's affected systems and operations back into normal service as quickly as possible. This can impact the ability to secure evidence associated with the incident because evidence may be lost while returning to service. A detailed incident response plan and regular testing that involves the business will increase awareness and ensure the appropriate time is granted for evidence collection and analysis. If the business does not understand the need to collect evidence or the incident response team does not know how to collect and preserve evidence, the enterprise is at a greater risk to be liable for the event, and the attacker has a greater chance to avoid prosecution.

Each incident must be examined to extract the lessons learned to improve the prevention, detection and recovery from future incidents of a similar nature. A thorough review of an incident can identify weak controls, poor detection, inappropriate or ineffective response and lack of training of staff. In addition, threats, vulnerabilities and impact can be extracted from the review of incident reports.

5.3.2 Business Continuity Planning

Business continuity refers to preventing, mitigating and recovering from disruption. Having an effective business continuity plan is an example of risk mitigation.

All systems will fail from time to time. The purpose of business continuity planning is to enable a business to continue critical services in the event of a disruption, up to and including the ability to survive a disastrous interruption. Rigorous planning and commitment of resources is necessary to adequately plan for such an event.

Business continuity plans include controls that reduce the risk of losing critical processes to acceptable levels. A business continuity plan should address the level of risk that it is meant to address. The risk associated with a particular process depends on the magnitude of impact to the business should it be interrupted and the probability of an interruption.

Business continuity plans may be established at the enterprise level, by each department or for each process. When there is an overarching plan, it is usually divided into multiple annexes that relate to the division and process-level activities that must be carried out to continue operations. It is highly desirable to have a single integrated plan to ensure that:

- There is proper coordination among various plan components.
- Resources committed are used in the most effective way and there is reasonable confidence that, through its application, the enterprise will survive a disruption.

The goal of a business continuity plan is to provide a reduced but sufficient level of functionality in the business operations immediately after encountering an interruption and while recovery is taking place, so the plan should address all functions and assets required to continue as a viable enterprise. A business continuity plan includes the continuity procedures determined by the enterprise as necessary to survive and minimize the consequences of business interruption. The business continuity plan also lists the people needed to carry out the continuity procedures. The recovery of critical business processes may be through an alternate process, including:

- A manual process or outsourced support
- Having sufficient inventory on hand to support operations
- Using facilities available at another office or location
- Displacing less critical work with more critical functions

5.3.3 Disaster Recovery

Disaster recovery includes the activities and programs designed to return the enterprise to an acceptable condition. Disaster recovery refers to the reestablishment of business and IT services following a disaster or incident within a predefined schedule and budget. The term is commonly associated with IT rather than business, but disaster recovery can be considered a relative of overall business continuity. Time frames for recovery are based on the cost of recovery and length of time that management is willing to accept.

A disaster recovery plan should be kept current to ensure that it reflects risk scenarios and business priorities. A comprehensive disaster recovery plan includes specific information on:

- Hardware and software requirements for restoration
- Which, and in what order that systems and applications should be restored
- How to accomplish the restorations under multiple scenarios
- How many, and in what time frame user logins are required

The plan should also be rigorously tested, which can uncover any vulnerabilities and provide the experience needed for team members to enact the plan effectively.

5.4 Risk States

Risk can be differentiated by its state of risk (inherent, current and residual).

Inherent risk is the risk state (or exposure) that exists without considering the actions that management has taken or might take (e.g., implementing controls) to mitigate risk. Inherent risk is present because of the nature of the situation, for example, the 'out of the box' state of risk before any processes, technologies or controls are put in place.

Current risk is the risk state that exists in the moment, taking into account those actions that have already been taken but not actions that are anticipated or have been proposed. Current risk represents inherent risk with existing risk responses applied. When risk is referenced in I&T-related risk, it generally refers to current risk. I&T-related risk rarely uses the concept of inherent risk.

Residual risk is the risk state that remains after management has implemented a risk response, which is typically a mitigation activity but may also include risk transfer. Risk transfer (also known as risk sharing) is the process of assigning risk to another enterprise, such as through the purchase of an insurance policy or by outsourcing a service to a third-party provider. Residual risk is calculated by subtracting the effectiveness of all risk responses (typically controls) (see **figure 5.4**).

Figure 5.4—Risk States

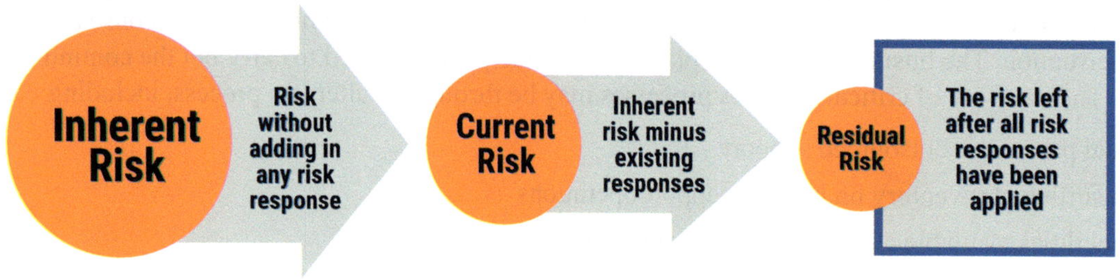

Source: ISACA, *COBIT® 5 for Risk*, USA, 2013, pg. 18, *www.isaca.org/COBIT/Pages/Risk-product-page.aspx*

If the residual risk associated with a particular control is within the enterprise risk appetite, the residual risk should be accepted. Otherwise, an additional response is needed.

Residual risk can be used by management to determine:

- Which areas require more controls
- Whether the benefits of such controls outweigh the control costs

5.4.1 Risk and Control

Risk and control are strongly connected and introduce other types of risk such as control risk and detection risk.

Control risk was introduced in section 1.4 and is the risk that a material error exists that would not be prevented or detected on a timely basis by the system of internal controls (ordinarily low for I&T, as processes are applied consistently). The selection of the wrong control, the incorrect configuration of the control, the improper operation of the control, the failure to monitor and review the control, or the inadequacy of the control to address new threats may each introduce the risk of control failure. If risk is mitigated through the use of controls, control risk must also be considered (i.e., control risk is the probability the control will fail or be inadequate).

Detection risk is the risk that the prescribed controls, substantive testing procedures or monitoring will not detect an error that could be material—individually or in combination with other errors.

For example, the detection risk associated with:

- Identifying breaches of security in an application system is ordinarily high because logs for the entire period of the investigation are not available at the time when the investigation is made.
- Identification of lack of disaster recovery plans (DRPs) is ordinarily low because existence is easily verified.

Figure 5.5 outlines how residual risk relates to inherent risk and provides pervasive and detailed I&T control and detection risk areas that should be considered.

<table>
<tr><th colspan="3">Figure 5.5—How Residual Risk Relates to Inherent Risk</th></tr>
<tr><th>Components of Risk</th><th colspan="2">Description</th></tr>
<tr><td>Residual risk</td><td colspan="2">The risk remaining after management has implemented a risk response</td></tr>
<tr><td rowspan="4">Inherent risk</td><td colspan="2">The risk level without any controls or other management actions
Example:
Operating system (OS) security usually involves a high inherent risk because changes to, or even disclosure of, data or programs through OS security weaknesses could result in system failure, security breach or regulatory penalties.
Inherent risk for most areas of IT is ordinarily high. Because IT is integral to many business processes, the potential effect of errors spans several business systems and many users. Assessing the inherent risk should consider pervasive and specific I&T controls, as outlined in the following table.</td></tr>
<tr><th>Control Type</th><th>Investigation Area</th></tr>
<tr><td>Pervasive I&T controls</td><td>• Integrity of IT management and IT management experience and knowledge
• Pressures on IT management that may predispose it to conceal or misstate information (e.g., large business-critical overruns, hacker activity)
• Nature of the enterprise's business and systems (e.g., plans for electronic commerce [e-commerce], complexity of the systems, lack of integrated systems)
• Factors affecting the enterprise's industry as a whole (e.g., changes in technology, IT staff availability)</td></tr>
<tr><td>Specific I&T controls</td><td>• Complexity of the systems involved
• Level of manual intervention required
• Susceptibility to loss or misappropriation of the assets controlled by the system (e.g., inventory, payroll)
• Likelihood of activity peaks at certain times in the period of investigation
• Poor change control procedures
• Integrity, experience and skills of the management and staff involved in applying the I&T controls</td></tr>
<tr><td>Control risk</td><td colspan="2">The risk of failure of the inner control systems to prevent, detect or correct an incident in a timely manner
Example:
Manual reviews of computer logs can have a high associated control risk due to the volume of logged information. Activities requiring investigation can be easily missed.
Because automated data validation procedures are applied consistently, their associated control risk is usually low.</td></tr>
</table>

Figure 5.5—How Residual Risk Relates to Inherent Risk *(cont.)*	
Components of Risk	**Description**
Detection risk	The risk of an inability of the prescribed controls, substantive testing procedures or monitoring to detect an error that could be material, individually or in combination with other errors Example: An intrusion detection system (IDS), such as an antivirus system or firewall, does not detect an adverse condition and trigger an adequate response (sometimes called a false negative—an indication that everything is fine when there is actually a problem).

5.5 Risk Response Selection, Prioritization and Communication

The determination of the appropriate risk response is often based on the evaluation of several possible response options. If there are risk that fall outside the risk tolerance limits for an enterprise—and there most certainly will be—then risk responses will be required to bring the risk under control and the residual risk to an appropriate level. This ongoing effort is part of the risk management cycle. It might not be possible or cost effective to remediate all risk at the same time; therefore, a risk prioritization strategy should be used to create a risk response plan and implementation schedule.

5.5.1 Risk Response Selection Parameters

A comprehensive examination of all factors influencing the risk decision will determine the most appropriate strategy for an enterprise's response to risk. The following parameters should be taken into account when choosing the best response to a given situation:

- **Cost of the response**—In the case of risk transfer, consider the cost of the insurance premium; in the case of risk mitigation, consider the cost of implementing, maintaining and testing controls.
- **Importance of the risk addressed by the response**—Consider priority or rank on the risk register.
- **Capability to implement and maintain the response over time**—The more mature an enterprise is in its risk management capability, the better the responses that can be implemented; when the enterprise is rather immature, some very basic responses may be used and improved over time.
- **Effectiveness of the response**—Consider the extent to which risk response activities will reduce the frequency or impact of the risk, should it materialize.
- **Efficiency of the response**—Consider the extent to which risk response activities will be reduced compared to other responses and other IT-related investments
- **Other I&T-related investments**—Investing in risk response measures always competes with other I&T-related investments, and requires careful deliberation.
- **Other responses**—One response may address several risk types while another may not; risk may be aggregated and subsequently addressed with a common response.

Sometimes the effort or resources required for responses (e.g., the collection of controls that need to be implemented or strengthened) will exceed the available capability of the enterprise. In this case, decisions on prioritization requires skill and expertise.

5.5.2 Risk Response Options

Possible risk response options can be grouped as follows:

- **Quick wins**—Quick wins include very short-term, time-efficient and effective responses to high-impact risk.
- **Compliance obligations for which there is a nonnegotiable requirement**—Managing the risk of noncompliance should be done in conjunction with other risk responses to avoid duplicative or overlapping work.

An example of a quick win and one that addresses compliance obligations is where an enterprise that is missing a number of relatively simple, but critical, IT procedures and is at risk of regulatory non-compliance, creates and implements the missing procedures.

- **Business case required**—More expensive or difficult responses to high-impact risk require careful analysis and management decisions prior to investment. Responses in this category may also include outsourcing the management of risk that the enterprise cannot address internally.
- **Deferring and/or continued monitoring of conditions**—Enterprises may defer the response and continue monitoring to determine if changes to the identified risk or environment warrant a different response.

An example of where a business case is likely to be required is where an enterprise that has a complex IT architecture is nearing capacity and extending capacity and maintaining existing software will be very expensive. Response options available to mitigate this risk involve either a complete overhaul of the IT architecture through a large project or the purchase of a completely new system. Because of the complexity and cost associated with each option, an appropriate business case will be required to support any business decision.

Figure 5.6 outlines the broad process for selecting and prioritizing risk responses.

Figure 5.6—Risk Response Selection and Prioritization

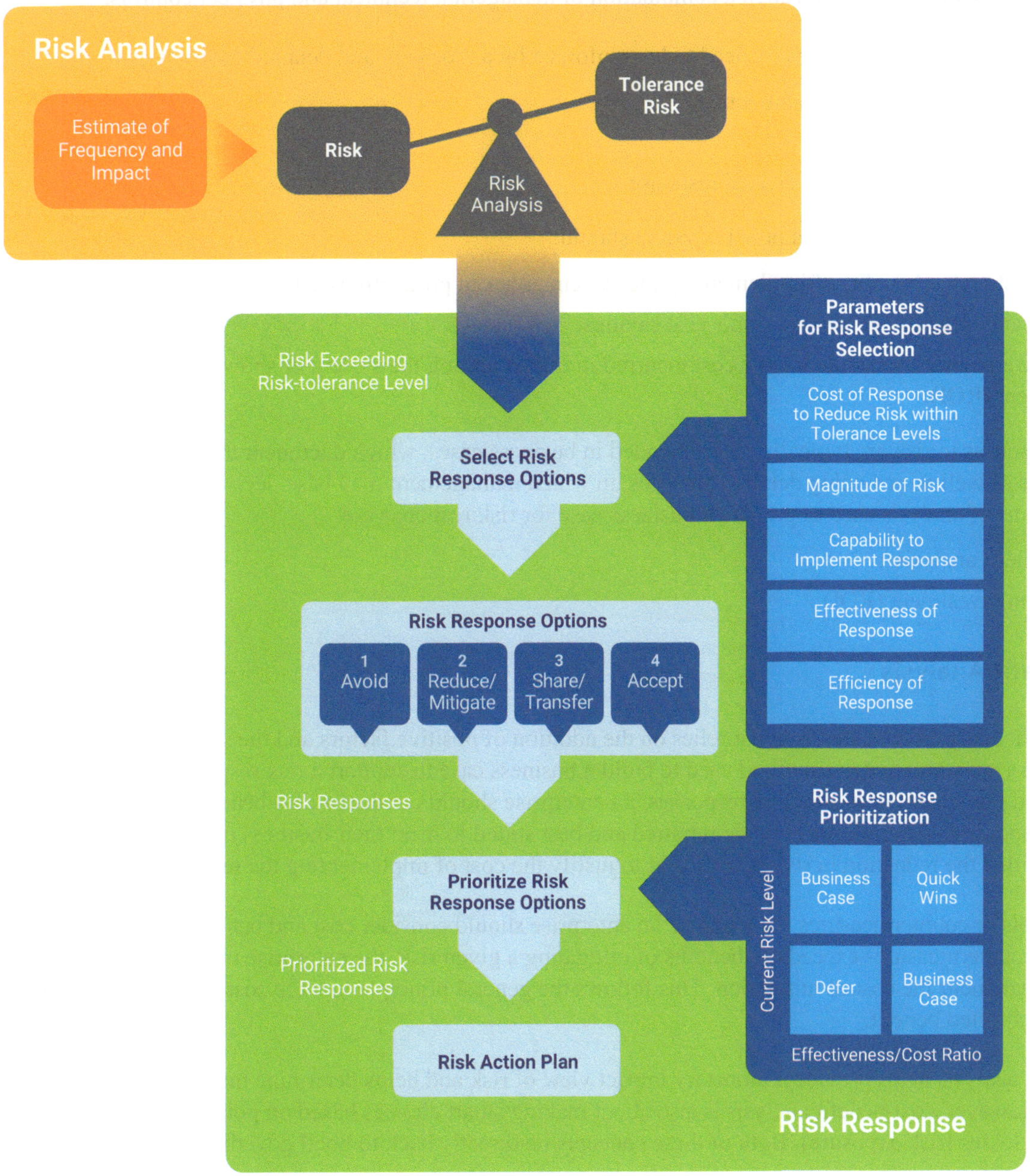

Source: ISACA, *Risk IT Framework, 2nd Edition*, USA, 2020, figure 8.1, *https://www.isaca.org/bookstore/bookstore-risk-digital/ritf2*

5.5.3 Business Case Development

A business case documents the rationale for making a business investment, used both to support a business decision on whether to proceed with the investment and as an operational tool to support management of the investment through its full economic life cycle.

The use of a business case in the selection of the appropriate risk response is based primarily on the calculation of value obtained from a risk response for cost incurred. In other words, does the cost of implementing a specific risk response provide enough value to the enterprise for it to be a wise decision? In the end, the decision may be to accept the risk or to respond to the risk through a combination of managerial, technical and physical controls.

Risk responses that involve investment need to be reinforced by a thorough and detailed business case, which:

- Justifies the expense of the investment
- Outlines alternatives
- Explains the rationale for the selected response

A business case for implementing a new IT system should:

- State the strategic benefits of implementing the system either in productivity gains or in future cost avoidance.
- Identify and quantify the new system's cost savings.
- Estimate a payback schedule for the cost incurred in implementing the system or show the projected return on investment (ROI).

Specific responses to risk are typically recommended in business cases, which document the problems and one or more options as well as providing detailed analyses on which management may base decisions. Two of the most common forms of analysis used to prepare a business case for risk response are:

- Cost-benefit analysis
- Return on investment (ROI)

Cost-benefit Analysis

A cost-benefit analysis is an analysis that relies on the addition of positive factors and the subtraction of negative ones to determine a net result and is a method used to build a business case to support a risk response. In order to allocate resources and implement cost-effective responses, an enterprise should conduct a cost/benefit analysis for each proposed response to determine which are required and best suited to meet their business objectives. The purpose is to demonstrate that the reduction in risk is sufficient to justify the cost of implementing the response.

When controls or countermeasures are planned, an enterprise should consider cost and benefits. If the cost of specific controls or countermeasures exceed the benefits of mitigating a given risk, the enterprise may choose to accept the risk rather than incur the cost of mitigation. This follows the general principle that the cost of a control should never exceed the expected benefit.

Cost-benefit analysis helps provide a monetary impact view of risk and helps determine the cost of protecting what is important. However, cost-benefit analysis is also about making smart choices based on potential risk mitigation costs vs. potential losses (risk exposure). Both of these concepts tie directly back to good governance practices.

Return on Investment

Return on investment (ROI) is a measure of operating performance and efficiency, computed in its simplest form by dividing net income by the total investment over the period being considered. Many enterprises justify an investment in projects, tools or new ventures using ROI, which calculates how long it takes to recoup its cost through value added or other savings produced. For example, a new computer system might pay for itself over three years as a result of better productivity, lower numbers of staff required or increased sales.

In determining the ROI of a specific risk response, the enterprise is trying to forecast the likelihood and impact of an incident and decide on an adequate level of investment based on its appetite for risk and the amount of exposure that will be mitigated or eliminated by the investment.

5.5.4 Risk Response Prioritization

The prioritization of a response to risk should be based on a number of factors, including:

- **The enterprise's mission and strategic objectives**—Which risk, if realized, will have the greatest impact on the enterprise?
- **The criticality of an asset**—Which I&T asset is most critical in the context of the enterprise mission and strategy?
- **The criticality of third-party resources**—Which vendors, service providers, suppliers, or third parties are critical in the context of the enterprise mission and strategy?
- **The probability, or likelihood, of a certain scenario materializing**—Subject matter experts inside and outside the enterprise as well as research can help determine the probability, or likelihood, of a certain risk scenario materializing.
- **The largest potential impact on the enterprise**—Which risk, if realized, will have the greatest impact on the ability of the enterprise to continue to deliver its products and services?
- **The ability of the enterprise to respond to a given scenario or set of scenarios**—Which risk scenario will the enterprise have difficulty responding to? This is a real problem for many enterprises, which do not have adequate technology or resources to respond to certain risk scenarios.

The main drivers for risk management include the need to improve decision making in enterprises, align risk management resources to address the risk with the greatest potential impact on the enterprise, and build the capabilities and gather the resources towards detecting and responding to realized risk.

The ultimate decision on risk response lies with the risk owner but is subject to the strategic direction and technological direction of the enterprise.

5.5.5 Risk Response Communication

As projects are completed and residual levels of risk are accepted by risk owners, the risk register (see Section 4.5) should be updated to reflect the changes. The risk register should also show the progress of testing and the attainment of milestones during the progress of a mitigation project. By keeping the risk register accurate and up-to-date, it ensures that it is consistently available as a resource for risk management activities.

The risk response process integrates with the other risk management processes to ensure that management is provided accurate reports on:

- The level of risk faced by the enterprise
- The types of incidents that have occurred
- Any change to the enterprise's risk profile based on changes in the (internal and external) risk environment

Benefits of open communication of risk responses taken by the enterprise include:

- Management understanding of the actual I&T-related risk exposures, enabling informed risk decisions
- Raised awareness within the enterprise and motivation for the integration of risk mindfulness into daily duties
- Ability of external stakeholders to see that good risk management practices are in use

Inadequate communication of risk response actions taken can result in:

- A false sense of confidence about the levels of risk
- Lack of direction of strategic risk planning
- Poor communication of risk levels to clients, investors and regulators
- A perception that the enterprise is trying to cover up known risk from stakeholders

5.5.6 Risk Response Plan

A risk response plan is developed after the risk response strategy has been approved. A risk response plan should be run as a project, with a defined start and end date. The end date is often used to determine the critical path of the project, which refers to those elements of the project that may have a direct impact on whether the end date can be met. A risk response plan should be run by a project manager that understands that change in the delivery of any project element on the critical path affects the delivery of the entire project. For example, a project that does not receive its equipment from the supplier on time may not be able to meet the scheduled project dates. Critical path elements should be given special consideration for timeliness, because delays in these elements increase overall project risk. Careful and informed consideration should be given on the:

- Feasibility of project dates
- Expected workload associated with the project
- Costs of the project
- Overall success of the project according to risk management and business goals

A risk response plan should outline the requirements for implementing the approved risk response strategy, including:

- Detailed steps and tasks
- Timelines
- Budgets
- Resources
- Tools

A risk response plan should include:

- Name and explanation of risk
- Risk rating
- Planned action for mitigation
- Entity or person performing the mitigation
- Mitigation completion date
- Risk rating after mitigation has been put in place

The risk registry should be updated at the completion of the risk response plan in order to communicate risk.

5.6 Summary of Terminology

It is important to recognize and understand I&T-related risk terminology. The following terms were introduced in this chapter.

Figure 5.7—Chapter 5 Terminology

Term	Definition
Business case	Documents the rationale for making a business investment, used both to support a business decision on whether to proceed with the investment and as an operational tool to support management of the investment through its full economic life cycle
Business continuity	Preventing, mitigating and recovering from disruption
Compensating control	An internal control that reduces the risk of an existing or potential control weakness resulting in errors and omissions
Cost-benefit analysis	An analysis that relies on the addition of positive factors and the subtraction of negative ones to determine a net result and is a method used to build a business case to support a risk response
Countermeasure	Any process that directly reduces a threat or vulnerability
Current risk	The risk state that exists in the moment, taking into account those actions that have already been taken but not actions that are anticipated or have been proposed
Detection risk	The risk that the prescribed controls, substantive testing procedures or monitoring will not detect an error that could be material—individually or in combination with other errors
Disaster recovery	The activities and programs designed to return the enterprise to an acceptable condition
Inherent risk	The risk level or exposure without taking into account the actions that management has taken or might take (e.g., implementing controls)
IT-related incident	An IT-related event that causes an operational, developmental and/or strategic business impact
Residual risk	The remaining risk after management has implemented a risk response
Return on investment (ROI)	A measure of operating performance and efficiency, computed in its simplest form by dividing net income by the total investment over the period being considered
Risk acceptance	Decision to accept a risk made according to the risk appetite and risk tolerance set by senior management where the enterprise can assume the risk and absorb any losses
Risk avoidance	The process for systematically avoiding risk, constituting one approach to managing risk
Risk mitigation	The management of risk through the use of countermeasures and controls
Risk response	Risk avoidance, risk acceptance, risk sharing/transfer, risk mitigation, leading to a situation that as much future residual risk (current risk with the risk response defined and implemented) as possible (usually depending on budgets available) falls within risk appetite limits
Risk sharing	See risk transfer.
Risk transfer	The process of assigning risk to another enterprise, usually through the purchase of an insurance policy or by outsourcing the service Also known as risk sharing
Safeguard	A practice, procedure or mechanism that reduces risk

Page intentionally left blank

Chapter 5 Knowledge Check

Review questions are provided as a means to support the content presented within this study guide and serve as a gauge or assessment of knowledge of I&T-related risk topics. One question is provided for each topic.

For individuals intending to earn the ISACA IT Risk Fundamentals Certificate, these questions are written to depict the type of questions that may appear on the exam. These questions will not specifically appear on the exam, but similar ones may appear.

REVIEW QUESTIONS

1. A risk response strategy that embeds risk awareness activities into the regular business workflow, so that they become part of the regular course of daily activities is an example of risk:

   A. Mitigation
   B. Transfer
   C. Avoidance

2. Which of the following is the **MOST** important consideration when choosing to implement a new control?

   A. The type of controls that the enterprise currently utilizes
   B. The intended effectiveness of the new control.
   C. The number of business processes that the new control will address.

3. Which of the following is **MOST** likely to have a negative impact on an enterprise's ability to secure evidence after an incident has occurred?

   A. Attempting to get affected systems and operations back into normal service as quickly as possible.
   B. Using an internal response team to collect and secure evidence.
   C. Using external resources to collect and secure evidence.

4. Residual risk is risk that exists:

   A. After management has implemented a response to new risk.
   B. In the moment with existing risk responses applied.
   C. Before any risk response has been applied.

5. A quick win risk response option will **MOST** likely be chosen when addressing:

   A. Long-term, high-impact risk
   B. Short-term, low-impact risk
   C. Short-term, high-impact risk

Answers on page 162

Chapter 5 ANSWER KEY

Review Questions

1. **A. Embedding risk awareness activities into the regular business workflow, so that they become part of the regular course of daily activities is an example of a risk mitigation strategy. This allows staff to better understand and recognize risky behaviors before an incident occurs.**
B. Risk transfer means reducing the impact by transferring or otherwise sharing a portion of the risk. In this case, the embedding of risk awareness activities into regular enterprise activities does not transfer risk. Taking out insurance coverage to protect the enterprise from the impact of risk is an example of risk transfer.
C. Risk avoidance is where a risk cannot be shared or transferred. In this case, the embedding of risk awareness activities into regular enterprise activities does not avoid risk. An example of risk avoidance is when an enterprise moves a data center away from a geographical area or region that has had significant natural hazards.

2. A. The type of controls that the enterprise currently utilizes should not be an important factor in implementing a new control unless a specific type of control is missing or mandated, because as it is important that an enterprise maintain a correct balance between technical, managerial (administrative) and physical control types.
B. When implementing a new control, it is important that the control effectively prevent, detect and/or correct damage resulting from an incident and enable recovery from a risk event.
C. The number of business processes that the new control will address may be an important factor in implementing a new control, but what is most important is the effectiveness of the new control.

3. **A. The primary focus of incident management is to get the enterprise's affected systems and operations back into normal service as quickly as possible. However, this can impact the ability to secure evidence associated with the incident, because evidence may be lost while returning to service.**
B. Incident response teams generally consist of employees assigned specific roles during various types of incidents. Using properly trained internal resources should have a positive impact on an enterprise's ability to secure evidence. However, if the business does not understand the need to collect evidence or the incident response team does not know how to collect and preserve evidence, the enterprise is at a greater risk to be liable for the event, and the attacker has a greater chance to avoid prosecution.
C. Incident response can utilize external resources. Using properly trained and experienced external resources should only have positive impact on the enterprise's ability to secure evidence. However, if external resources do not understand the need to collect evidence or are not properly experienced and trained on how to collect and preserve evidence, the enterprise is at a greater risk to be liable for the event, and the attacker has a greater chance to avoid prosecution.

4. **A. Residual risk is risk that remains after management has implemented a risk response, which is typically a mitigation activity, but may also include risk transfer.**
B. Risk that exists in the moment, taking into account those actions that have already been taken, but not actions that are anticipated or have been proposed, is known as current risk. Current risk represents inherent risk with existing risk responses applied.
C. Risk that exists without considering the actions that management has taken or might take (e.g., implementing controls) to mitigate risk is known as inherent risk. Inherent risk is present because of the nature of the situation, for example, the out-of-the-box state of risk before any processes, technologies or controls are put in place.

5. A. Anything long-term is by its nature not a quick win. Long-term, high-impact risk is likely to require a more difficult and detailed response, which better lends itself to utilizing a business case approach.
B. Low-impact risk does not require a quick win risk response, and most likely does not require a response at all.
C. Quick wins include very short-term, time-efficient and effective responses to high-impact risk. An example of a quick win is where an enterprise that is missing a number of relatively simple, but critical, IT procedures, creates and implements the missing procedures.

Page intentionally left blank

Chapter 6:

Risk Monitoring, Reporting and Communication

Learning Objectives 166

Risk Monitoring, Reporting and Communication

6.1 Risk Monitoring Process 167
6.2 Key Risk Indicators 168
6.3 Key Performance Indicators 175
6.4 Risk and Control Monitoring and Testing 176
6.5 Risk Reporting and Communication 179
6.6 Summary of Terminology 181

Chapter 6 Knowledge Check 187

Learning Objectives

The monitoring and reporting of risk play an important role in the risk management process. Indicators for risk and performance should be considered carefully and chosen deliberately, based on their alignment with enterprise goals. Because of the changing nature of risk and associated controls, ongoing monitoring and reporting is an essential step of the risk management process.

Learning objectives include the following:

- Gather available sources of data to monitor and report on risk.
- Articulate how to monitor risk through the use of key risk indicators (KRIs) and key performance indicators (KPIs).
- Describe how to monitor existing controls.
- Explain risk reporting guidelines and types.
- Outline the importance of an ongoing risk monitoring process and a proactive and continuous approach to risk management.

Risk Monitoring, Reporting and Communication

6.1 Risk Monitoring Process

An important component of risk management is continuously monitoring, evaluating, assessing and reporting risk. In order to prevent an acceptance of risk that exceeds the risk acceptance criteria set by the business, risk monitoring and evaluation should be integrated with enterprise performance management systems to ensure alignment between I&T-related risk and business risk.

Risk monitoring and evaluation are processes performed to:

- Collect, validate and evaluate business, IT, and process goals and metrics
- Monitor processes to ensure that they are performed in line with established performance metrics
- Provide reports that are systematic and timely

To accomplish these tasks, data related to risk management must be gathered from various sources in a timely and accurate manner. After the data have been validated for integrity, analysis can be performed against specific performance targets. Properly done, this process provides a succinct, all-around view of IT performance within the enterprise monitoring system.

An enterprise should be aware of changes in risk over time and the impact of changes in the risk environment. As the goals and strategies of the enterprise evolve, it is natural for the risk environment to also evolve. Risk should be taken into account as part of strategic planning so that changes can be anticipated and mitigated as new strategic plans are unveiled, designed and implemented, rather than attempting to address these retroactively as part of the risk response and mitigation process.

Risk monitoring involves observing and assessing potential risk events, threat events and vulnerability events, and to make sure that current and emerging risk remains within the enterprise's risk tolerance levels. Risk reporting schedules and KRI monitoring are some of the processes used to keep stakeholders aware of current risk and ensure that risk responses are effective in mitigating enterprise risk.

Risk is dynamic; therefore, risk monitoring is necessary to determine if risk responses have been implemented as planned and how the effectiveness of those responses are at mitigating risk. Monitoring provides indicators of whether risk exposure has changed from its prior state as trends are analyzed or if any new risk has occurred that was not previously identified.

Over time, risk monitoring can:

- Provide an early warning (forward-looking) signal that high risk is emerging.
- Provide a backward-looking review of past risk events, enabling improvement.
- Enable the documentation and analysis of trends.
- Provide indication of risk appetite/tolerance through metric setting.
- Increase the likelihood of achieving enterprise objectives.
- Assist in the continual optimization of risk governance and risk management.

Monitoring should be conducted both before and after a risk treatment plan is completed. This includes:

- Monitoring the status of identified risk, risk treatment plans and measures of the risk management process. In some enterprises, the project management function can be leveraged to embed the risk management processes into daily business routines.

- Periodically revisiting areas of concern, watch items and identified risk as conditions change. This includes updating the risk register, as needed.
- Reporting the progress of risk management activities to all relevant stakeholders.

6.1.1 Risk Monitoring Stakeholders

Many stakeholders are responsible for, or interested in, the results of I&T-related risk activities. Among them are:

- Process and system owners
- Chief information officer (CIO) or chief technology officer (CTO)
- I&T governance board
- Chief risk officer
- Audit and risk committees
- External regulators (if an enterprise is subject to such regulation)
- Project/program steering committee

6.1.2 Risk Monitoring Status

An enterprise uses a risk register as a central repository for tracking, monitoring and reporting the status of risk from a single source (see Section 4.5 for information on the development and use of a risk register). Risk entered into the register should be described in common business terms. This provides the enterprise with a standardized view of its overall risk landscape, that is used to monitor the status of all enterprise risk that is faced by the enterprise being monitored to ensure relevancy and the status of the risk response. It is important that the enterprise has the ability to track, monitor and report on the risk register (list of risk), because as the general nature of IT, internal and external business drivers, and regulatory requirements that impact and influence an enterprise are all dynamic.

The risk register should include risk statements that are actionable. It is important that the risk register is kept current and does not simply contain a list of vulnerabilities or past audit findings. For example, the risk register should not include deficiencies discovered during an audit or the results of a vulnerability assessment that are not associated with risk.

6.2 Key Risk Indicators

An enterprise may develop an extensive set of metrics to serve as risk indicators. A key risk indicator is a subset of risk indicators that are highly relevant and possess a high probability of predicting or indicating important risk.

Key risk indicators (KRIs) are metrics capable of showing that the enterprise is subject to—or has a high probability of being subject to—a risk that exceeds the defined risk appetite or tolerance. KRIs are the metrics or pieces of data that signal:

- Something is not operating as expected
- Increased exposure to risk in one or more areas of the enterprise

KRIs are used to measure risk levels in comparison to defined risk thresholds (trigger levels), so that the enterprise receives an alert when a risk level approaches an unacceptable level. By putting tracking and reporting mechanisms in place that alert staff to a developing or potential risk, the enterprise gains the opportunity to quickly respond to the risk before it produces unacceptable outcomes.

KRIs are only indicators of risk and not direct measures of risk and are specific to each enterprise. Development and selection of KRIs depend on many parameters in the internal and external environments, including:

- Size and complexity of the enterprise
- Regulatory and operating environment (e.g., whether it is operating in a highly regulated market)
- Strategic objectives of the enterprise

The identification of KRIs should take into account:

- The different stakeholders in the enterprise. Risk indicators should be identified for stakeholders depending on their unique information needs. Involving the right stakeholders in the selection of risk indicators ensures greater buy-in and ownership.
- The need to tie directly to the stated risk appetite and risk tolerance statements. This provides the most meaningful way to track desired outcomes of the risk management program.
- The need for lag and lead indicators. An enterprise should take a balanced selection of risk indicators.

6.2.1 Types of Key Risk Indicators

Lag Risk Indicator

A lag risk indicator is a backward-looking metric that indicates risk has been realized after an event has occurred.

Lag indicators include data, information or capabilities that are measured after an event or condition occurs— e.g., meeting a performance target or service level availability goal. Analyzing root causes from realized risk, failed controls or processes, and missed targets over time can help enterprises develop new indicators, trends or correlating conditions to gain insights.

Lead Risk Indicator

A lead risk indicator is a forward-looking metric that provides an early warning that risk may soon be realized before an event has occurred. Lead risk indicators include pieces of data, information or capabilities that are in place to prevent events from occurring. Lead risk indicators may have upper and lower limits to help an enterprise understand when a condition requires attention before the risk is realized.

Because a lead risk indicator is based on data relating to risk that has not yet been realized, it may not be completely reliable or there may be alerts that turn out to be false positive indicators.

6.2.2 Developing Risk Indicators

A variety of risk indicators can be developed for various parts of an enterprise as a means of ongoing monitoring. A common method used for developing risk indicators, some of which might result in key risk indicators, is root cause analysis.

Root Cause Analysis

Root cause analysis was introduced in section 4.3 as one of many risk analysis methods. Root cause analysis is a process of diagnosis to establish the origins of events, which can be used for learning from consequences, typically from errors and problems.

After root causes are identified, root causes they can be used to develop needed controls to accurately address root causes that lead to system failures and deficiencies. Root cause analysis enables an enterprise to learn from consequences, typically from errors and problems, in the effort to not repeat undesired actions or results.

The actions that an enterprise takes in response to risk are often based on the lessons learned from previous events. A root cause of an incident is examined to discover the conditions and factors that led to the event, rather than reacting to the symptoms of the problem. These underlying conditions, which comprise the root (core) of a problem, are the conditions against which action must be taken in order to prevent the problem from recurring. For example, if a review of a business process finds that users are not compliant with the procedures and policies in place, an examination should be conducted to determine why the users are not compliant before recommending enforcement of the procedure. It may be that the procedure is outdated, flawed or unworkable when aligned with the objectives of the enterprise, in which case, it is the procedure and not the behavior that should be corrected. Root cause analysis examines the reasons why a problem exists or a breach has occurred and seeks to identify and resolve these underlying issues.

In many cases, a risk event may be the result of coinciding events—several issues that act in combination to create what appears to be a single result. Root cause analysis can be used as a means of identifying coinciding events, which cannot be traced to a single common cause. In this case, the solution is more than just a single response activity or implementation of a single control.

KRIs should drill down to the root cause of the events (indicative of root cause and not just symptoms). Analyzing root causes from realized risk, failed controls or processes, and missed targets over time can help enterprises develop new indicators, trends or correlating conditions to gain insights.

6.2.3 KRI Selection

In addition to experience, the selection of KRIs can be based on sources such as industry benchmarks, external threat reporting services, or any other factor that can be monitored that indicates changes in risk to the enterprise.

KRIs should be selected carefully and sparingly. Common mistakes made when selecting KRIs include choosing too many KRIs and choosing KRIs that are flawed in some way. These include KRIs that:

- Are not linked to a specific risk
- Are not linked to business goals
- Are incomplete or inaccurate due to unclear specifications
- Are difficult to measure, aggregate, compare and interpret
- Provide results that cannot be compared over time

Criteria to select KRIs include:

- **Impact**—Indicators for risk with high business impact or tied directly to risk tolerance statements are more likely to be KRIs.
- **Effort (to implement, measure and report)**—For different indicators that are equivalent in sensitivity, the one for which data collection is easier may be a good starting point.
- **Reliability**—The indicator must possess a high correlation with the risk and be a good predictor or outcome measure.
- **Sensitivity**—The indicator must be representative of the risk factors and capable of accurately indicating variances in the risk factors.

KRI Attributes

The effectiveness of KRIs depend in large part on the strength of their metrics. Good metrics should be SMART.[23] That is, they should be:

- **Specific**—Based on a clearly understood goal; clear and concise
- **Measurable**—Able to be measured; quantifiable (objective), not subjective
- **Attainable**—Realistic; based on important goals and values
- **Relevant**—Directly related to a specific activity or goal
- **Timely**—Grounded in a specific time frame

KRI Selection Benefits

The selection of the appropriate KRIs provides the following benefits to the enterprise:

- Early warning, forward-looking signals to the enterprise that a risk may be soon realized, enabling a proactive response before the risk becomes a loss
- Backward-looking historical context on risk that has been realized, further informing future risk responses, driving improvement, and supporting documentation and analysis of trends
- Feedback on risk appetite and tolerances to facilitate improvements in risk management strategy and processes, and optimize risk governance and oversight

KRI Selection Challenges

Some common challenges associated with the selection of KRIs include:

- Undefined measurement objectives, absence of stated/expected outcomes, or lack of definitive questions that can be answered with data from KRIs
- Rote collection of data that is easy to obtain or already on hand, as opposed to data that correlates significantly to specific risk or risk types
- Lack of clear logical relationship between KRIs and specific risk or business objectives
- Excess metrics without a clear measurement objective or purpose
- Cumbersome processes of aggregation
- Excess complexity in synthesizing and/or interpreting results from KRIs at an enterprise level

Figure 6.1 provides KRI selection guidance.

[23] Doran, George T.; Management Review, November 1981

Figure 6.1—KRI Selection Guidance

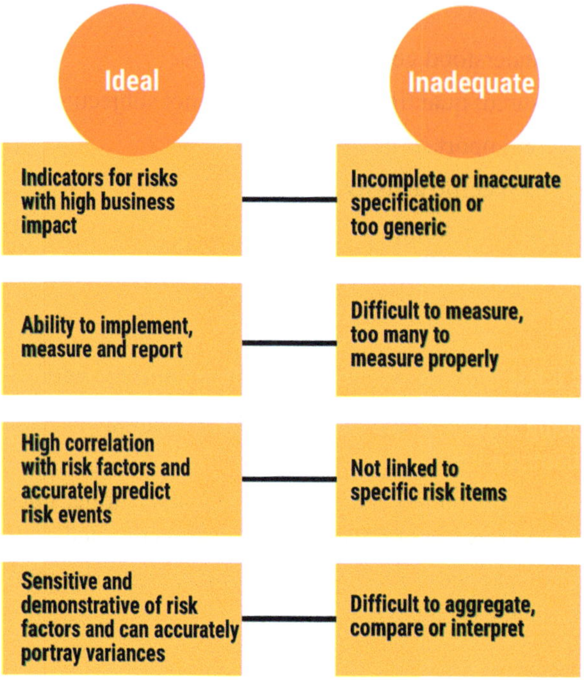

Because the internal and external environments are constantly changing, the risk environment is also highly dynamic, and the set of KRIs needs to be changed over time. Each KRI should be clearly related to the risk appetite and tolerance, so that trigger levels can be defined in support of appropriate, timely action.

6.2.4 Examples of Key Risk Indicators

KRIs may be different for different stakeholders and their view of I&T-related risk. For example, the:

- Chief executive officer (CEO)/board of directors requires a high-level view of risk and I&T-related risk
- Chief information officer (CIO) requires an IT department view on I&T-related risk, which is limited to its own personnel and resources
- Chief risk officer (CRO) requires a broader view on I&T-related risk from across the business, but can be considered operational

Figure 6.2 provides examples of KRIs for these different stakeholders (not intended to be a complete list).

Figure 6.2—Stakeholder KRIs (Example)

Event Category	CIO	CRO	CEO/Board of Directors
Investments/project decision-related events	Percent of projects on time, on budget Number and type of deviations from technology infrastructure plan	Percent of IT projects reviewed and signed off on by quality assurance (QA) that meet target quality goals and objectives Percent of projects with benefit defined up front	Percent of IT investments exceeding or meeting the correct business benefit Percent of IT expenditures that have direct traceability to the business strategy
Business involvement-related events	Degree of approval of business owners of the IT strategic/tactical plans	Frequency of meetings with enterprise leadership involvement where IT's contribution to value is discussed	Frequency of CIO reporting to or attending executive board meetings at which IT's contribution to enterprise goals is discussed
Security	Percent of users who do not comply with password standard	Number and type of suspected and actual access violations	Number of (security) incidents with business impact
Involuntary staff act: Destruction	Number of service levels impacted by operational incidents Percent of IT staff who complete annual IT training plan	Number of incidents caused by deficient user and operational documentation and training Number of business-critical processes relying on IT not covered by IT continuity plan	Cost of IT noncompliance, including settlements and fines Number of noncompliance issues reported to the board or causing public comment or embarrassment

Source: ISACA, *CGEIT Review Manual, 8th Edition*, USA, 2020, figure 6.2, *https://www.isaca.org/bookstore/cgeit-exam-resources/cgm8ed*

Other examples of enterprise KRIs include:

- Percent of critical business areas that have completed a risk assessment in the past 12 months
- Percent of compliance or controls testing regime for critical assets completed in past 12 months
- Percent of unmitigated risk in the risk register for which no response plan exists
- Percent of business processes where customer personal data is used
- Percent of incidents where customer personal data is lost/stolen
- Percent of lost or delayed product deliveries due to IT failure
- Percent of suppliers providing critical IT systems who have implemented an approved security control framework
- Percent of disaster recovery plans successfully tested in the past 12 months (leading)
- Percent of disaster recovery plans scheduled to be tested in the next 12 months (lagging)

I&T-related risk metrics should be aligned with other enterprise metrics to the greatest extent possible, and relevant stakeholders should be involved in the process.

6.2.5 Using KRIs for Gap Analysis

A risk gap exists when the acceptable level of risk and the current risk are different. Actions may be needed to close the gap. Gap analysis can be used in iteration to devise deliverables, projects and milestones. This process is illustrated in **figure 6.3**.

Figure 6.3—Reducing the Gap

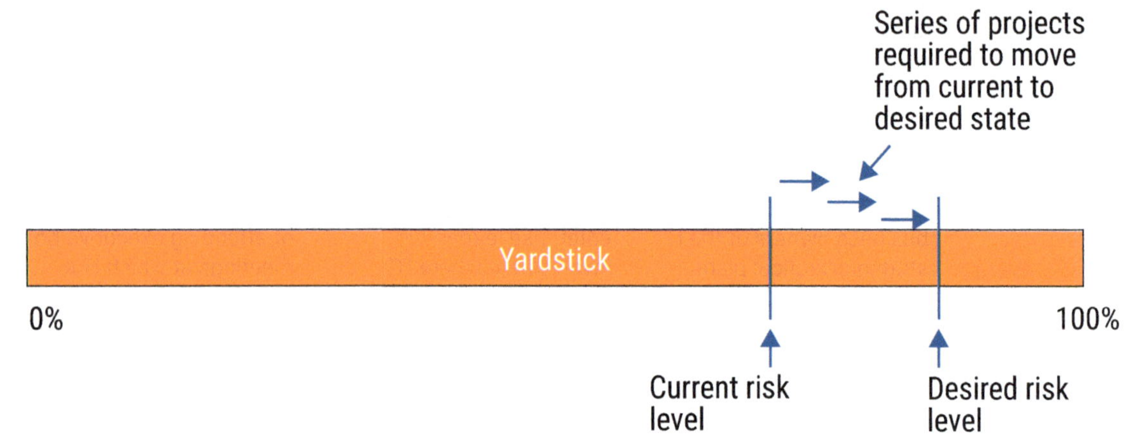

Source: ISACA, *CRISC Review Manual, 6th Edition*, USA, 2015, figure 2.8, *https://www.isaca.org/bookstore/crisc-exam-resources/crr6ed*

Using the gap analysis method to plan projects, along with milestones, can help the enterprise initiate and execute projects in an orderly and logical manner that takes into account their dependencies among each other.

To measure the current state, it is beneficial to identify one or more key goal indicators (KGIs) or key performance indicators (KPIs), which may be internal to the enterprise to relate to identified standards, frameworks or good practices. Desired states are typically linked to risk (i.e., KRIs). KPIs are presented in **section 6.3**.

6.2.6 KRI Optimization, Communication and Maintenance

To ensure accurate and meaningful reporting, KRIs must be optimized to ensure that the:

- Correct data are being collected and reported on.
- KRI thresholds are set correctly. KRIs that report on data points that either cannot be controlled by the enterprise or are not alerting management at the correct time to an adverse condition should be adjusted to be more precise, relevant or accurate.

KRIs are particularly important during the communication on risk. They facilitate a dialogue on risk within the enterprise, based on clear and measurable facts. This results in a less emotion-based or not overly intuitive discussion on where to place priorities for risk management. At the same time, KRIs can be used to improve risk awareness throughout the enterprise due to the factual nature of these indicators.

KRIs should be evaluated on a regular basis to verify that each KRI remains properly related to the risk appetite and tolerance levels of the enterprise, and that KRI trigger levels should be defined at a point that enables stakeholders to take appropriate action in a timely manner. Any KRIs that are no longer related to the risk appetite and tolerance should be replaced;, while any KRIs whose trigger levels are found to be out of alignment with the requirements of the enterprise should be optimized.

6.3 Key Performance Indicators

Performance indicators measure how well a process is performing in terms of its stated goal. Like risk indicators, performance indicators are put in place in order to provide insight into whether action may be required.

A key performance indicator (KPI) is an indicator that is effective in predicting whether a goal will be reached and indicates the capabilities, practices and skills of value to the enterprise. KPIs measure activity goals, which are actions that process owners must take to achieve effective process performance. KPIs are used to set benchmarks for risk management goals and to monitor whether those goals are being attained. Management sets its risk management goals according to its risk acceptance level and desired cost-benefit analysis. For example, a KPI may indicate that an error rate of five percent is acceptable, which implies that an error rate higher than five percent is unacceptable and requires escalation with some form of response.

KPIs are designed to provide a high-level overview of past performance and are almost always derived from historical data. KPIs are known as lagging indicators and provide information on whether or not targets were met for a compliance requirement or expenses were controlled on a project at the completion of the project.

Like KGIs, a KPI should be based on SMART metrics and should be:

- Valuable to the business
- Tied to a business function or service
- Under the control of management
- Quantitatively measured
- Used repeatedly in different reporting periods

Examples of potential KPIs include metrics associated with:

- Network availability
- Customer satisfaction
- Number of complaints resolved on first contact
- Time between data request and presentation
- Number of employees that attended awareness sessions

KPIs place emphasis on processes that should be good indicators of the health of the overall process. For example, the time required to deploy security patches is controllable by management, which can set policies, manage the change control process, mandate objectives and control resourcing. It is also quantitative and easily measured on a monthly or semiannual basis, so the results can be compared over time. KPIs are often used on charts or graphs to report compliance to management in a clear, easily understood manner.

6.3.1 Using KPIs with KRIs

KPIs and KRIs are often used in conjunction with one another to measure and monitor performance and mitigate risk. Using both KRIs and KPIs when getting started with risk management measurements may be necessary until there is enough data to improve the process.

- KPIs help to identify underperforming aspects of the enterprise and business functions that may require additional resources and attention.
- KRIs provide early warnings of increased risk and are forward-looking signals of risk to the enterprise.

Failing to meet performance goals is a risk, so KPIs and KRIs can be used together in risk management or combined with indicators specific to controls that may foreshadow an increase in risk due to a decrease in the effectiveness of mitigation.

KPI and KRI Example

To illustrate the difference, consider the risk that unpatched systems may lead to a serious breach of customer data, loss of availability and financial loss.

In response to this risk, the enterprise:

- Develops a policy to apply all critical patches within 30 days. The enterprise now has a clear, measurable standard of what constitutes proper performance. This business goal is an example of a KPI.
- Sets an alert at 25 days to indicate when the patch policy threshold is getting dangerously close to exceeding the KPI, but has not yet done so. The alert is an example of a KRI.

On a scheduled basis, the enterprise tracks and reports to senior management on the average time to deploy critical security patches on its UNIX, Windows and other systems (see chart in **figure 6.4**).

Figure 6.4—Example of KRI and KPI Use

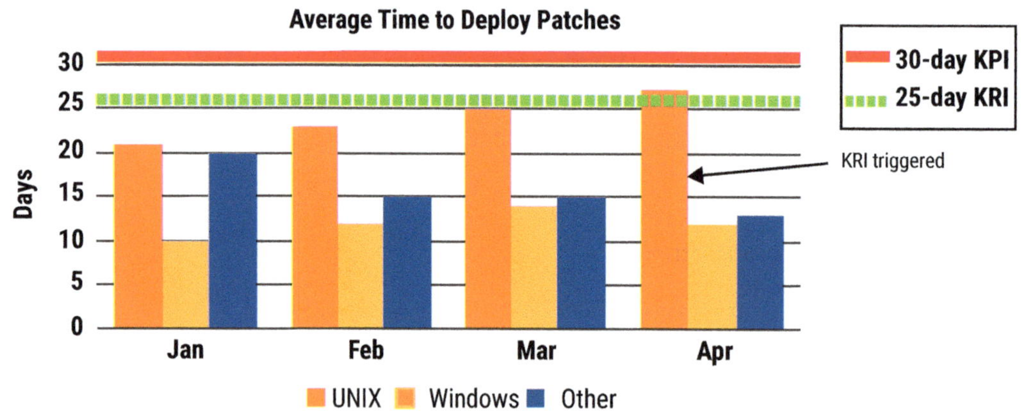

Source: ISACA, *CRISC Review Manual, 6th Edition*, USA, 2015, figure 4.3, *https://www.isaca.org/bookstore/crisc-exam-resources/crr6ed*

The chart shows that the enterprise UNIX system is increasing each month and is in danger of exceeding the 30-day KPI threshold. It also shows that, for the month of April, the KRI was triggered. This alert precipitated a review of patching procedures. Management investigated the situation to enable preventive action and addressed the slow deployment process before the deployment of the UNIX patches violated the policy.

This example shows how KRIs and KPIs can be used to monitor and track the attainment of goals and risk. When measuring the success of a risk management program, KPIs must be based on meaningful criteria that can help management track the overall success of the controls put in place to support risk response.

6.4 Risk and Control Monitoring and Testing

6.4.1 Continuous Monitoring

Risk management is an ongoing, cyclical process that recognizes the dynamic nature of risk and the need for continuous monitoring and assessment. Continuous risk and control monitoring is a process that includes:

- Developing a strategy to regularly evaluate selected I&T-related controls/metrics
- Recording and evaluating I&T-related events and the effectiveness of the enterprise in dealing with those events

- Recording changes to I&T-related controls, or changes that affect I&T-related risk
- Communicating the current risk and control status to enable information-sharing decisions involving the enterprise.

Continuous monitoring involves the monitoring of risk by every manager and every department, coupled with a robust risk culture that emphasizes local ownership and accountability. It aids in timely reporting and response to risk events and facilitates the development of more effective and efficient risk management processes.

6.4.2 Control Monitoring

It is important to have proven methods that can measure and ascertain the extent to which I&T-related activities contribute to, or support, business success. By having such methods, active monitoring and corrective action can be taken to reduce the risk that I&T-related activities deviate from the expected business contributions they are supposed to be making.

Control monitoring ensures that:

- Control requirements are being met.
- Standards are being followed.
- Staff is complying with enterprise policies, practices and procedures.

The purpose of control monitoring is to verify whether the control is effectively addressing the risk, not to see whether the control itself is working. For example, a firewall that is configured in a way that does not regulate traffic between two networks may be ineffective even if the firewall is operational and processing traffic.

The monitoring and associated metrics of managing a control must be based on data relevant to the risk and overall performance. I&T-related controls should be continuously monitored, benchmarked and improved. When the results of monitoring indicate an area of noncompliance or unacceptable performance, mitigation activities should be employed including:

- Implementation of new controls
- Adjustment or enforcement of existing controls
- Changes to a business process to address the risk environment

The monitoring of controls and the risk management framework may be done through self-assessment or independent assurance reviews. When risk action plans are required to address a risk, the plans should be monitored to ensure appropriate risk management practices are in alignment with the enterprise's risk appetite and tolerance. Assurance activities performed by entities which are independent from the function, group or enterprise being monitored, and these entities should have the necessary skills and competence to perform assurance and adhere to codes of ethics and professional standards.

Any exceptions to risk monitoring and control activities should be promptly reported, analyzed and addressed with properly prioritized corrective actions. As the risk environment changes and internal control systems are affected by changes in business and I&T-related risk, gaps in the risk environment must be evaluated and changes made where necessary.

6.4.3 Control Assessment and Testing

Effective control monitoring relies on the accuracy and completeness of the data provided for monitoring and evaluation. Data must be genuine and free from errors or misstatements. There are many types of control assessment and testing activities that include:

- Control self-assessment
- Internal audit control review
- Vulnerability assessment
- Vulnerability scan
- Penetration test

Control Self-Assessment

Each business process owner should take ownership of control monitoring and improvement through a continuing program of self-assessment to evaluate the completeness and effectiveness of management's control over processes, policies and contracts. An explicit acknowledgement by management that all monitoring activities are functioning as designed should be recorded in the risk register. For more information on control self-assessment (also see Section 4.6).

Internal Audit Control Review

Audit teams provide independent and objective review of the effectiveness and appropriateness of the control environment. Information provided by IT auditors can underscore the need for control enhancement and bring risk to the attention of management. Recommendations provided by IT audit often result in the updating of risk action plans and the risk register as well an enhancement of I&T-related controls.

Vulnerability Assessment

Vulnerability assessments (also see Section 3.6) deliver information to management that can be used both to understand the effectiveness of the risk management program and make decisions regarding treatment of identified vulnerability, such as deploying new controls.

Vulnerability Scan

Vulnerability scanning is the process of using proprietary or open source tools to search for known vulnerabilities. Often the same tools used by adversaries to identify vulnerabilities are used by enterprises to locate vulnerabilities proactively. Vulnerability scans should be conducted regularly to identify new vulnerabilities and ensure that previously identified vulnerabilities have been properly corrected.

Penetration Test

A penetration test (also see Section 3.6) is a live test of the effectiveness of security defenses through mimicking the actions of real-life attackers. A penetration test is a targeted attempt to break into an environment. As with a vulnerability assessment, the target of a penetration test may be a system, application, facility or end-to-end business process.

If the goal of a penetration test is to validate a vulnerability assessment, the tester is typically given the results of the assessment in order to focus on attempts to exploit the vulnerabilities that have already been identified. If the penetration tester is able to break in, then the vulnerability is real and must be mitigated; otherwise, there is a good chance that the vulnerability may be a false positive and not require mitigation. This validation-centric approach is typically called a white hat penetration test.

Penetration tests can also be undertaken against systems believed to be secure. In order to test the effectiveness of the security associated with such a system, the tester is generally given no information beyond a limited number of ground rules for the engagement and a definition of what constitutes a successful compromise of the system. This approach closely approximates the circumstances of someone attempting to break into a system maliciously and is typically called a black hat penetration test.

To perform a penetration test, the same tools used by malicious hackers to try to break into systems are often used. This approach provides meaningful results, but methods used for penetration testing may pose a risk to enterprise in the form of system failure or data compromise. Therefore, it is of utmost importance that such tests—whether white hat or black hat—are conducted only with management approval, using a defined methodology and under proper oversight. The results of the penetration test should be provided to management for follow up and review.

Third-party Assurance

Third-party attestation may be based on an external audit or a certification of compliance with an internationally recognized standard. The third party is responsible for evaluating the processes of the subject enterprise and validating compliance with the requirements of the standard.

6.4.4 Risk and Control Monitoring Effectiveness

Monitoring controls is a method of providing assurance that the controls are working correctly or effectively mitigating risk. Regular monitoring and reporting on risk are essential to management, and the use of KPIs and KRIs assists management in the monitoring of trends, compliance and issues related to risk.

Risk management is a never-ending process. I&T-related risk and controls should be continuously monitored and reported on to relevant stakeholders to ensure the continued efficiency and effectiveness of the I&T-related risk management strategy and its alignment to business objectives.

The effectiveness of monitoring is dependent on:

- **Timeliness of the reporting**—Are data received in time to take corrective action?
- **Skill of the data analyst**—Does the analyst have the skills to properly evaluate controls?
- **Quality of monitoring data available**—Are the monitoring data accurate and complete?
- **Quantity of data to be analyzed**—Can important data be identified in the midst of all the other data available?

An enterprise's risk profile reflects its enterprise attentiveness to monitoring the effectiveness of controls;, proactivity in identifying and addressing, or preventing, risk; and development of a risk culture. Changes in an enterprise's risk profile can occur for many reasons, including:

- New technologies
- Changes to business procedures
- Mergers or acquisitions
- New or revised regulations
- Changes in customer expectations
- Actions of competitors
- Effectiveness of risk awareness programs

To evaluate the effectiveness of controls and determine the I&T-related risk profile of the enterprise, numerous indicators should be monitored, including:

- New assets
- Changes to the scope of risk assessment

- Changes in business priorities, assets, services, products and operations
- Risk acceptance levels
- New threats (internal and external)
- Newly discovered vulnerabilities
- Possibility of increased risk due to aggregation of threats and vulnerabilities
- Incidents
- Logs and other data sources
- People and the morale of the enterprise
- Regulations and legal changes

Other monitoring areas include:

- Actions of competitors (benchmarking and standards)
- Changes in the supply chain (e.g., mergers, political turmoil, transportation problems, natural events, bankruptcies of vendors)
- Changes in the financial markets
- Total cost of ownership (TCO)
- Impact from external events
- Availability of staff/resources

I&T-related risk management goals and objectives should be reviewed to ensure that they continue to be aligned with the goals and objectives of senior management on a regular basis. Many enterprises find it beneficial to perform the review on an annual basis and to include criteria for monitoring, thresholds used for KPIs and KRIs, policies and strategies of risk, the reporting schedule, and the list of key stakeholders to be notified when KPIs or KRIs exceed their thresholds.

The review also provides a valuable opportunity to review the risk management program in terms of increasing maturity, including:

- The completion of risk response and mitigation activities
- The training of staff
- The success of risk awareness programs
- Improved response time to incidents
- Timely rollout of patches
- Better alignment and communication among management, audit, business continuity, physical security and information security departments

Throughout the I&T-related risk management process, risk owners, IT staff, third parties, incident response teams and auditors should work together to monitor risk and evaluate the effectiveness and efficiency of controls. As incidents occur, lessons learned are used to improve the risk management process through better knowledge, staffing, technical controls, procedures, monitoring and response programs. These benefits can help avoid future problems, enable the impact of future incidents to be minimized and sustain business operations.

6.4.5 Monitoring Control Exceptions

An important aspect of risk monitoring is clearly defining procedures for handling exceptions to monitored controls. While these controls manage risk, they also frequently cross enterprise objectives and business functions, making exception management essential to smooth enterprise operation. Exceptions can be required for a variety of reasons, including compensating for deficiencies in technology or associated skill set and enabling testing of a new application.

Before an exception is approved and implemented, it must be evaluated for its potential impact on risk levels. Exceptions to rules governing controls should be made as infrequently as possible, and only when necessary. The occurrence of frequent exceptions may indicate that the control being excepted may be misaligned with business priorities or improperly implemented, or that the policy governing this control is inappropriate.

Periodic documentation and review of exceptions to policy—along with any changes required to the I&T-related control's configuration— must be conducted to determine whether the exception is still necessary and removed if it is not.

If exceptions are undocumented and uncontrolled, the level of risk is unknown and may represent a hidden vulnerability. Therefore, exceptions should only be allowed through a documented, formal process that requires approval of the exception at the proper management level.

6.5 Risk Reporting and Communication

Risk reporting and communication is a key part of the risk management process. It is critical for decision-makers and stakeholders (including boards) to receive timely and accurate information on risk that can be acted upon.

Risk monitoring is essential, but its effectiveness depends in large part on its successful integration with reporting. Consistent, repeatable methods of reporting provide management with a means of assessing the efficiency of the risk response and mitigation activities and justify the expense of supporting controls. Reports also assist management in exercising due care and due diligence in protecting enterprise assets and meeting regulatory requirements.

Because risk reporting and communication is such an important part of the risk management process, it is covered in several chapters within this study guide, where it best applies.

6.5.1 Reporting Principles

This chapter provides risk reporting and communication principles, types of reports and communication, and report inputs and outputs.

To be effective, risk reporting and communication should adhere to the risk reporting principles provided in **figure 6.5**.

Figure 6.5—Risk Reporting Principles

Communication must be:	To:
Clear	Enable understanding by all stakeholders.
Concise	Focus the reader on the key points. Concise information is well structured and complete and avoids peripheral information, jargon and technical terms, except where necessary.
Useful	Enable decision making. Useful information is relevant and presented at the appropriate level of detail. Usefulness includes consideration of the target audience because information that may be useful to one party may not be useful to another party.
Timely	Allow action at the appropriate moment to identify and treat the risk. For each risk, critical moments exist between its origination and its potential business consequence; a delay in reporting may increase the level of impact. Example: Communicating a potential problem too late to undertake corrective or preventive action serves no useful purpose

Figure 6.5—Risk Reporting Principles *(cont.)*	
Communication must be:	To:
Aimed at the correct target audience	Enable informed decisions. Information must be communicated at the right level of aggregation and adapted for the audience. Aggregation must not hide root causes of risk. Example: A security officer may need technical data on intrusions and viruses to deploy solutions. An IT steering committee may not need this level of detail, but it does need aggregated information to decide on policy changes or additional budgets to treat the same risk.
Available on a need-to-know basis	Ensure that information related to IT risk is known and communicated to only those parties with a genuine need. Example: A risk register with all documented risk is not public information and should be properly protected against internal and external parties with no need for it.
Source: ISACA, *CGEIT Review Manual, 8th Edition*, USA, 2020, figure 4.26, *https://www.isaca.org/bookstore/cgeit-exam-resources/cgm8ed*	

6.5.2 Risk Report/Communication Types

To ensure the timely and appropriate response to I&T-related exposures and opportunities, the status of I&T-related risk should be reported to the appropriate stakeholders. Guidelines for developing a risk report includes:

- Using a format, and expressing risk in a manner that is useful to support business decisions
- Clearly depicting risk/return, and providing the supporting results of any analysis
- Providing probabilities of loss and/or gain, ranges and confidence levels so management can balance risk and return
- Identifying negative impacts to drive response decisions and positive impacts that represent opportunities
- Providing worst-case and most-probable scenarios, due diligence exposures, and reputation, legal or regulatory factors.

Risk reporting schedules and KRI monitoring are some of the processes used to keep stakeholders aware of current risk and ensure that risk responses are effective in mitigating enterprise risk. Other types of risk reporting and communication types are provided and described in **figure 6.6**.

Figure 6.6—Types of Risk Reports/Communication	
Reporting Content	Function
Expectation	Essential communication that defines the enterprise's overall strategy toward risk. This drives all subsequent risk management efforts. **Example:** Risk strategy, policies, procedures, awareness training, continuous reinforcement of principles, etc.

Figure 6.6—Types of Risk Reports/Communication *(cont.)*

Reporting Content	Function
Status	This includes information on the enterprise's actual risk status, such as: • The risk profile of the enterprise, i.e., the overall portfolio of (identified) risk to which the enterprise is exposed • The root cause of loss events • Thresholds for risk • Options to mitigate (cost and benefits) risk • Event/loss data • KRIs to support management reporting on risk
Risk management capability	A key indicator for effective risk management, this information allows evaluation and monitoring of the risk management activities at work in the enterprise. It has predictive value for the effectiveness of the enterprise's risk management and exposure reduction.
Actionable items	Including actionable items and risk owners' roles and responsibilities in the risk reporting matrix allows the risk report to overlap with the risk response plan.

To facilitate risk status reporting, visual aids, such as spreadsheets, graphs or charts, and summarized overviews can be useful. **Figure 6.7** shows an example of a risk report summary overview format from *COBIT® 5 for Risk.*

A risk report includes information on current risk management capabilities and actual status and trends with regard to risk. This report will be based on the risk profile and will be tailored to the requirements of recipients.

Figure 6.7—Risk Report

	Life Cycle Stage	Internal Stakeholder	External Stakeholder	Description/Stake
Life Cycle and Stakeholders	**Information planning**	Risk function		Risk management capabilities, actual status and trends are communicated timely and accurately to the right people, based on their needs and requirements
	Information design	Risk function		Risk management capabilities, actual status and trends are communicated timely and accurately to the right people, based on their needs and requirements
	Information build/acquire	Risk function, business process owners/CIO		Ensure that the risk report includes the latest information on risk management capabilities, latest status and trends with regard to risk of the entire organization
	Information use/operate: store, share, use	Board, executive management, CIO, risk function, business process owners/CIO, compliance, internal audit	External audit, regulator	Effective utilization and availability of information item by all involved stakeholders
	Information monitor	Board, risk committee, audit committee, risk function, business process owners/CIO	External audit	Verifies that information remains actual and alerts on changes
	Information disposal	Risk function		Ensures information is disposed of in a timely, secure and appropriate manner

Figure 6.7—Risk Report *(cont.)*

	Quality Subdimension and Goals		Description—The extent to which information is:	Relevance	Goal—The risk report:
Goals	Intrinsic	Accuracy	• Correct and reliable	• High	• Should accurately define the risk management capabilities and actual status and trends
		Objectivity	• Unbiased, unprejudiced and impartial	• High	• Information is based on the enterprise's risk culture and confirmed by observations
		Believability	• Regarded as true and credible	• Medium	• Should be realistic and accurate
		Reputation	• Regarded as coming from a true and credible source	• High	• Source information is collected from competent and recognized sources

Source: ISACA, *COBIT® 5 for Risk*, USA, 2013, figure 64, *https://www.isaca.org/bookstore/cobit-5/wcb5rk*

Risk reporting should also include information on the effectiveness of current controls and countermeasures and whether controls are functioning properly to reduce the amount of risk. Reports should indicate whether the residual risk levels are appropriate.

Reports can be customized to an enterprise's needs and should include such information as:

- The overall portfolio of risk to which the enterprise is exposed
- Root causes of loss events
- Risk thresholds
- Options to mitigate (cost/benefit) risk
- Event loss data or probable future gain
- Relevant risk indicators to support the conclusions and recommendations of the analysis

6.5.3 Risk Reporting Channels

Risk reports must be useful and accessible to the proper stakeholders. **Figure 6.8** details reporting channels for risk monitoring and the types of outputs that are generated in this stage of the risk management process.

Figure 6.8—Risk Reporting Channels

Input	Stakeholder	Output
• Executive summary risk reports • Current risk exposure/profile • KRIs	Executive management and board	• Enterprise appetite for I&T-related risk • Key performance objectives • I&T-related risk Responsible, Accountable, Consulted and/or Informed (RACI) charts • I&T-related risk policies that express management's I&T-related risk tolerance • Risk awareness expectations • Risk culture • Risk analysis request
• Risk management scope and plan • Risk register • Risk analysis results • Executive summary risk reports • Integrated/aggregated risk report • KRIs • Risk analysis request	Chief risk officer (CRO) and enterprise risk committee	• Enterprise appetite for I&T-related risk • Residual I&T-related risk exposure • I&T-related risk action plan
• Enterprise appetite for risk • Risk management scope and plan • Key performance objectives • Risk RACI charts • Risk framework and scoring methodology • Risk register	Chief information officer (CIO)	• Residual risk exposures • Operational risk information • Business impact of the risk and impacted business units • Ongoing changes to risk factors
• Key performance objectives	Chief financial officer (CFO)	• Financial information with regard to programs and projects (e.g., budget, actual, trends, etc.)
• Risk management scope • Plans for ongoing business and risk communication • Risk culture • Business impact of I&T-related business risk and impacted business unites • Ongoing changes to I&T-related risk factors	Business management and business process owners	• Control and compliance monitoring • Risk analysis request

Figure 6.8—Risk Reporting Channels *(cont.)*		
Input	**Stakeholder**	**Output**
• Key performance objectives • Risk management plan • Risk framework and scoring methodology • Risk register • Risk culture	IT management (including security, service management)	• Residual I&T-related risk exposure
• Key performance objectives • RACI charts • Risk management plan • Control and compliance monitoring	Compliance and audit	• Audit findings
• Key performance objectives • Risk management plan • Risk framework and scoring methodology • Risk register • Audit findings	Risk control functions	• Residual risk exposures • Risk reports
• Risk awareness expectations • Risk culture	Human resources (HR)	• Potential risk • Support on risk awareness initiatives

6.6 Summary of Terminology

It is important to recognize and understand I&T-related risk terminology. The following terms were introduced in this chapter.

Figure 6.9—Chapter 6 Terminology	
Term	**Definition**
Continuous risk and control monitoring	A process that includes: • Developing a strategy to regularly evaluate selected I&T-related controls/metrics • Recording and evaluating I&T-related events and the effectiveness of the enterprise in dealing with those events • Recording changes to I&T-related controls, or changes that affect I&T-related risk • Communicating the current risk and control status to enable information-sharing decisions involving the enterprise
Key performance indictor (KPI)	An indicator that is effective in predicting whether a goal will be reached and indicates the capabilities, practices and skills of value to the enterprise
Key risk indicator (KRI)	A subset of risk indicators that are highly relevant and possess a high probability of predicting or indicating important risk
Lag risk indicator	A backward-looking metric that indicates risk has been realized after an event has occurred
Lead risk indicator	A lead risk indicator is a forward-looking metric that provides an early warning that risk may soon be realized before an event has occurred

Figure 6.9—Chapter 6 Terminology *(cont.)*	
Term	Definition
Penetration test	A live test of the effectiveness of security defenses through mimicking the actions of real-life attackers
Risk gap	A gap that exists when the acceptable level of risk and the current state of risk are different
Root cause analysis	A process of diagnosis to establish the origins of events, which can be used for learning from consequences, typically from errors and problems

Chapter 6 Knowledge Check

Review questions are provided as a means to support the content presented within this study guide and serve as a gauge or assessment of knowledge of I&T-related risk topics. One question is provided for each topic.

For individuals intending to earn the ISACA IT Risk Fundamentals Certificate, these questions are written to depict the type of questions that may appear on the exam. These questions will not specifically appear on the exam, but similar ones may appear.

REVIEW QUESTIONS

1. Risk monitoring focuses on:

   A. Measuring and assessing inherent risk.
   B. Observing and assessing potential risk events.
   C. Selecting metrics that exceed risk tolerance.

2. A lead key risk indicator collects and measures data:

   A. Relating to risk that has not yet been realized.
   B. Pertaining to meeting a performance target.
   C. Pertaining to a service level availability goal.

3. Key performance indicators are:

   A. Are qualitative and thus hard to measure over time.
   B. Are used to provide a high-level overview and measure of past performance.
   C. Provide information on whether or not a target will be met.

4. The purpose of control monitoring is to:

   A. Determine whether controls are functioning as designed.
   B. Verify whether controls are effectively addressing risk.
   C. Determine the type of controls needed to address risk.

5. The status of I&T-related risk should be reported to the appropriate stakeholders and:

   A. Should focus on best-case and least-probable scenarios.
   B. Be as concise as possible and as such exclude probabilities of gain and loss.
   C. Express risk in a manner that is useful to support business decisions.

Answers on page 190

Chapter 6 ANSWER KEY

Review Questions

1. A. Risk monitoring is a process used to keep stakeholders aware of current risk (not inherent) and ensure that risk responses are effective in mitigating enterprise risk.
   B. Risk monitoring involves observing and assessing potential risk events, threat events and vulnerability events.
   C. Risk monitoring involves making sure that current and emerging risk remains within the enterprise's risk tolerance levels. As such, metrics should be chosen at, or below, the risk tolerance level.

2. **A. A lead key risk indicator is a forward-looking metric that provides an early warning that risk may soon be realized before an event has occurred.**
   B. Meeting a performance target is an example of a lag key risk indicator.
   C. Service level availability goal is an example of a lag key risk indicator.

3. A. Key performance indicators are quantitative and easily measured on a monthly or semiannual basis, so the results can be compared over time.
   B. Key performance indicators are designed to provide a high-level overview of past performance.
   C. Key performance indicators are lag indicators that provide information on whether or not targets were met.

4. A. The purpose of control monitoring is not to determine whether controls are functioning as designed, but instead, to verify whether the control is effectively addressing the risk. Controls may have been designed with flaws that lead to them not effectively addressing risk.
   B. The purpose of control monitoring is to verify whether controls are effectively addressing risk and if not, corrective action can be taken to reduce risk.
   C. The type of controls needed to address risk should be determined early, on as part of the risk management process and not during the control monitoring process. However, the results of control monitoring may indicate that a specific type of control is not effectively addressing risk and should be replaced by another type of control.
5. A. A risk report should report on all possible outcomes, but should focus on worst-case and most-probable scenarios.
   B. A risk report should provide probabilities of loss and/or gain, ranges and confidence levels so management can balance risk and return.
   C. A risk report should use a format and express risk in a manner that is useful to support business decisions.

APPENDIX A: Glossary

Term	Definition
Access risk	The risk that information may be divulged or made available to recipients without authorized access by the information owner, reflecting a loss of confidentiality
Advanced persistent threat (APT)	An adversary that possesses sophisticated levels of expertise and significant resources which allow it to create opportunities to achieve its objectives using multiple attack vectors (NIST SP800-61)
Asset	Something of either tangible or intangible value that is worth protecting
Asset inventory	A register used to record all relevant assets
Asset value	The value of an asset to both the business and to competitors
Attack	An event or attempt to gain unauthorized access or use of an asset
Attack vector	A path or route used by the adversary to gain access to the target (asset)
Audit	A formal inspection and verification to check whether a standard or set of guidelines is being followed, records are accurate, or efficiency and effectiveness targets are being met
Availability risk	The risk that service may be lost or data are not accessible when needed
Business case	Documents the rationale for making a business investment, used both to support a business decision on whether to proceed with the investment and as an operational tool to support management of the investment through its full economic life cycle
Business continuity	Preventing, mitigating and recovering from disruption
Business impact	The net effect, positive or negative, on the achievement of business objectives
Business impact analysis (BIA)	A process to determine the impact of losing the support of any resource
Business process	An interrelated set of cross-functional activities or events that result in the delivery of a specific product or service to a customer
Business risk	Business risk is the probability a situation with uncertain frequency and magnitude of loss (or gain) that could prevent the enterprise from meeting its business objectives
Change risk	A change in technology, regulation, business process, functionality, architecture, user and other variables that affect the enterprise business and technical environments and the level of risk associated with systems in operation
Compensating control	An internal control that reduces the risk of an existing or potential control weakness resulting in errors and omissions
Compliance risk	The probability and consequences of an enterprise failing to comply with laws, regulations or the ethical standards or codes of conduct applicable to the enterprise's industry
Consequence	The magnitude of loss resulting from a threat exploiting a vulnerability (used interchangeably with impact

Term	Definition
Continuous risk and control monitoring	A process that includes: • Developing a strategy to regularly evaluate selected I&T-related controls/metrics • Recording and evaluating I&T-related events and the effectiveness of the enterprise in dealing with those events • Recording changes to I&T-related controls, or changes that affect I&T-related risk • Communicating the current risk and control status to enable information-sharing decisions involving the enterprise
Control	The means of managing risk, including policies, procedures, guidelines, practices or organizational structures
Control objective	A statement of the desired result or purpose to be achieved by implementing control procedures in a particular process
Control owner	A person in whom the enterprise has invested the authority and accountability for making control-related decisions and is responsible to ensure the control is implemented and is operating effectively and efficiently
Control risk self-assessment	A method/process by which management and staff of all levels collectively identify and evaluate risk and controls with their business areas. This may be under the guidance of a facilitator such as an auditor or risk manager
Control self-assessment	An assessment of controls made by the staff and management of the unit or units involved
Control weakness	A deficiency in the design or operation of a control procedure. Control weaknesses can potentially result in risk relevant to the area of activity not being reduced to an acceptable level (relevant risk threatens achievement of the objectives relevant to the area of activity being examined). Control weaknesses can be material when the design or operation of one or more control procedures does not reduce to a relatively low level the risk that misstatements caused by illegal acts or irregularities may occur and not be detected by the related control procedures
Corrective control	Designed to correct errors, omissions and unauthorized uses and intrusions, once they are detected
Cost-benefit analysis	An analysis that relies on the addition of positive factors and the subtraction of negative ones to determine a net result and is a method used to build a business case to support a risk response
Countermeasure	Any process that directly reduces a threat or vulnerability
Credit risk	The potential that a borrower or creditor will fail to meet financial obligations in accordance with agreed terms
Current risk	The risk state that exists in the moment, taking into account those actions that have already been taken but not actions that are anticipated or have been proposed
Cyber and information security risk	The danger, harm or loss related to the use of, or dependence on, information and communications technology, electronic data, and digital or electronic communications

Term	Definition
Detection risk	The risk that the prescribed controls, substantive testing procedures or monitoring will not detect an error that could be material—individually or in combination with other errors
Detective control	Designed to detect and report when errors, omissions and unauthorized uses or entries occur
Disaster recovery	The activities and programs designed to return the enterprise to an acceptable condition. The ability to respond to an interruption in services by implementing a disaster recovery plan (DRP) to restore an enterprise's critical business functions
Environmental risk	Threats to natural resources, human health and wildlife
Event	Something that happens at a specific place and/or time
Exploit	An event where the attacker takes advantage of a vulnerability
Frequency	A measure of the rate by which events occur over a certain period of time
Frequency analysis	Determines how often a particular risk scenario might be expected to occur during a specified period of time
Governance	Ensures that stakeholder needs, conditions and options are evaluated to determine balanced, agreed on enterprise objectives to be achieved; setting direction through prioritization and decision making; and monitoring performance and compliance against agreed-on direction and objectives
I&T operations and service delivery risk	Risk related to the performance of IT systems and services. A poorly performing IT operation can bring destruction or reduction of value to the enterprise
I&T risk governance and management	The implementation of a risk strategy that reflects the culture, appetite and tolerance levels of enterprise management, considers technology and budgets and addresses the requirements of regulation and compliance
I&T-related risk	A part of overall business risk associated with the use, ownership, operation involvement, influence and adoption of I&T within an enterprise
Impact	Magnitude of loss resulting from a threat exploiting a vulnerability
Incident	Any event that is not part of the ordinary operation of a service that causes, or may cause, an interruption to, or a reduction in, the quality of that service
Infrastructure risk	The risk that I&T infrastructure and systems may be unable to effectively support the current and future needs of the business in an efficient, cost-effective and well-controlled fashion
Inherent risk	The risk level or exposure without taking into account the actions that management has taken or might take (e.g., implementing controls)
Integrity risk	The risk that data may be unavailable due to incompleteness or inaccuracy
Investment (or expense) risk	The risk that I&T investment fails to provide value commensurate with its cost or is otherwise excessive or wasteful, including the overall I&T investment portfolio
IT risk register	A repository of the key attributes of potential and known IT risk issues. Attributes may include name, description, owner, expected/actual frequency, potential/actual magnitude, potential/actual business impact, disposition
IT-related incident	An IT-related event that causes an operational, developmental and/or strategic business impact

Term	Definition
Key performance indictor (KPI)	An indicator that is effective in predicting whether a goal will be reached and indicates the capabilities, practices and skills of value to the enterprise
Key risk indicator (KRI)	A subset of risk indicators that are highly relevant and possess a high probability of predicting or indicating important risk
Lag risk indicator	A backward-looking metric that indicates risk has been realized after an event has occurred
Lead risk indicator	A lead risk indicator is a forward-looking metric that provides an early warning that risk may soon be realized before an event has occurred
Likelihood	The probability of something happening
Magnitude	A measure of the potential severity of loss or the potential gain from realized events/scenarios
Market risk	Pressures on an asset class
Operational risk	The potential for losses caused by inadequate systems or controls, human error or mismanagement and natural disasters
Penetration test	A live test of the effectiveness of security defenses through mimicking the actions of real-life attackers
Policy	A document that records a high-level principle or course of action that has been decided on
Preventive control	An internal control that is used to avoid undesirable events, errors and other occurrences that an enterprise has determined could have a negative material effect on a process or end product
Probability	A mathematical driven measure of the possibility of a specific outcome as a ratio of all possible outcomes
Procedure	A document containing a detailed description of the steps necessary to perform specific operations in conformance with applicable standards
Project ownership risk	The risk that I&T projects fail to meet objectives through lack of accountability and commitment
Project risk	A failed IT project that poses a significant risk to an enterprise, manifesting as lost market share, failure to seize new opportunities or other adverse impacts on customers, shareholders and staff
Qualitative risk analysis	Approach based on expert opinion, judgement, intuition and experience
Quantitative risk analysis	Approach based on a calculation of a risk's likelihood and impact using numerical and statistical techniques
RACI chart	Illustrates who is Responsible, Accountable, Consulted and Informed within an enterprise framework
RACI model	A method to define and depict roles and responsibilities
Relevance risk	The risk that the right information may not get to the right recipients at the right time to allow the right action to be taken or the right decisions to be made
Residual risk	The remaining risk after management has implemented a risk response
Resource (IT)	Anything that helps to achieve I&T goals

Term	Definition
Return on investment (ROI)	A measure of operating performance and efficiency, computed in its simplest form by dividing net income by the total investment over the period being considered
Risk	The combination of the likelihood of an event and its impact
Risk acceptance	Decision to accept a risk made according to the risk appetite and risk tolerance set by senior management where the enterprise can assume the risk and absorb any losses
Risk aggregation	The process of integrating risk assessments at a corporate level to obtain a complete view on the overall risk for the enterprise
Risk analysis	A process by which frequency and magnitude of IT risk scenarios are estimated
Risk appetite	The amount of risk, on a broad level, that an enterprise or other entity is willing to accept in pursuit of its mission (or vision) and the achievement of business objectives
Risk assessment	A process used to identify and evaluate risk and its potential effects
Risk avoidance	The process for systematically avoiding risk, constituting one approach to managing risk
Risk awareness program	A program that creates an understanding of risk, risk factors and the various types of risk that an enterprise faces
Risk capacity	The objective magnitude or amount of loss that an enterprise can tolerate without risking its continued existence
Risk culture	The set of shared values and beliefs that governs attitudes toward risk-taking, care and integrity, and determines how openly risk and losses are reported and discussed
Risk evaluation	The process of comparing the estimated risk against given risk criteria to determine the significance of the risk. [ISO/IEC Guide 73:2002]
Risk gap	A gap that exists when the acceptable level of risk and the current state of risk are different
Risk governance	Sets the direction and strategy of risk management efforts, defines risk culture and acceptable levels of risk, makes risk-aware business decisions and ensures that the risk management function is operating effectively to identify, manage, monitor and report on current and potential risk facing the enterprise
Risk identification	Risk identification is the process for determining and documenting the risk an enterprise faces
Risk management	The coordinated activities to direct and control an enterprise with regard to risk
Risk map	A (graphic) tool for ranking and displaying risk by defined ranges for frequency and magnitude
Risk mitigation	The management of risk through the use of countermeasures and controls
Risk owner	The person in whom the enterprise has invested the authority and accountability for making risk-based decisions and who owns the loss associated with a realized risk scenario
Risk register	A list of risk that have been identified, analyzed and prioritized

Term	Definition
Risk response	Risk avoidance, risk acceptance, risk sharing/transfer, risk mitigation, leading to a situation that as much future residual risk (current risk with the risk response defined and implemented) as possible (usually depending on budgets available) falls within risk appetite limits
Risk scenario	The tangible and assessable representation of risk
Risk scope	The selection of items included in the risk activities based upon understanding the full risk universe and then down-selecting the specific part of the enterprise to which the risk activities will be applied
Risk sharing	See Risk transfer.
Risk statement	A description of the current conditions that may lead to the loss; and a description of the loss. Source: Software Engineering Institute (SEI)
Risk taxonomy	A scheme for classifying sources and categories of risk that provides a common language for discussing and communicating risk to stakeholders
Risk tolerance	The acceptable level of variation that management is willing to allow for any particular risk as the enterprise pursues its objectives
Risk transfer	The process of assigning risk to another enterprise, usually through the purchase of an insurance policy or by outsourcing the service Also known as risk sharing
Risk universe	Encompasses the overall risk environment, defines the areas risk management activities will address and provides a structure for I&T-related risk management
Root cause analysis	A process of diagnosis to establish the origins of events, which can be used for learning from consequences, typically from errors and problems
Safeguard	A practice, procedure or mechanism that reduces risk
Schedule risk	The risk that I&T projects take longer than expected
Stakeholder	Anyone who has a responsibility for, an expectation from or some other interest in the enterprise
Standard	A mandatory requirement, code of practice or specification approved by a recognized external standards organization
Strategic risk	The risk associated with an enterprise's future business plans and strategies
Threat	Anything that is capable of acting against an asset in a manner that can result in harm. Threats are aimed at exploiting enterprise vulnerabilities.
Threat actor	Any person, thing or entity that acts or carries out a threat and is responsible for a threat event
Threat agent	Methods and things used to exploit a vulnerability
Threat assessment/analysis	An evaluation of the type, scope and nature of events or actions that can result in adverse consequences; identification of the threats that exist against enterprise assets
Threat event	Any event during which a threat actor acts against an asset in a manner that has the potential to directly result in harm
Uncertainty	The difficulty of predicting an outcome due to limited knowledge of all components

Term	Definition
Vulnerability	Control condition that is deemed to be deficient relative to requirements of the threat levels being faced by the enterprise. Vulnerabilities represent a weakness in the design, implementation, operation or internal control of a process that could expose the system to adverse threats from threat events
Vulnerability assessment/analysis	A process of identifying and classifying vulnerabilities

Page intentionally left blank

9781604207262